MW00978266

Employment Cr[...]
and Social Protection in the
Middle East and North Africa

Mediterranean Development Forum

The Economic Research Forum
for the Arab Countries, Iran and Turkey
Cairo, Egypt

The World Bank
Washington, DC

Employment Creation and Social Protection in the Middle East and North Africa

Edited by

Heba Handoussa
Zafiris Tzannatos

An Economic Research Forum Edition

The American University in Cairo Press
Cairo • New York

First published in 2002 by
The American University in Cairo Press
113 Sharia Kasr el Aini, Cairo, Egypt
420 Fifth Avenue, New York 10018
www.aucpress.com

in association with
The Economic Research Forum for the Arab Countries, Iran and Turkey
7 Boulos Hanna Street, Dokki, 11123 Cairo www.erf.org.eg
and The International Bank for Reconstruction and Development / THE WORLD BANK
1818 H Street, N.W., Washington, D.C. 20433, USA

Dar el Kutub No. 16710/01
ISBN 977 424 700 0

Printed in Egypt

Contents

Contributors

Ali Abdel Gadir Ali is Economic Advisor, Arab Planning Institute, Kuwait.

Alan Abrahart is former State Director of the Department of Employment, Education and Training, Australia.

Victor Billeh is Regional Director, UNESCO Regional Office for Education in the Arab States, Beirut, Lebanon.

Moez Doraid is Coordinator, Sub-Regional Resource Facility for Arab States, United Nations Development Program (UNDP).

Ibrahim A. Elbadawi is Lead Economist at the Development Economics Research Group (DECRG), the World Bank.

Maurice Girgis is Managing Director, LTC Techno-Economics Research Group, Inc.

Iqbal Kaur is a social protection specialist at the World Bank, Middle East and North Africa Region, Human Development Network.

Noha El-Mikawy is Senior Research Fellow, Center for Development Research, University of Bonn.

Valentine Moghadam is Director of Women's Studies and Associate Professor of Sociology, Illinois State University.

Marsha Pripstein Posusney is Associate Professor of Political Science at Bryant College and an adjunct associate professor of international relations (research) at Brown University.

Zafiris Tzannatos was formerly Sector Manager, Social Protection in the Middle East and North Africa Region, at the World Bank, where he is currently Adviser to the Managing Director.

Abbreviations and Acronyms

ALMP	Active Labor Market Policies
CDD	Community Driven Development
CDF	Comprehensive Development Framework
CFS	Consumer Food Subsidies
CNAC	Caisse Nationale d' Assurance et de Chomage
CREDIF	Center for Research, Study, and Documentation of Information on Women
DE	Diversified Economies
ECA	Europe and Central Asia
EN	Entraide Nationale (Morocco)
ERF	Economic Research Forum
ERSAP	Economic Reforms and Structural Adjustment Programs
ESA	Employee Shareholders Associations
ESCWA	Economic and Social Commission for West Asia
ETUF	Egyptian Trade Union Federation
EU	European Union
FDI	Foreign Direct Investment
GCC	Gulf Cooperation Council
GDI	Gender Development Index
GDP	Gross Domestic Product
GEM	Gender Empowerment Measure
GNP	Gross National Product
HDI	Human Development Index
HPI	Human Poverty Index
ILO	International Labour Organization
IMF	International Monetary Fund
JD	Jordanian Dinar
JNCW	Jordanian National Committee for Women
KD	Kuwaiti Dinar
LAC	Latin America and Caribbean
LCHR	Land Center for Human Rights
LIC	Learning and Innovation Credit
LIL	Learning and Innovation Loan
LMIS	Labor Market Information System
MDF	Mediterranean Development Forum
MENA	Middle East and North Africa
MOE	Ministry of Education
MOHE	Ministry of Higher Education
MOP	Mixed Oil Producers
MOP	Ministry of Planning

NDP	National Democratic Party
NGO	Non-Governmental Organization
NHDR	National Human Development Reports
NICs	Newly Industrialized Countries
OECD	Organization for Economic Cooperation and Development
OED	Operation Evaluation Department
ORT	Oral Rehydration Therapy
PAYG	Pay As You Go
PN	Promotion Nationale
PP	Primary Producers
PPP	Purchasing Power Parity
PRSP	Poverty Reduction Strategy Paper
PWP	Public Works Program
SEWA	Self-Employed Women's Association
SFD	Social Fund for Development
SME	Small and Medium-sized Enterprise
SOE	State-Owned Enterprise
TFP	Total Factor Productivity
UAE	United Arab Emirates
UN	United Nations
UNDP	United Nations Development Program
UNESCO	United Nations Educational, Scientific, and Cultural Organization
UNICEF	United Nations Children's Fund
VET	Vocational Education and Training
VT	Vocational Training
VTC	Vocational Training Corporation (Jordan)
WBG	West Bank and Gaza
WDI	World Development Indicators
WID	Women in Development
WSSD	World Summit for Social Development
YR	Yemeni Rials

About MDF

The Mediterranean Development Forum (MDF), launched in 1997, is a partnership of ten Middle East and North Africa region (MENA) think tanks and the World Bank Institute. The partnership is dedicated to providing policy support for development actors, research, and the capacity-building of think tanks, and to creating networks in the MENA region. The partnership's work culminates in a forum held every eighteen months.

The forum is a crucial component of the MDF initiative because it provides a rare opportunity for MENA experts, high-level government officials, and civil society representatives to meet and engage in a dialogue to set the region's development agenda. MDF already makes a unique impact on the region. Its first conference, held in Marrakech, Morocco, in May 1997, focused on the interplay of civil society, business, and government as they engage in efforts to boost the region's competitiveness. The discussions that took place at its second conference, held in September 1998 also in Marrakech, broke new ground on the most crucial issue facing the developing world: how to enhance public participation in the development process. Its third conference, held in Cairo, Egypt, in March 2000 under the title "Voices for Change, Partners in Prosperity," examined the relationship between economic growth, employment, and poverty, and forms the background to this book. The September 2002 forum is planned to take place in Amman, Jordan.

As a direct result of the MDF partnership, the following projects have emerged in the past few years: programs on decentralization and governance in the West Bank and Gaza; programs on quality education emphasizing gender; the Network on Women Evaluators; the Network of Lawyers Reforming NGO Laws; the "Meet the Civil Society" Initiative; the MENA Data Initiative; and the MDF publication series.

Foreword

This is the third book published on behalf of the Mediterranean Development Forum (MDF), a partnership of ten Middle East and North Africa region (MENA) think tanks and the World Bank Institute. The volume is a joint publication with the Economic Research Forum for the Arab Countries, Iran and Turkey (ERF).

The MDF publication series is based on conferences that the MDF partnership holds every eighteen months. This particular volume, *Employment Creation and Social Protection in the Middle East and North Africa*, includes papers originally presented at the Third Mediterranean Development Forum, which took place in Cairo, Egypt, in March 2000.

This publication, by presenting some of the most noteworthy contributions, hopes to capture the spirit and magnitude of the conference. More than 125 speakers debated innovative and cutting-edge development issues with an audience of over 600 of the region's most influential thinkers and practitioners, including high-level government officials, think tank representatives, private sector leaders, academics, and civil society representatives.

We would like to express our thanks to all those think tank representatives who ensured the smooth running of the conference, in which ERF played a major role; to all those who contributed to the sessions; and to the authors of this volume, who have provided a unique perspective on a crucial area of the ongoing debate on the development opportunities and challenges facing the countries of the MENA region.

Heba Handoussa, Managing Director
Economic Research Forum for
the Arab Countries, Iran and Turkey

Vinod Thomas, Vice President
World Bank Institute

Preface

The Mediterranean Development Forum (MDF) is a partnership of ten Middle Eastern and North African think tanks that began working together in 1997 to support development throughout the region. It operates by increasing research capacity, creating and maintaining regional networks, encouraging debate, exploring new ideas, and influencing policy. MDF conferences are an opportunity to put forward policy recommendations.

The third MDF conference, held in Cairo on March 5–8, 2000, hosted 42 separate workshop sessions under seven themes. One of these themes was the social implications of job creation, which was discussed in a workshop entitled "Employment Creation and Social Protection." The papers presented at this workshop form the basis of the present volume.

The workshop was concerned with the interrelationship between labor, human development, and, above all, social well-being in the Middle East and North Africa (MENA) region. These issues were discussed against the backdrop of globalization that is shaping country and international economic relations. Workshop participants tackled the question of how to protect the labor force from new forms of insecurity being ushered in by the globalization era. One way to achieve this is through the concept of "decent work," which comprises the right to work and to do so under reasonable conditions. This brings to the forefront the issue of social protection, which in itself creates a number of dilemmas for policy-makers, as formal social security covers only a small percentage of the labor force. The idea of "social reinsurance," which would integrate the informal sector and allow for social dialogue, emerged at the conference. The new social contract should include the government, the private sector, and civil society.

In this collection, Victor Billeh (Chapter 1) argues that upgrading the quantity, quality, and relevance of learning through comprehensive country-specific reforms of education and training systems should be a major priority for economic policy-makers in MENA countries. He writes of the need to synchronize the education and training programs with the demands of the constantly evolving job market. Billeh argues that globalization threatens to widen the gap even further between the knowledge and skills of the labor force and the requirements of the marketplace. The future of the region and its share in the fruits of globalization will depend on each country's ability to empower its labor force with the necessary skills to compete in the world economy.

In Chapter 2, Alan Abrahart, Iqbal Kaur, and Zafiris Tzannatos examine government employment and active labor market policies in the MENA region in a comparative international context. MENA countries have undertaken economic adjustment programs in order to create an efficient public sector and a dynamic private sector. However, as the authors point out, these policies have resulted in winners and losers, and policy-makers now face the challenge of achieving economic growth and integration into the world economy, while simultaneously minimizing social dislocation.

Noha El-Mikawy and Marsha Pripstein Posusney (Chapter 3) employ a political economy approach in their analysis of labor-government and labor-business relations. Urban workers, they argue, although privileged relative to the rural poor, are likely to be among the first "losers" when price controls are removed, government budgets are cut, or the public sector is rationalized or privatized. At the same time, however, these workers are in a position of strength to organize and protest against policies that harm their interests. El-Mikawy and Posusney examine the ways in which organized labor may influence economic reforms on the one hand, and how the reform process impacts labor representation, on the other.

In Chapter 4, Maurice Girgis investigates the recent emergence of unemployment in the Gulf Cooperation Council (GCC) region. Past policies in the GCC have provided nationals with ample employment opportunities, job security, high salaries, and generous fringe benefit packages, but mostly in the public sector. Over the past two decades, increased employment of expatriates has resulted in an unemployment problem for national workers.

Zafiris Tzannatos (Chapter 5) analyzes the impact of several macroeconomic trends (i.e., fluctuations in oil markets and patterns of labor migration) on the MENA economies. He then evaluates a wide range of social policies in the MENA region—including public works programs, safety net programs, and pension plans—in terms of their respective abilities to reduce vulnerability and insulate their beneficiaries from poverty. Tzannatos concludes with recommendations for revamping some of these programs, while using more sparingly those with unproven effects, and for increasing the synergy between public and private social protection mechanisms.

Ali A. G. Ali and Ibrahim A. Elbadawi (Chapter 6) explore the relationship between growth and distribution in order to develop an analysis of poverty in six Arab countries—Algeria, Egypt, Jordan, Mauritania, Morocco, and Tunisia. Using a nontechnical framework, the two authors suggest tentative, country-specific strategies for tackling poverty and income inequality.

In his study of Arab human development and poverty (Chapter 7), Moez Doraid argues that the ultimate goal of growth and development in the MENA region should be the elimination of poverty. He emphasizes that the political commitment to narrowing the gap between rich and poor should emanate from ethical, social, political, and moral imperatives as well as from the region's religious and cultural traditions.

Finally, in Chapter 8, Valentine Moghadam stresses the need for proactive policies to encourage women's economic participation in the MENA region. These include an integration of gender issues—including women's employment—into policies and projects at all levels and in all sectors. In addition, large investments are required in girls' education. National policies aimed at making the private sector more friendly to women should be pursued (i.e., maternity leave and the provision of support services to working women should be financed through contributions from employers, employees, and the government). Lastly, NGO support and extension services are needed for women-owned or -managed businesses. Moghadam identifies several related trends: an increase, in most countries, in the supply of job-seeking women, along with very high unemployment rates among women; increased activity by poor and working-class women in the urban informal sector; and the "feminization" of government employment.

Papers have been revised and edited for inclusion in this volume.

Heba Handoussa
Zafiris Tzannatos

August 2001

1

Matching Education to Demand for Labor in the MENA Region

Victor Billeh

Context

Never before in the history of mankind have all countries and regions been so globally threatened by forces of change as now, when we are transiting to the twenty-first century. These forces are generated with good intentions, but like the cyber-nation of science fiction, have grown beyond the control of their creators. Under the onslaught of such formidable global forces, individual nations and groups of countries allied into regions have to formulate their national and regional strategies to meet the challenges posed by the forces of change. In such cases, an ancient Chinese proverb says: *"When the winds of change blow, some build walls, others build windmills."*

In the current situation of rapidly expanding globalization and prevailing social, economic, and political conditions in the MENA region, the opinions of the pundits seem to converge on the strategy of building windmills to harvest the benefits of the winds of change. There are voices, however, to caution us against the far-reaching consequences of globalization, such as disintegration of cultural and social values, a climate of insecurity, poverty, inequality, marginalism, pollution, and irreversible devastation of many delicate ecological balances (Carmeliau 1997; Ratinoff 1995).

In order to construct adequate, appropriate, and effective strategies to cope with the challenges posed by the winds of change, it is imperative to analyze and understand the various dimensions of globalization which include: deregula-tion, liberalization, privatization, and structural adjustments. The national economies that are not accustomed to brisk structural adjustments are caught unaware in the whirlpool generated by the rapidly increasing speed of global-ization.

Dramatic developments in information and communication technologies have revolutionized the decision-making process. On the other hand, innovations in production technologies have been introducing spectacular changes in the pro-duction processes. National economies are finding difficulties in adjusting to the new requirements of the world economy and global trade, especially with respect to product specialization, quality standards, competitiveness, and macroeconom-ic shifts. Structural changes have adversely affected the labor force, resulting in increased unemployment, particularly of the educated and young work force, and thus highlighted the mismatch between the demand and supply sides of skilled labor.

With this backdrop, I will present first an overview of the current education and labor situation in the MENA region. Then I will discuss the need for struc-tural reform of education and training systems in general, illustrating my argu-ment by a detailed case study of one country as a typical example. This will be followed by situation analysis of education and training in the MENA region. The final section of the chapter presents the main goals and strategies needed to equip the MENA workers in a changing world.

Overview of the Education and Employment Situation in the MENA Region

Educational, Social, and Economic Situation
Despite some common features like the Arabic language and predominantly Islamic culture, MENA countries vary in many important dimensions. There is wide variation in the type and amount of natural resources. While more than half of the MENA countries have significant oil reserves, some countries, like Jordan, lack nearly all kinds of natural resources except potential human resources. There are wide differences in the levels of economic and social devel-opment. Also, there is a diversity of political systems and ethnic composition.

Different countries have adopted varying approaches and followed their own paths to development. Given the non-renewable nature of exhaustible oil and mineral resources and the variable nature of low returns from agricultural and other raw commodities, all countries in the region will have to rely, sooner or later, on harnessing their human resources for sustainable social and economic development.

Education

All countries recognize the importance of education in the sustainable social and economic development of a nation. Quality education and training is a key to raising economic productivity and social well-being. Sustainable development and competitive capacity largely depends upon building a broad base of flexible, educated, and technologically skilled workers equipped with marketable knowledge, skills, attitudes, and competencies.

Since the global economy is characterized by fast-changing technologies, innovative administration and management, and creative production methods, the modern labor force has to be prepared to embrace innovations and to be retrained on a continuous basis. Lifelong education and training, as well as multiple job changes and career shifts are going to be facts of life. During the past few decades general education systems have undergone fast expansion in the MENA countries. Access to education is almost universal, as provision of free public general education has been generally accepted as a canon of the social contract in almost all the MENA countries. In most countries education is publicly financed and centrally administered. This expansion of the education system carried out to provide universal access to basic education depleted the quality of its output and eroded its efficiency. Although the average per capita income is significantly higher than the average per capita income in the developing world, this was not translated into human development. Levels of human development in the Arab countries are generally lower than what would be expected given their per capita income.

Governments, however, have been spending a considerable portion of their national budgets on education and health. In 1996 MENA countries devoted 5.2% of their GNP to education. This was more than any other region in the developing world barring Eastern Europe and Central Asia. Even those countries that are implementing structural adjustment programs and are reducing public spending (e.g., Egypt and Tunisia) have increased their expenditures on education.

Despite considerable effort in this direction, misguided policies have resulted in misallocation and maldistribution of resources across the education sector. Public spending has been over-concentrated on higher education. For example, in Egypt, Jordan, and Kuwait, about one third of the education budget is spent on the tertiary level. Unit cost of tertiary education in the Arab states (at US$1588) is higher than in any other developing country. Relatively higher spending on tertiary education has been at the cost of broad-based expansion and quality of general education. Moreover, subsidies to higher education have proven inequitable because students in universities and colleges come typically from higher income groups.

As a result of such policies, education and training systems have become grossly discordant with the demands of the labor market. This phenomenon—prevalent to varying degrees in all the MENA countries—has created the dilemma of rising unemployment of young educated job seekers on the one hand, and, on the other, a shortage of workers needed for the technology-driven knowledge-based market economy and spiraling modern services employment sector.

Education policy analysts and labor economists commonly agree that rising unemployment among the educated first-time job seekers in the MENA region is a reflection of a mismatch, between an excessive supply of tertiary graduates in the conventional fields of study and the new knowledge, skill, and competency requirements of the globalizing economy.

The Need for Structural Reform of Education and Training Systems
Emphasizing the prospect of structural reform, to which matching education and training to labor market demands is the key, El-Naggar (1996) has aptly concluded that "[t]here is still a long way to go before we achieve the levels of productivity and competitiveness required … economic reform has become an absolute necessity for transforming an unsustainable situation into a sustainable one." Structural economic reform implies the demand for new types of knowledge, skills, and expertise in the transition stage and post-structural stage entirely different from what the labor forces presently possess. This scenario evidently and emphatically calls for reform of the education and Vocational Education and Training (VET) systems in the MENA countries. If no such reform of education and training is undertaken, the labor market will be unable to cope with the emerging modes of production and styles of management and administration.

An alternative strategy that the production sector may employ would be to substitute capital for labor by employing capital-intensive hypertechnologies. The consequences of such a policy are evident: higher rates of unemployment and increasing poverty, which could lead to social unrest.

Therefore, there is no viable alternative *to preparing and equipping the labor force* to effectively deal with the challenges of structural changes and globalization. In this regard, top priority should be given to mobilization of human resources and developing the potential by providing access and incentives to state-of-the-art general education integrated with pertinent VET, and relevant higher education.

Problems of Education and Labor in the MENA Region
A number of independent studies of the conditions of the labor and education/training situations in the MENA countries have reached the following general conclusions.

- There is a chronic problem of unemployment and underemployment in the MENA region.
- Unemployment is more acute in the educated, young, first-time job-seekers, the unskilled, and the poor.
- Unemployment among youth is higher than average.
- Unemployment is inversely related to level of education, it tends to be lower among illiterates and those with primary education, and higher among those with intermediate and secondary education.
- There is a lack of labor mobility.
- There is heavy reliance on the public sector.
- The quality of education is generally poor.
- Education and training are traditional, and have lost touch with the knowledge and skill requirements of the changing world of work.
- There are limited linkages and dialogue between employers and producers of the work force (education professionals).
- There is a lack of guidance and counseling in education and training.
- There are limited opportunities for retraining, skills-upgrading and life-long education.
- The education system has encouraged rote learning and cramming of irrelevant facts at the cost of developing critical thinking, problem solving, and creative application of integrated knowledge and experience to solve real-life problems.

Infrastructure for Education and Training

Institutionalized infrastructure of education and training exists in all the MENA countries. The education and VET systems of different countries vary considerably in terms of quality, efficiency, effectiveness, and relevance to societal needs.

In the face of challenges posed by globalization, openness, free trade, privatization, and structural adjustment of the economy, education and training systems need to be reviewed and appropriately restructured in order to make them responsive to the changing skill needs of knowledge-driven competitive labor markets. In order to better understand the proposed strategies for reforming and restructuring the education and training systems, I have found it necessary and useful to take a case study of one country—Jordan—whose infrastructure and problems associated with it are more or less typical of several other countries in the region. This case study will be followed by a general analysis of the problems of education and training in the MENA region.

Box 1

Jordanian Reform: A Case Study

This section presents a brief overview of Jordan's Vocational Education and Training (VET) system as a typical case. It examines its weaknesses, which are to some extent shared by many countries in the region, and outlines its reform endeavor, highlighting the key components. VET is provided by three different public organizations with an increasing number of private community colleges and training centers. The Ministry of Education provides vocational education and training in its comprehensive, multi-purpose and specialized vocational schools. The Vocational Training Corporation provides applied secondary vocational training in its training centers. At the post-secondary level, both public and private community colleges under the supervision of the Council of Higher Education, provide various types of vocational education and training.

The Institutional Setting
Jordan has achieved a relatively strong system of VET. Institutional coverage is widespread and facilities are typically of good quality. Staff are well educated and dedicated.

The Ministry of Education has a good tradition of academic teaching with broad-based education and tends to recruit more capable students than in "applied" vocational training. It has a large network of institutions, including comprehensive schools, multipurpose and specialized vocational training schools.

The Vocational Training Corporation (VTC) is unusual in the developing world in its apprenticeship system and use of modular training. The VTC has a solid organization dedicated to training with a long (twenty-year) tradition in industrial training

The Community College System, by offering some practical subjects in short (two-year) programs, tends to alleviate pressure for enrollments in longer and more expensive study programs at the universities, thereby saving on public expenditures. The technical fields in community colleges apparently have a strong employment demand for those who complete its programs. There is a broad range of practical and academic subjects offered, some 95 specializations. There is a tradition of accreditation and comprehensive national examinations for graduates which can enhance achievement of quality standards and provide information on system performance. The existence of private community colleges offers advantages in terms of their relatively close attention to labor market needs, quality training and incentives for efficient use of resources, and reduction in the burden on public finances.

Mismatch Maladies
The foregoing suggests that the basic elements exist for high-quality training. However, despite the strengths, the system outlined above does not appear to be efficient in using available staff or physical resources. Equally important, the system lacks adequate information on employment demands. Little or no attempt is made to deduce the training directions and implications from overall economic strategies and policies. Informal coordination exists, but the functions of the system tend to overlap. Formal coordination, with the authority to direct

the development of various parts of the system, does not exist. Management tends to be overly centralized; insufficient initiative is allowed for the managers of individual institutions. The articulation between the parts of the system is inadequate. Students lack possibilities for vertical and horizontal mobility while employer partnership is basically lacking. I return to these issues after an examination of the labor market that provides the acid test for human resources development policies.

Unemployment

While there are differences in the incidence of unemployment by level of educational attainment, and the unemployment rates of the more educated have shown some tendency to decline over time (see Table 1.1), these differences are not pronounced and seem to depend on the year of estimation. Unemployment has been and still is particularly acute among first-time job-seekers who are relatively well educated.

Table 1.1 Unemployment Rates by Education Level

Education Level	1987	1996
Illiterate	1	5
Read and Write	13	10
Primary	16	13
Preparatory	15	13
Secondary	16	13
Diploma (CC)	22	20
Bachelor's	14	12
MA/PhD	9	6
All (Average)	8	13

Source: Department of Statistics *Survey of Health, Nutrition and Manpower*

Linkages Between Public Training Providers and Industry

Linkages between public training and vocational education are weak. This is partly explained by the fact that almost half of private employment consists of foreign, guest workers, while Jordanian citizens have a relatively sufficient level of general education and high unemployment rates. Thus, on the demand side, firms enjoy "outside opportunities," that is, they can with relative ease recruit locals for the more skilled jobs and foreigners for the unskilled ones. On the supply side, public institutions are not under great pressure to accommodate employers, given the relative availability of public funds for human resources development, and the willingness of Jordanian youth to enroll in whatever is available and publicly subsidized.

Jordan is a labor surplus economy, as the economy and labor market have been unable to create jobs at the speed required to absorb the increase in the labor force due to high population growth. To a significant extent, the high educational attainment of Jordanians and the employment opportunities in neighboring countries acts as a buffer for the surplus labor and puts little pressure to adopt labor-intensive policies in the past. The public sector has been a high-cost employer with spillover effects on the private sector. Capital intensity has been unduly high. Immigration policy has been laissez faire.

Education and Training Issues

Though in aggregate the supply of human capital is relatively abundant, and Jordan "exports" workers to neighboring countries, each of the three main actors in VET face some serious problems that impede the overall system in terms of relevance to market economy requirements, efficacy (the degree to which objectives are met), management effectiveness, quality of training, and efficiency in the use of resources.

Ministry of Education

Relevance

The vocational education and training schools of the MoE tend not to be well linked with business, industry, and labor market demand. Some inertia is evident in adjusting teaching content to conform with local business practices. For example:

- Plumbing instruction uses cast iron pipe, while most plumbing firms use plastic PVC pipe;
- Computer courses teach programming, whereas the vast majority of demand is for training in applications (databases);
- TV repair includes black and white televisions, while virtually all sets delivered for repair are now color sets.

Follow-up

Moreover, schools do little systematic follow-up on graduates. There is little or no help given to students in job counseling and placement. Lack of knowledge of what graduates do reduces the effectiveness of the activities of the MoE. Its institutions tend to operate in an environment which values academic achievement and undervalues vocational training. The directorate responsible for VET must report to a Directorate General in charge of all academic matters. Thus, VET managers operate inside a MoE where they are unable to impose the priorities of trade training vis-à-vis the predominant rules of academic education. The low esteem of VET is reinforced by compelling about half the students to enter vocational schooling against their wishes.

Quality

In terms of quality, students in the MoE program tend to receive little reinforcement of the vocational content from the academic programs. For example, mathematics is a diluted version of academic mathematics rather than applied to the occupations being taught. Instrumental mathematics, e.g. teaching of examples from occupational programs, is not used. The quality of instruction in some industrial trades is poor. The main reason is the lack of practical training and industrial work experience among the instructors. Little or no use is made of specialized crafts people on a part-time basis for instructional purposes.

Internal Efficiency

Efficiency is low, as evidenced by the high dropout rates for apprentices (20% in the first year in some places), which is largely traced to low levels of student interest. This contributes to small class sizes and under-utilization of staff and workshop facilities. In general, the available facilities could handle substantially more trainees without significant additional costs.

Vocational Training Corporation (VTC)

The VTC have employer councils for each institution but these rarely function regularly or effectively as intended. Problems exist in several other areas that affect relevance. Students tend to specialize relatively quickly upon entry into training centers and, as a result, they lack broad-based general training. This contributes to some lack of flexibility among graduates. The VTC is constrained in increasing its intake of students by several factors:

- The number of enterprises willing to accept apprentices (this is mainly because of the limited size of Jordanian industry);
- The VTC does not have enough staff for developing an apprenticeship placement program;
- Low interest in vocational training (especially females).

The VTC suffers from a lack of capacity to provide training for some target groups and in some areas of the country, e.g., for females and in the south. There are social pressures on VTC to open new facilities in areas without employment prospects.

Effectiveness
Effectiveness is adversely affected by weak standards of training in several industrial fields. A good training ethos and environment is lacking. Tolerance of mediocre quality by enterprises accounts for much of the lack of incentive to provide quality craftsmanship. Another major factor is the lack of practical technical expertise by instructors. They often tend to be undemanding and satisfied with low levels of workmanship by students. In addition there are localized problems of equipment shortages, or resources either inadequate for instructional purposes or in disrepair. All of these factors reduce the quality of instruction. Supervision of trainees in apprenticeship programs is also reportedly inadequate.

Community Colleges/Technical Post-Secondary Institutes
The largest lack of relevance of the course offered by the three agencies is found in community colleges that tend to be unconnected with enterprises. As a consequence, the content of programs is sometimes not well linked with the actual needs of employers. The system is not addressed to the local labor market, but rather serves national programs. Owing to central financing and control, the community colleges are not particularly responsive to the needs and requirements of the communities in which they are located. Another reflection of lack of flexibility is the length of training (two years) where shorter programs would be more appropriate, and the narrow specializations offered, which add up to about 95 specializations. The recent precipitous decline in enrollment suggests problems in the availability of jobs for this level of education, idle capacity and unemployment of graduates in general fields.

An overriding issue is the lack of clear purpose and mandate, hence effectiveness, of the community colleges. In all, community colleges have serious problems in the quality of practical instruction offered in workshops. These stem in part from a lack of clear conception of technician training. There is a shortage of craftsmanship in institutions. Teaching is dominated by academically trained instructors. There is little, if any, use of part-time instructors with industrial experience and existing teaching staff have few opportunities for upgrading. There are difficulties in placing students in meaningful internships.

Situation Analysis of Education and Training in the MENA Region

Following this detailed analysis of the case of Jordan, I will now attempt to provide an overview of the generalized situation analysis of education and training in the MENA region. Despite the fact that the region is vast and diverse in many ways, most countries in it share similar problems. These problems, however, do not all exist in every country or in every institution in each country. There are exceptions and bright spots here and there, but the general scene is outlined below.

Enrollment Rates in Education
MENA countries achieved significant progress in the last two decades where enrollment rates doubled. General education has undergone rapid expansion and most MENA countries have nearly achieved the goal of universal primary enrollment. Secondary enrollments have also increased significantly, but there is much room for further improvement. The number of out-of-school children (nearly eleven million) is expected to grow by more than 40% in coming years, with larger shares of girls and rural poor.

Average gross enrollment in secondary education is less than 60%, compared with 100% in industrialized countries. Average gross enrollment in tertiary education ranges from 9% to 35%, compared with 60% in industrialized countries.

High rates of illiteracy are still dominant features in several countries in the region, especially those with relatively large populations. (The total number of illiterates in Arab countries alone amounts to 68 million, according to 1999 estimates).

Poor Quality and Low Efficiency
In general, the quality of education and student achievement levels are low. With rapid quantitative expansion of the education system the quality of teaching and learning and, in turn, the quality of school output declined. Curricula and textbooks, instructional methods and materials are generally outdated. Vocational and technical programs generally offer narrow specializations. This phenomenon leads to increased unemployment. Furthermore, high dropout and repetition rates add to the inefficiencies of the system.

Low Participation of the Private Sector
Almost all systems of education and training in the region are centralized, and rigid, and ministries of education, technical, and vocational education, and

higher education are the major providers of education and training services. The regional/local authorities have limited control, and the private sector has a marginal role and input in the training process. Moreover, lack of facilitatory, legal, statutory, and accreditation regulations and frameworks hinder the participation of the private sector in education, particularly in post-compulsory, intermediate, and university education. Moreover, programs almost invariably are of fixed length (e.g., two years in technical institutions). Short courses are limited.

Low Social Prestige of Vocational Training Programs and Absence of Career Guidance Counseling
Generally, the students who dropped out of the general education system for academic reasons join vocational training programs. Such trainers generally lack basic learning skills. Those who complete the vocational training are often ill prepared to meet the knowledge and skills requirements of the modern labor markets and swell the ranks of the unemployed. Moreover, students and trainees do not have clear ideas about the future prospects of vocational programs offered by public and private training centers.

Absence of Comprehensive National VET Strategies
In most MENA countries vocational training systems are sprawling, without coherent or comprehensive national strategies. Training systems are expanding without consideration for labor market needs analysis. In many countries vocational training systems offer large numbers of different specializations with little or no relevance to the requirements of the job market. Moreover, course materials, methods of training, and tools and equipment used for training are often outdated and no longer used in industry. There are not reliable methods of standard practices to assess and evaluate the standard, quality, and relevance of the training courses, programs, and product.

Supply-Driven Rather than Demand-Driven Training Programs Do Not Correspond to Realities of the Modern Labor Market
In public-funded vocational/technical education and training systems, curricula are often traditional, outdated, and outmoded. Programs and courses have a tendency to be offered year after year without review, revision, or evaluation of their quality or relevance.

Absence of Accreditation Standards, and Quality-Control Systems
There is a nearly total absence of authentic accreditation systems for testing of knowledge, skills, and competencies related to different types of jobs.

Labor Market Information System (LMIS) and Manpower Requirement Forecasting
In the absence of LMIS, vocational training institutions produce workers for occupations in which there are no job openings.

Higher Education Still Follows its 'Ivory-Tower' Traditions, Unconcerned with the Real World of Work
Higher education in almost all the MENA countries has expanded quickly, enjoying a disproportionately large share of resources, and has been biased in favor of socioeconomically more privileged groups and urban communities. Returns from higher education are low. Universities have not fulfilled their promise of research and development. Unemployment among university graduates is high and relatively higher among female graduates. Programs are overly theoretical and unrelated to modern technological developments and the changing requirements of industry, trade, and the economy. There are limited links between universities and industry and other sectors of the economy. Within the universities, various disciplines of study work in isolation from each other and follow narrow specializations. There is a general shortage, if not total absence, of applied technology programs and interdisciplinary and multidisciplinary programs of study. Moreover, there is no coordination between universities, community colleges, technical vocational education and training, and general education systems.

Relatively Higher Percentage of GDP Allocation to Education
Most MENA countries consistently allocate a large share of their GDP to education, but investment and current expenditures are neither used efficiently nor wisely. On the one hand, distribution of resources to different levels and types of education is distorted, and has generally resulted in low returns and increasing unemployment of educated young people. At the same time, a bureaucratic administration governed by archaic civil-service regulations of hiring, promotion, and termination of employees, has eroded the efficiency, cost-effectiveness, and overall quality of the education system and its product (the graduates). In general, about 90% of the education budget is spent on staff salaries.

In brief, one concludes that the general paradigm for a typical MENA education and training system is characterized as state-dominated, centralized, rigid, and supply-driven, in which education and training are separated, policy and delivery are combined, and the focus is on institutional training rather than workplace learning.

Table 1.2. Total Education Expenditure as Percentage of
GDP in Selected MENA Countries, 1993–95

	Fiscal Year		
Country	*1993*	*1994*	*1995*
Algeria	7.0	7.0	7.0
Egypt	4.5	5.1	4.7
Iran	5.3	4.5	4.5
Jordan	4.1	3.7	6.0
Morocco	5.9	5.4	5.5
Tunisia	6.1	6.2	6.5
Yemen	6.2	6.4	5.1

Sources: *WDI*, 1998; *UNESCO Statistical Yearbook 1997.*

How to Equip Workers in the MENA Region in a Changing World: The Search for a New Paradigm

Effective broad-based education integrated with appropriate skills training is the key to enabling and empowering workers in the MENA region to cope with the challenges of the rapidly changing world. The challenge is posed not so much by change as by the unprecedented acceleration of the change. Speed has never been at a high premium in the MENA countries, but now the whole region seems to have no choice but to quickly adapt to the climate of globalization and the technology-driven open economy.

There is no uncertainty about the pressing need for equipping the work force of MENA countries with the necessary knowledge, skills, competencies, and strategies to cope with rapidly occurring changes not only in the world of work, but in their lifestyles as well. The question is "how"?

Effective and easily implemented strategies must be grounded in the contextual realities of each country and the region in general.

Restructuring and reformulation of the education and training system is the call of the day throughout the region. Some countries like Egypt, Jordan, Morocco, Algeria and Tunisia have already embarked upon structural reform. Many others are engaged in reforming their education and training systems. Egypt, Jordan, Morocco, Qatar, Tunisia and United Arab Emirates have joined the World Trade Organization, and others are expected in the near future.

Radical structural reform of education and vocational training systems is imperative for the MENA region. Matching education and training with the needs of the labor markets is a dire necessity. This is perhaps the only measure that might be able to correct existing policy distortions, structural imbalances, and growing unemployment, while preparing the region for the increasingly knowledge-based cyber-economy of the twenty-first century.

Comprehensive structural reform of education and the VET system should address all the issues listed in the foregoing section. The aim of the reform is to improve the quality, efficiency, and pertinence of the education and training systems. Pertinence here refers to alignment of education and vocational training with the requirements of the labor market.

In any society undergoing structural reform, close coordination between education and training is extremely important. The basic education system should not only incorporate pre-vocational education, but it must also lay a solid broad-based foundation for diversified generic vocational skills rather than narrow job specialization.

Therefore, the new paradigm for the MENA Education and Training System which is sought should be characterized by the following features:

(a) participatory governance with the private sector taking an active role;
(b) decentralization with flexibility for multiple entry/exit points;
(c) policy formulation and delivery separated with more delivery at local levels with private sector participation and training in the workplace;
(d) multi-skill training to replace narrow specializations; and
(e) lifelong learning and vocational training.

Developing a Comprehensive Policy Framework

Most MENA countries have well-defined goals of education and training, and some have reviewed and redefined their goals in light of the twenty-first century challenges to education. Some countries have started to establish national policies on education and training. Without sound policy frameworks, priorities have a tendency to shift while goals of education remain the same. Policy frameworks anchored in goals generally protect the education system from major policy shifts occurring due to different orientations of individual policy makers. Therefore, strategic policy frameworks should be grounded in long-term goals, objective-driven, interlinked with macroeconomic policies, realistic and fully owned by the country.

Goals and Strategies
The following section presents a new vision of a desired VET system for the MENA region, in terms of two broad goals and strategies for achieving these goals.

Goal I: Improve the quality of the system graduates and adjust their knowledge, skills, attitudes, and competencies to accommodate the requirements of changing labor markets and globalization.

The achievement of this goal can be realized through the following strategies:

- Establish and maintain world-class standards of quality by setting high expectations for instruction and rigorous requirements for graduation.
- Ensure that programs, curricula, facilities, equipment, and instruction are modern, effective, and appropriate.
- Ensure that VET graduates are employable, self-reliant members of society equipped with knowledge, practical skills and attitudes, and the communication skills required for lifelong education and training:
    (a) Learn how to be flexible;
    (b) Learn how to adjust to changing requirements;
    (c) Learn how to adapt to changing work conditions and environments; and
    (d) Learn how to acquire new skills.
- Establish *meaningful linkages* with business, trade, industry, and the service sector in order to continuously adapt the pertinence and relevance of the program's content, knowledge, skills, attitudes, and competencies to fit the needs of the market economy and a globalizing society.
- Strengthen links between schools and industry. The development of human resources is not the responsibility of VET alone. The general education system, tertiary education, and universities—including the private sector, industry, trade, and commerce—are all involved. However, there is a strong need to forge policies and plans of action for their participation as active partners in equipping the work force to meet the growing challenges of globalization.

    The general basic education curricula should be revised to emphasize broader basic education skills, skill training, and core competencies rather than specialized education.

    Secondary education should provide more diversified education and wider selection. This can enable students to satisfy requirements of further education while at the same time acquiring professional knowledge and skills to enter the world of work.

    Preparation for the transition from school to work should be gradual and smooth. It should start from primary cycle. Learning incorporates efforts in educational improvement integrated with skills and attitudes related to the world of work and economic development.

- Equip workers with flexibility and adaptability to changing jobs. With rapidly changing production technologies, work conditions, and administration and management systems, knowledge and skills become outdated and obsolete within a few years. Workers have to change jobs or learn new methods of doing the same job. To be able to adjust to changing conditions workers must have access to resources and information without losing their accrued experience and capabilities in the process of re-adjustment and relocation. Their situation demands the availability of specifically designed, effective short-term retraining programs, for well defined target groups, geared to improve the employability, job prospects, and/or earnings of the participants.
- Lifelong Learning and Training for All. This was one of the themes of the Second International Congress on Technical and Vocational Education held in Seoul on August 26–30, 1999. The congress emphasized the need for the development and improvement of education and training systems that provide for lifelong learning and training.

The conference recommended the adoption of a holistic approach that transcends the boundaries compartmentalizing education and training into categories such as academic vs. vocational, theoretical vs. applied, and intellectual vs. manual. Effective collaboration and partnerships are needed between education and training systems, in addition to linkages between industrial and other sectors of the economy.

Lifelong education and training involve continuously upgrading the skills and competencies of workers, particularly of the unskilled, through on-the-job teaching of technical know-how, as well as in-service training and re-training in order to build flexibility in skills needed for mobility.

- Enterprise Training. Enterprise training based upon a solid foundation of general education is needed in order to enhance the quality and efficiency of production and maintenance. Enterprises function in the marketplace and can be quick to adapt to the new production technologies. Employers can train workers very quickly by providing hands-on training, and then put them to work immediately. Therefore, it is more cost-effective and efficient. Enterprises, particularly those that invested in high technology, require continuous updating of skills and knowledge for which formal schools are inadequately equipped. Enterprises should be encouraged to become places of learning as well as places of work.

Under the influence of expanding globalization, liberalization and privatization are becoming the instruments of structural adjustment programs in many MENA countries. Under structural adjustment programs the role of the public sector as the largest employer is shrinking. Vocational Education and Training systems are called upon to incorporate entrepreneurship education and training into VET and educational policy goals at all levels. There is a dire need to integrate these programs into pre-vocational and vocational education and training. Entrepreneurship education and training programs should focus on the key competencies required for initiatives in establishing sustainable small- and medium-sized enterprises. These programs should target women and youth. The training should cover all aspects of small- and medium-sized business development and maintenance—managerial, legal, fiscal, marketing, and accounting. The goal is to encourage some of the trainees to be job creators rather than job hunters.

Goal II: Improve the efficiency and effectiveness of the VET system.

The achievement of this goal can be realized through the following strategies:

- Establish *clear mandates* for all agencies involved in VET, and for each VET institution.
- Create a *seamless* system by removing the age barriers for adult entry into VET, and develop an education and training ladder on which adults may progress according to their knowledge, skills, and performance.
- Establish competency-based equivalency and requirements for entry into all VET programs.
- Establish a *council on admissions and transfers* to develop course and program equivalencies that allow for transfers between institutions and subsystems.
- Establish policies to permit VET institutions to offer short-term bridging and upgrading programs and courses, to levy fees, and to retain these fees as revenues to re-invest in the institutions.
- Establish a management information system and a system for vocational guidance and services.
- Establish and institutionalize accreditation and certification systems and a regulatory framework. Accreditation and certification of knowledge and competency levels in various occupations on the basis of reliable, valid and credible assessment procedures and standards are requirements for mobility and flexibility of workers, as well as for flexibility and responsiveness of education and training programs needed to meet the challenges of an expanding global economy and competitive free trade.

Establishment of such standardized systems would facilitate immensely the mobility of labor across levels, occupations, sub-regions, and regions. Moreover, it would facilitate the assessment and comparison of certificates and qualifications awarded by different institutions for different programs of training. In addition, these systems would help enforce standards for such courses and training programs, and would inform the selection, recruitment, and promotion decisions of the employers and managers.

- Ensure public participation in education, training, and accreditation systems. Traditional government control policies and labor market mechanisms were unable to create the desired knowledge, skills, attitudes, and behavioral changes essential for adaptability to labor market demands and sustainable development.

  Social participation in education and training decision-making should include all actors and sectors of production—labor, education, the formal and informal economies, as well as public and private sectors.

- Establish and operationalize comprehensive and efficient Labor Management Information Systems to supply much-needed, timely information about labor market forecasts and changing skill requirements to the VET system and to the incumbent labor force, in order to enable them to match education and training with the demands of the market.

  At present, there are almost no Labor Management Information Systems in the MENA countries to supply timely, relevant, and reliable labor market information to all the concerned stakeholders—the planners and managers of VET on one side, and the employers, industry, trade, social services, and the public sector on the other.

  Establishment of integrated, efficient, and effective Labor Market Information Systems interfaced with VET and Education Management Information Systems is a necessary prerequisite to matching VET with the changing needs and skill requirements of the modern labor markets of increasingly knowledge-driven economies.

- Establish vocational guidance and counseling centers for trainees, and job placement services. Information about expected trends in labor markets, short-term and long-term job prospects, expected earnings in various occupations, and assessment of the training potential of individual candidates—in conjunction with the right guidance—is the key to making good choices of training programs and vocational careers. Information about training, upgrading opportunities, and career advancement training, are equally important for those seeking employment, re-employment, a career change, or advancement. The provision of such ancillary but vital services, as well as access to easily understandable information, is essential to enabling workers to cope with the requirements of changing employment conditions in the globalizing economies of the region.

References

Comeliau, Christian. March 1997. "The challenges of globalization." *Prospects* 27 (1). Paris.

Economic Research Forum for the Arab Countries, Iran, and Turkey. 1998. *Economic Trends in the MENA Region 1998.*

El-Naggar, S. January 1996. Opening remarks in a seminar on the social effect of economic adjustment on Arab countries.

ESCWA. 1999. "Labor Markets in the ESCWA Region During the Past Twenty-Five Years." Unpublished paper.

ESCWA. 1999. *Social Impact of Restructuring with Special Reference to Employment.*

Fergany, Nader. 1998a. *The Challenge of Full Employment in Arab Countries.*

Haddad, Wadi D. March 1997. "Globalization of the Economy: The Implication for Education and Skill Formation." *Prospects* 27 (1). Paris.

Ratinoff, Luis. June 1995. "Global Insecurity and Education: The Culture of Globalization." *Prospects* 25 (2): 147–74.

The World Bank. 1995. *Regional Perspectives on World Development Report 1995. Will Arab Workers Prosper or Be Left out in the Twenty-First Century?*

The World Bank. 1999. Education Sector Strategy. Washington, DC: The World Bank Group, The Human Devlopment Network.

Tzannatos, Zafiris, and Victor Billeh. 1997. *Vocational Education and Training in Jordan. Performance, Issues and Prospects.*

UNDP. November 1999. "Human Development and Poverty in the Arab Region." Draft.

UNESCO. 1998. *World Conference on Higher Education : Higher Education in The Twenty-First Century: Vision and Action.* Paris.

UNESCO. 1999. *Second International Congress on Technical and Vocational Education Final Report.* Paris.

2

Government Employment and Active Labor Market Policies in MENA in a Comparative International Context

Alan Abrahart[*]
Iqbal Kaur[†]
Zafiris Tzannatos[†]

Introduction

Countries in the Middle East and North Africa (MENA) are engaging in economic adjustment with a view to creating an efficient public sector and a dynamic private economy. But adjustment creates political economy considerations as it results in winners and losers, and a major challenge which policy makers face is how to bring the size and performance of the public sector to levels commensurate with the broader objectives of achieving economic growth and integration into the world economy. Ideally, they aim to achieve this goal with minimal dislocation in the social sectors. Addressing the effects of job losses among public sector employees, both in central government and in parastatals, becomes a critical issue. This chapter reviews issues of the public sector in the region, paying particular attention to its size and wage levels. It then examines the experience of OECD and East European countries with active labor market programs during periods of adjustment, and compares them to MENA countries, showing (in graphical form) demographic and labor force

[*] Former State Director of the Department of Employment, Education and Training, Australia; † World Bank. The chapter and its findings, interpretations, and conclusions should not be attributed in any manner to the World Bank, to its affiliated organizations, or to the members of its Board of Executive Directors or the countries they represent.

data for more than 40 countries. This comparison is a valid one as MENA has similar characteristics with these two groups of countries, that is, an initially large public sector and sizeable government involvement in the area of social protection in general, and labor markets in particular. This chapter includes options for efficient adjustment of the public sector and the role active labor market policies can play in the region for providing transitory relief to affected workers, while equipping them for future employment in the private sector.

The Two Phases of Public Sector Employment

Phase I: Growth
The MENA region entered the 1990s with a high share of government employment in the labor force, high wages, and extensive involvement of the state in economic production. The rise in government employment was initially associated with significant increases in social services (education, health, social protection) and great improvement in social indicators. Living standards and health status in the region have improved significantly in the past 30 years, and the MENA region has now the lowest poverty rates in the developing world. Universal enrollment in basic education is within reach in MENA and, though child labor exists, it lacks the scale and general conditions found elsewhere. By 1995, except in Yemen and Morocco, over 90% of the population had access to health services. Mortality and morbidity rates have declined substantially.

Following the drop in oil prices and low, even negative, economic growth rates, public sector employment started creating "deficit-financed" jobs to absorb the excess supply of labor, thereby acting as a welfare program for those who could be absorbed into the private sector. The role of government in economic production (through parastatals) became significant, and MENA now stands out in world statistics.

First, the share of civilian government employment worldwide accounts for about 11% of total employment, but for MENA countries it stands at 17.5%. This figure is much lower for other developing regions: 9% for LAC, 7% for Africa, and 6% for Asia. Only in Morocco and Lebanon is this share lower than the world average (Table 2.1). Among developing regions, central administration is also largest in the Middle East and North Africa.

Second, also in the early 1990s, the share of the government wage bill to GDP was the highest in MENA, averaging almost 10%—compared to a worldwide average of less than half that figure. Public sector wages in MENA are significantly higher than private sector wages (Table 2.2).

Third, the share of public enterprises in economic production was high (Figure 2.1). While it is generally below 10% for middle-income economies, it

Table 2.1. Public Sector Employment
(% of total employment)

| | General Civilian Government Employment | | | | | |
| | Government Administration | | Social Sectors | | Total | |
	Central Government	Non Central Government	Education	Health	General Civilian Government	Armed Forces
Algeria	8.7	4.9	7.5	3.8	24.8	2.7
Bahrain	5.9	0.0	4.0	2.6	12.5	n.a.
Egypt	**7.2**	**11.1**	**3.8**	**3.0**	**25.8**	**3.1**
Jordan	3.3	3.3	6.5	2.0	15.2	10.3
Lebanon	1.1	1.6	5.0	0.5	8.1	6.9
Morocco	2.9	1.7	3.2	0.5	8.3	2.7
Syria	4.2	1.2	7.1	1.1	13.7	n.a.
Tunisia	5.2	0.9	5.4	1.9	13.5	1.5
WB–Gaza	16.6	n.a.	7.6	2.0	16.6	n.a.
Yemen	14.5	4.4	1.9	1.3	22.1	1.9
Average	6.6	3.9	5.1	1.9	17.5	3.2

Source: Salvatore Schiavo-Campo, Guilio de Tommaso, and Amitabha Mukherjee. 1997. *An International Survey of Government Employment and Wages.* Policy Research Working Paper No. 1806. The World Bank.

Table 2.2. Central Government Wages, Early 1990s

Region	Central Government Wages and Salaries as % of GDP	Average Central Ratio of Government Wage as Multiple of per capita GDP	Public as Private Sector wages
AFRICA	6.7	5.7	1.0
ASIA	4.7	3.0	0.8
ECA	3.7	1.3	0.7
LAC	4.9	2.5	0.9
MENA	**9.8**	**3.4**	**1.3**
OECD	4.5	1.6	0.9
World Average	5.4	3.0	0.8

Source: Salvatore Schiavo-Campo, Guilio de Tommaso, and Amitabha Mukherjee. 1997. *An International Survey of Government Employment and Wages.* Policy Research Working Paper No. 1806. The World Bank.

reached high levels in MENA—such as more than 30% in Egypt and Tunisia, and nearly 60% in Algeria. Combining government employment and employment in public enterprises brings the share of employment in the broader public sector among wage employees to as much as 35% in Egypt, 50% in Jordan, and almost 60% in Algeria.

Figure 2.1. The Share of Public Enterprises in Economic Activity*

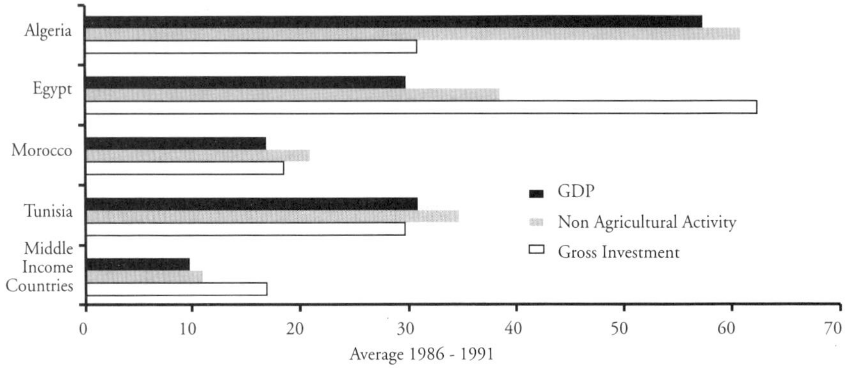

Source: Anderson and Martinez 1995

In short, the region reached the end of the twentieth century with:

• A sizeable and rigid public sector, a marginalized—rather than leading—private sector, and economies relatively isolated from global trade.
  Following the decline in the price of oil, investment and growth rates collapsed, as did regional capital and labor markets. Over the last 30 years, growth of economy-wide productivity, or Total Factor Productivity (TFP), declined while population growth has remained high. Declining productivity, high population growth, and falling oil prices contributed to an average regional decline in real per capita incomes of 2% per year since 1986, the largest decline in any developing region during this period. In some oil-exporting countries the decline was more than 4% per year.
• Labor market characteristics which have been shaped by the macroeconomic and trade policies implemented during the oil boom, which are now out of tune with economic reality.
  Expansion of the public sector has been partly fueled by an expansion of the activities of state-owned enterprises (SOEs), while public administration has played a substitute role for "social protection" through over-recruitment. These rigid institutional structures have led to a rather inflexible response to labor market pressures.

_____

* All subsequent figures appear at the end of the chapter.

- High urban unemployment, which is still rising in many MENA countries.
  The incidence of unemployment in countries with major labor market imbalances, such as Egypt and Morocco, seems to be worsening more quickly among older workers, thus shifting the center of the problem away from one of unemployed dependents towards one of unemployed household heads. Rising unemployment among the less-educated, as seen in Algeria and Morocco, is also of great concern, particularly from a poverty perspective.

Phase II: Rationalization
Though the onset of the new millennium provides a picture not drastically different in terms of basic magnitudes than the one outlined above, this picture also masks significant underlying changes. These changes are being induced by an evolving role of the state and its associated reforms. A series of adjustment and liberalization programs have been introduced which aim to enhance the efficiency of the economy by creating an environment for market mechanisms to work more properly, and to facilitate the positioning of the economy in the context of globalization. Reforms are gathering momentum despite a slow start in the early 1990s.

During the early 1990s privatization proceeds were creating negligible amounts of public revenue (e.g., less than US$25 million before 1992), but this had reached more than US$2 billion towards the end of the decade. Tunisia has been the regional pioneer in this area and Algeria, despite its stop-go record with privatization, has effectively sold or liquidated almost one-third of its public enterprises, and the government is expected to put another half of the remaining ones up for privatization. Significant changes are also underway in Morocco, Yemen, Jordan, Egypt, and Lebanon.

All this creates efficiency gains in the economic sphere, but results also in social dislocation. The issue goes beyond the question of winners and losers and individual interests. It relates also to the fact that the high share of government employment in MENA is partly explained by the fact that due attention is paid in general to health, education, and social protection policies. The new role of the state therefore calls for an adjustment of broad government employment in a way that will provide some compensatory mechanisms in the short-run for those who lose their jobs. It also must create an environment that will enable faster labor absorption while preserving and developing human capital in the long run, through effective but fiscally affordable social policies.

Given the large size of government employment, efficient public sector downsizing requires a great number of labor redundancies. For example, in

Egypt the initial estimate for labor redundancies in public enterprises was around 10%, but in practice this figure proved to be closer to 35%. In Morocco, 23% of public enterprises had very small returns (lower than 5%), 36% made losses, and the fourteen largest public enterprises produced an annual average loss that reached more than 2% of GDP by 1992. In Algeria, more than 500,000 employees have been retrenched during 1990–98, and the pace of adjustment has accelerated recently. Still, the restructuring of the large public sector remains to be done despite the fact that the official unemployment rate has risen to 29%.

Any downsizing of this magnitude requires political consensus, as voluntary separations reflecting compensation for actually accrued rights could amount to several thousand dollars per worker. A single downsizing operation may therefore go beyond the ability of the economy to bear such costs, because the countries where public sector downsizing is most needed tend to be cash-strapped. It is in this context that multilateral agencies have increased their support towards mass retrenchment, often by modifying their rules to allow lending for severance pay—provided it is aimed at restructuring the public sector, allows to quickly reduce budget deficits, and severance pay is treated as investment and not recurrent expenditure.

The challenge of unemployment remains a significant one. Though increased labor-market flexibility facilitates the efficient deployment of labor and reduces unemployment in the longer run, unemployment remains high in most MENA countries—generally above 10%.

Most regional forecasts of unemployment indicate that it is likely to rise (and in some cases significantly). By some accounts, unemployment is not expected to start declining before 2010. This is only partly due to the underlying demographic transition. The key to enhanced labor absorption will be an increase in effective investment and in economic growth. In this respect the role of government is to ensure that, while the drive to increase efficiency through adjustment continues, employment programs are not over-designed (see "Active Labor Market Programs," below) and informal employment keeps expanding as it has generally done in the region in the recent past. For example, in Morocco, about half of all new employment has come from an expansion of the informal sector, and in Egypt the figure is even higher. Though little is known about the behavior of informal wages over time, it is likely that these have fallen as the formal sector became increasingly less able to absorb new labor-market entrants. For example, in Egypt, agricultural wages fell by almost half between 1982–95. Still, as long as opportunities for the expansion of the informal exist, this reduces unemployment and allows government budgets to be more effectively directed at measures targeted at the employed poor and those unable to work. This will also enable governments to continue playing its useful role in the areas of education, health, and social protection which have proven critical in raising social indicators fast and to commendable rates.

In addition to offering compensation to retrenched workers, other policies have been called upon to ease the cost of adjustment and enable the redeployment of affected workers. These policies, often lumped under the heading of active labor market policies (ALMPs), include the setup of counseling and placement services, training/retraining of displaced workers, support for entry into self-employment, public works, and wage subsidies. In some cases, as in Algeria, the introduction of ALMPs was accompanied by an unemployment-assistance scheme.

An alternative approach to public-enterprise restructuring is the Employee Shareholders Associations (ESAs), which were formed in Egypt to enable workers to buy stakes in their companies. This approach was expected to create an interest in the privatization program and also give incentives to improve productivity. Some empirical evidence suggests that this led to greater efficiency: in seven of the ten companies that were sold to ESAs. In 1994, profits improved by over 60% on average.

ALMPs and ESAs are not, however, panaceas for the problem of low employment-creation in the region. A survey of the evidence from more than 100 evaluations of ALMPs in OECD and developing countries showed that such policies can only marginally mitigate structural problems in the labor and product markets and the macroeconomy at large, while some, if inappropriately designed, can actually produce overall negative economic effects in terms of fiscal implications and deadweight loss (see "Active Labor Market Programs," below). Equally, ESAs are not necessarily the most effective form of privatization. For example, in the case of Hungary, the decision to privatize to strategic investors and to welcome foreigners has been largely successful, while privatization by sale to workers in some other transition economies had much less of an effect on corporate governance and company performance. A critical factor in deciding whether to liquidate, privatize, or go the ESAs route is the presence of investor interest in the companies under question.

In addition to the introduction of the aforementioned programs, governments in MENA have started reforming labor laws and regulations in areas such as job security, separation awards, and wage regulations (such as collective bargaining and minimum wages). For example, in Tunisia, the labor code was revised both in the early and also in the late 1990s. Measures have been taken to revise the representation of workers in the firm and conflict resolution procedures. The costs of individual firings have been fixed between one or two months of wage bill per year of service, with a maximum ceiling of 36 months of the wage bill. Lay-off procedures in labor legislation are simplified and their time frame is fixed—at a maximum of 33 days from the time a retrenchment request has been submitted to the inspectors of employment. Additional measures have been introduced, such as a distinction between abusive lay-offs and the maximum amount of fines to be paid upon breach of contract; fixed-term contracts for apparently permanent employment are set at a maximum of four years; the recruitment procedure is simplified by allowing firms to advertise vacancies without the approval of the employment bureau; and a guaranteed fund has been created to finance severance packages for workers at bankrupt firms.

The Task Before Active Labor Market Policies are Introduced: Efficient Public Sector Restructuring

Efforts to improve the efficiency of the public sector—through outsourcing or as a result of functional reviews—are likely to identify a potentially large pool of redundant labor. As state-owned enterprises and parastatals are perceived to be overstaffed, their privatization may be preceded by, or lead to, a reduction in employment levels. Social and political constraints limit the ability of the government to reduce employment levels, however, especially in an environment of high unemployment. In this context, cutting public sector jobs risks popular criticism as a violation of the social contract. The potential social and political implications suggest that any viable strategy to address over-staffing must take these constraints into consideration: ALMPs are simply not enough to address political or structural issues.

If the public sector in MENA is to move toward a results-oriented system, its work force needs to be deployed more flexibly than now. Given the large size of the public sector, such a move would undoubtedly entail a reduction in its scale, particularly in some parts. This reduction needs to take into account differences in the public-servants' opportunity costs, with appropriate compensation for downsized public sector employees combining voluntary with mandatory separations, and measures for the redeployment of still-productive workers. For example, if some redundant workers receive generous compensation or assistance, then other workers will not settle for less, regardless of their actual losses in case of separation, thereby raising the total costs of public sector reform. In the extreme, such a shift from over-staffing to over-spending does not improve economic efficiency. The comprehensive nature of the required reform effort implies that restructuring or privatization cannot happen overnight. A consistent and comprehensive approach to this restructuring is needed.

The first step consists of redefining the role of governments. This new role may entail

(a) skillful facilitation of private-sector-led economic growth;
(b) effective enforcement of property rights and private contracts;
(c) efficient and impartial regulation of private-sector activities to protect consumers from anticompetitive and fraudulent business practices, and
(d) protection of the most vulnerable group—the poor—through effective social services.

To achieve this goal while developing the design and implementation of a program to deal with overstaffing, the following main principles need be followed:[1]

- No involuntary separations. Social and political considerations restrict the use of layoffs and other mandatory separation mechanisms. Low attrition rates from the public sector (due to the age structure of the labor force) do not permit substantial reduction of employment in the medium term. Programs must therefore create incentives for public sector workers to leave their jobs voluntarily, such as through severance pay, early retirement, micro-enterprise support or training or other ALMPs, either in combination or offered as a "menu" of options.

- Targeting redundant workers only. To avoid an outflow of the most productive workers when voluntary separation packages are offered, packages should be given only to workers who are redundant. Whereas identifying the optimal level and composition of the work force may be straightforward, the difference between "good" and "bad" workers is often unobservable. An appropriately designed menu of separation packages and new contracts could induce self-selection, with good workers opting for new contracts and bad workers opting for separation packages.[2]

- Avoiding over-compensation. Providing "golden handshakes" to redundant public sector workers is neither equitable nor effective in alleviating poverty. Typically, households headed by a public sector worker are not among the poorest, and international experience suggests that poverty rates of public sector workers remain low even after separation. To ensure fairness and minimize waste, the total cost of the packages offered should not be (much) higher than the present value of the expected loss in earnings and benefits as a result of job separation.

- Allowing a choice between cash and training or other ALMPs. Setting up support services such as training, job placement, counseling, and wage subsidies makes sense, but experience in other countries indicates that some of these services are costly, ineffective, and shunned by workers. For a given value of the total separation package, each worker should freely choose whether to take cash or to use some or all of it to "buy" support services. The cash option minimizes potential waste and creates incentives for providers to design useful support services.

- *Ex ante* evaluation of gains. Reducing public sector employment may not increase efficiency. For example, if weak recruitment policies lead to massive hires following voluntary separations, or in small communities with few job opportunities. The costs and benefits of reducing public sector employment must be weighed against leaving the public sector untouched.

- Aligning public sector pay and benefits with the market. Excess demand for public sector jobs can partly be explained by the attractive compensation, particularly for low-skilled jobs. Aligning pay and benefits with compensation available outside the public sector would help dissipate some of this pressure, and would help retain highly skilled civil servants whose alternative earnings may be greater outside the public sector.

Box 1

Public/Private Differences in Employment Conditions in a MENA Country

Public sector jobs are highly prized for both concrete and intangible reasons, as evidenced by the disproportionate number of applicants in response to job announcements. Public sector pay is higher than in the private sector, especially for lower skilled jobs. Although civil service salaries have essentially been frozen for a decade, total compensation has increased, thanks to a variety of allowances (e.g., cost of living, hardship, responsibility) which currently amount to 70% or more of the basic salary. Sectoral guilds for engineers and accountants have created "technical" allowances for their members, and pay is even higher in state-owned enterprises, where over-time and bonuses are common, and higher still in parastatals such as banks and telecommunications. Non-wage features in the public sector such as a shorter working day (six hours instead of eight) and a lower income tax rate (2.5% instead of 5%), also widen the pay gap with the private sector. Other benefits associated with public-sector jobs are harder to measure but no less real, such as job security, prestige, and lower effort levels. Old-age security is a more tangible benefit, with civil servants entitled to pensions after 20 years of service (fifteen years for women). Although civil servants contribute 8.75% of their basic salary towards a pension, the pay-as-you-go pension system is not financially viable, indicating an implicit transfer of treasury resources to finance civil servant pensions.

A reform of the civil service law has now been introduced to align pay/employment conditions in the public sector to those in the labor market at large. All new recruitment is made under fixed-term contract appointments and lower benefits, with contract renewal dependent on individual performance. The pension system was replaced by enrollment with social security under terms identical to private-sector workers, and other benefits were reduced as well.

- Establishing management capacity through the creation of a modern, well-functioning computerized personnel management system able to access information on personnel for policy purposes and manage information for routine administrative and financial purposes.
- Improving the process of selection, evaluation and advancement of highly qualified civil servants able to perform the tasks of a modern efficient public service. Focus personnel decisions on merit rather than other considerations and isolate the public service from political/other sort of pressures.

In preparation for an adjustment in public sector employment, analysis of individual records from household surveys is necessary to predict losses from job separation for workers with different characteristics. In order to achieve this, one must design appropriate separation packages that avoid over-compensating or under-compensating redundant public sector workers. Other preparatory steps are more difficult to implement because they require modification of existing legislation or entrenched government practices. The following policy recommendations are central to an effective public-sector downsizing strategy:

- Create or identify a unit in charge. Inconsistent employment-reduction efforts in different parts of the public sector risk undermining the reform process, for example through a perceived lack of fairness through variable treatment, or an excessively decentralized approach that results in the misuse of public funds, with "golden handshakes" used for political patronage. Key technical inputs (e.g., assessing the extent of labor redundancies and losses from job separation, designing a "menu" of options to be offered to public sector workers, setting up redeployment support services, and evaluating the overall costs and benefits of employment restructuring) should be provided by a central unit. This unit should rank "above" the ministries and departments to be restructured, have the authority to oppose employment-reduction plans, and not be limited in scope with respect to the occupations or levels to be handled.
- Freeze recruitment or recruit for rare skills and identified needs. An effective recruitment freeze and gradual suppression of existing positions as civil servants retire or quit would signal the government's commitment to correct over-staffing, and would dispel fears that reductions in public sector employment will be followed by new recruitment.
- Make public sector pensions portable. The loss of pension entitlement represents a major disincentive for civil servants to leave the public sector. This obstacle could be removed by compensating civil servants for this loss in the event of separation, or by recognizing years of service as

years of contribution to social security, with the treasury making available the corresponding funds. Current efforts to harmonize the old-age security benefits for "classified" and "contractual" civil servants should be assessed with caution, and enrollment of civil servants into the social security system should be preserved while the current pension system should be gradually phased out.

- Introduce separation packages. When not allowed, by-laws should be amended to allow voluntary separation packages for redundant public-sector workers, and should specify which government agency will oversee and authorize packages to be offered. Whereas voluntary separation packages can increase public sector efficiency, they risk becoming a pure transfer allocated as a political favor, much the same as public sector jobs. The central technical unit charged with managing the public-sector reform program should provide guidelines on the package amounts in line with worker characteristics, and should retain responsibility for clearing packages to avoid the departure of valued civil servants. It should also assess the ex-ante returns to large reductions in public-sector employment before granting clearance. Finally, civil servants who accept voluntary separation packages should be banned from public-sector jobs for many years in order to avoid the "revolving door" syndrome, with exceptions requiring a high level of clearance.
- Maintain labor market flexibility. The economic cost and social disruption associated with reductions in public-sector employment are minimized when job opportunities exist outside the public sector. Usually, labor markets are characterized by substantial flexibility, which is conducive to job creation in the long run. Attempts to undermine this flexibility should therefore be resisted. The importance of labor reforms was mentioned in the previous section.

Active Labor Market Programs: The International Experience

Many interventions in the labor market are clustered under the title "active labor market programs" (ALMP). Such programs may lead to direct job creation (through additional jobs offered by a new public works scheme), help the unemployed fill existing vacancies (through retraining to meet the new job requirements), or improve the functioning of the labor market (through employment information and labor offices). Expenditures on ALMPs vary (see Table 2.3), as do also the analytics of these programs. For example, public works are very much a demand-side intervention, training a supply-side one, while labor market intermediation can be seen as an attempt to bridge these two sides of the labor market.

Table 2.3. Public Expenditures on Active Labor Market Programs in
          OECD Countries (as % of GDP)

Country	1985/86	1992/93	1995/96
Australia	0.42	0.76	0.84
Austria	0.28	0.36	0.39
Belgium	1.23	1.21	1.41
Canada	0.63	0.67	0.56
Denmark	1.09	1.97	2.26
Finland	0.91	1.68	1.57
France	0.67	1.06	1.30
Germany	0.81	1.62	1.43
Greece	0.21	0.31	0.27
Ireland	1.58	1.31	1.75
Italy	0.45	1.88	1.08
Japan	NA	0.09	0.10
Netherlands	1.09	1.40	1.37
New Zealand	0.84	0.80	0.71
Norway	0.66	1.34	1.16
Portugal	0.41	0.87	0.83
Spain	0.34	0.59	0.67
Sweden	2.11	3.07	2.25
U.K.	0.75	0.59	0.46
U.S.A.	0.28	0.21	0.19
Unweighted Average	**0.77 (0.77)**	**1.08 (1.14)**	**1.03 (1.08)**
Eastern Europe			
Czech Republic	NA	0.18	0.14
Hungary	NA	0.61	0.43
Poland	NA	0.38	0.32

Note: Averages in parentheses exclude Japan.

In 1985/86, industrialized OECD countries spent about 0.75% of GDP on average on active labor market programs. There was significant variation across countries—while the U.S. spent 0.3% of GDP on ALMPs, Sweden spent over 2.1% of its GDP on these programs. By 1992/93, average expenditures on ALMPs had risen somewhat to about 1.1% of GDP, but the average has remained roughly constant since then. Since the late 1980s, transition economies have also instituted these programs. Expenditures on ALMPs in transition economies included in the previous table are lower on average than in industrialized countries, and have declined since the beginning of the decade.

In almost all OECD countries, training for the unemployed is "the largest category of active programs" (Table 2.4), and is often perceived as the principal alternative to regular unemployment benefits" (OECD 1994). In many countries, in fact, training—for those laid off en masse, for the long-term unemployed, and for youth—accounts for over 50% of the expenditure on active labor market programs. This is followed by expenditures on employment services and public works programs. Countries generally spend less than 10% of their expenditures on active programs, on micro-enterprise development, or wage subsidies. A notable exception is Poland, where over 30% of public expenditures on active programs go into these two programs.

Table 2.4. Distribution of Expenditures on ALMPs
(% of Total Active Expenditure on ALMP; 1995/96)

Country	Training	Public Works	Micro- Enterprises	Job Subsidies	Emp. Services	Total as % of GDP
Australia	33.7	26.5	3.6	7.2	28.9	0.84
Belgium	35.7	40.7	0.0	7.9	15.7	1.41
Canada	48.2	5.4	7.1	3.6	35.7	0.56
Denmark	77.0	12.8	3.5	1.3	5.3	2.26
France	55.8	17.1	3.1	12.4	11.6	1.30
Germany	55.2	21.0	2.1	4.9	16.8	1.43
Ireland	32.0	38.3	1.1	14.3	14.3	1.75
Netherlands	54.7	9.5	0.0	9.5	26.3	1.37
Sweden	59.1	19.1	3.1	7.6	11.1	2.25
U.K.	53.2	2.1	2.1	0.0	42.6	0.46
U.S.A.	57.9	5.3	0.0	0.0	36.8	0.19
Unweighted Avg	**51.1**	**18.0**	**2.2**	**6.2**	**22.3**	**1.3**
Eastern Europe						
Czech Republic	14.3	7.1	0.0	7.1	71.4	0.14
Hungary	30.2	25.6	0.0	14.0	30.2	0.43
Poland	40.6	21.9	6.3	25.0	6.3	0.32

Note: Training includes measures for youth and the disabled, some of which may be non-training-related.

Active programs vary in their aims. Some emphasize efficiency; reasoning that more information leads to better job matching. Others concern distributional aspects. For example, public works can be targeted to specific areas particularly hit by poverty. A third variety can be introduced or maintained based on political considerations. For example, retraining is offered to some groups of dismissed workers, while the already-unemployed could have filled these jobs.

These programs rest on the assumption that, for one reason or another, some market failure exists in the labor or other markets (for instance, existence of monopolies in product markets). Some also rest on the premise that certain market outcomes are socially unacceptable (as is the case with high unemployment leading to social unrest). Some people would argue, however, that the term "labor market program" is a contradiction in itself: if the market works, no program should be required. The policy emphasis instead should be on making markets work.

The theoretical debate on the need for active and passive programs is bound to continue, depending on the values and assumptions adopted by economists. However, given that many countries do implement these programs, a more pragmatic approach is not whether to have them, but whether the intended objective ("benefit") is met, and at what cost. Empirical evidence from evaluations of active programs is, in this respect, indispensable.

The evidence of more than 100 evaluations of active labor market programs has been surveyed in a recent paper (Dar and Tzannatos, 1999). Though most of the surveyed studies apply to OECD countries—mainly the U.S., Canada, U.K., Sweden, and Germany—some refer to developing and transition economies such as Hungary, Poland, the Czech Republic, Turkey, and Mexico. While it can be argued that the lessons from developed countries on the effectiveness of these programs may not be directly applicable to developing countries, it is unlikely that these programs will be more successful in developing countries, given the scarcity of administrative capacity to implement them, as well as the paucity of monitoring and evaluation experience to study their effectiveness.

Many of the evaluation studies have taken advantage of the recent advances made in model development and econometric analysis. However, a number of issues affecting the reliability of the findings of these studies for guiding public policy remain open. First, there are unresolved technical issues, such as handling selection bias and assessing deadweight and displacement/substitution effects. Second, there are a variety of data problems in the specific surveys. These include benchmarking pre-intervention profiles (employment history, human capital attributes, etc.) and the tracking of participants and non-participants for no more than one or at most two years while, in many cases, the full impact of policies is unlikely to play out in this short period of time (such as in the case of training and self-employment). Third, administrative data which may be called upon to provide supplementary information tend to be surprisingly poor, so that the nature or the intensity of the intervention received by the participant is often uncertain.

Table 2.5. Overall Impact of Public Service/Community Employment
Programs in Transition Economies

Indicator	Czech Republic	Hungary	Poland
Initial employment	No impact	Negative	Negative
Current employment	Negative	Negative	Negative
Initial earnings	n.a.	Positive	n.a.
Current earnings	No impact	Negative	No impact
Unemployment compensation	Negative	No impact	Positive
Memo items			
1. Cost per participant (US$)	625	1200	800
2. Cost per participant (PPP$)	1578	1867	1543
3. Per capita GDP (US$)	4740	4340	3230

Note: 1) Costs are per participant, not per year. For example, in the Czech Republic, the duration of participation is 6 months, which implies that annualized program costs were twice those reported.
2) The Purchasing Power Parity (PPP) conversion factor is defined as the number of units of a country's currency required to buy the same amount of goods and services in the domestic market as one dollar would buy in the United States.

Table 2.6. Annual Cost of Job Creation in Public Works

	Egypt	Honduras	Nicaragua	Madagascar	Bolivia	Senegal	Ghana
1. Cost/job (US$)	1401	2120	2580	786	2700	5445	2122
2. Cost/job (PPP)	7212	9759	14,302	3620	9388	12,100	10,610
3. Per capita GDP (US$)	790	600	380	230	800	600	390
4. Ratio (1/3)	1.77	3.53	6.79	3.42	3.38	9.08	5.44

While these remarks indicate that a definitive conclusion on which and under what conditions ALMP can be justified economically, the evidence points to some generalizations about active labor programs. These can be summarized as follows programmatically:

• Public works can help the more disadvantaged groups (older workers, the long-term unemployed, those in distressed regions) as a poverty/safety-net program. They are ineffective instruments as an escape route from permanent unemployment. Program participants are less likely to be employed in an unsubsidized job, and they earn less than individuals in the control group (Tables 2.5 and 2.6).

- Job-search assistance has a positive impact and is usually cost-effective relative to other ALMPs. Programs that have yielded positive results have generally been implemented under favorable macroeconomic conditions. However, job search assistance does not seem to significantly improve either the employment prospects or wages of youth.

- Training for the long-term unemployed can help when the economy is improving. Small-scale, tightly targeted on-the-job training programs, often aimed at women and older groups, offer the best returns. However, the cost-effectiveness of these programs is generally disappointing. The real rate of return is rarely positive, and they are no more successful than job search assistance programs in terms of post-program placement and wages. A caveat here is that job-search assistance may not be a direct substitute for training, as it may cater to different groups of the unemployed.

- Retraining for those laid off en masse usually has little positive impact and, as in case for the long-term unemployed, it is more expensive and no more effective than job-search assistance. Again, job search assistance may not be a direct substitute for retraining, as the target groups may be somewhat different.

- Training for youth generally has no positive impact on employment prospects or post-training earnings—it clearly cannot make up for the failures of the education system. Taking costs into account, the real rate of return of these programs in both the short- and long-run is usually negative.

- Micro-enterprise development programs are usually taken up by only a small fraction of the unemployed and are associated with high deadweight and displacement effects. The failure rate of these businesses is quite high. As in the case of training for the long-term unemployed, assistance targeted at particular groups—in this case, women and older individuals—seems to have a greater likelihood of success (Table 2.7).

- Wage-subsidy programs are unlikely to have a positive impact. They have substantial deadweight and substitution effects, and the wage and employment outcomes of participants are also generally negative as compared to a control group. Careful targeting can reduce, but not eliminate, substitution and deadweight effects, and further controls may be necessary to ensure that firms do not misuse this program as a permanent subsidy program (Table 2.8).

Table 2.7. Failure Rates of Businesses Support Programs

Program	Failure Rate
Australia in the late 1980's (New Enterprise Initiative)	58% of businesses failed within first year and 71% within two years.
Canada in the early 1990's (Self-Employment Assistance Program)	20% of businesses failed within first year
Denmark in the mid to late 1980's (Enterprise Allowance Schemes)	60% of businesses failed within first 12 months
France in the early 1980's (Micro-Enterprise Development)	50% of businesses failed within 4.5 years.
Hungary in the mid 1990's (MEDA)	20% of businesses failed within first 15 months.
Netherlands in the early 1990's	50% of businesses failed within four years.
Poland in the mid 1990's (MEDA)	15% of businesses failed within first two years.
U.S. in Washington in 1990 (Self-Employment Experiment)	37% of businesses failed within the first 15 months

There are polarized positions on the effectiveness of active labor market programs. On the one hand, their proponents argue that they are both necessary and useful, short only of a panacea for reducing unemployment and protecting workers. Opponents of the programs tend to summarily dismiss them as a waste of public money, with high opportunity costs to other social programs and labor market efficiency as a whole. Based on a thorough evaluation of the evidence, this chapter shows that some programs can be useful to some workers in some cases. There are also good design features for each program, but external (to the programs) conditions need to be taken into account (a good program in one country can prove to be a bad one for another; a program found to be useful in the past may no longer be needed). This calls for realism in setting the objectives of ALMP, and also setting standards against which active labor market programs should be evaluated. However, due to lack of evaluative evidence, the conditions under which programs will succeed have not been fully identified. A very *broad generalization* on the effectiveness of these programs (Table 2.9) leads to the conclusions that:

- Some of these programs—such as wage subsidies or training for youth— are unlikely to be cost-effective instruments in reducing unemployment.

Table 2.8. Effectiveness of Wage Subsidy Programs

Country	Deadweight and Substitution Effects (%)	Additionality (%)
Australia in mid 1980s (Jobstart Program)	Deadweight=65%	35%
Belgium in the early 1990s (Recruitment Subsidy)	Deadweight=53% Substitution=36%	11%
England 1986–1990 (Training and Employment Grant)	Deadweight=69%	31%
England late 1980s (Workstart I)	Deadweight=45% Substitution=30%	25%
England mid 1970s (Small Firms Employment Subsidy)	Deadweight=70%	30%
England early 1980s	Deadweight=63% Substitution=10%	27%
Germany in mid 1970s (Wage Subsidy Scheme)	Deadweight=75%	25%
Ireland in the 1980's (Employment Incentive Scheme)	Deadweight= 70% Substitution=21% Displacement=4%	4%
Netherlands during early 1980s (Vermeend–Moor Act)	Deadweight=25% Substitution=50%	25%
Netherlands during the late 1980s (JOB scheme)	Substitution =80%.	20%
Scotland 1989–1992 (Employment Subsidy)	Deadweight=20%. Substitution and Displacement=55%	25%
U.S. in mid 1980s (Targeted Job Tax Credit)	Deadweight=70% Substitution=10%	20%

Note: Additionality is the net employment effect after accounting for deadweight, displacement, and substitution effects.

- Some programs—such as job-search assistance—are likely to have positive impacts on the probability of finding employment if they are well-designed and implemented.
- However, the impact and cost-effectiveness of most of the active labor market programs depends not only on their design, but also on the overall macro and labor market framework in which they are designed.

These results suggest the following policy approach:

- If a country is going to institute labor market programs, a good practice is to start with modest programs.
- Sound impact evaluation techniques should be used to assess the instituted programs. Relying only on non-scientific evaluations may lead to incorrect policy conclusions. A good micro-evaluation will involve comparing labor market outcomes for individuals who have gone through a particular program with those of a control group of their peers, and will also utilize data on program costs. These will help to answer the important questions: (a) what is the impact of the program?; (b) are the impacts large and costs low enough to yield net social gains?; and (c) is this the best outcome that could have been achieved for the money spent?
- Based on these evaluations, the programs should be tightly targeted at those for whom they are found to be the most cost-effective, or, if the evaluations point towards these programs being ineffective, they should be amended or discarded.

MENA: International Comparisons

One final set of comments needs to be made about the relevance of active labor market programs in the region. Taking Egypt, the host country of this seminar, as an example, it is—like most MENA countries—still far removed from the prevailing economic circumstances and labor market characteristics in the OECD, especially with respect to the size of the formal labor market. And the labor market programs found in many OECD countries raise issues of the affordability of such programs. Most of the MENA countries are in some stage of transition to a market economy, like the other transition economies of Eastern Europe and Central Asia.

Just where, then does Egypt stand in comparison with these many countries? The graphs in the Appendix highlight some conditions in Egypt in comparison to other transition economies and to Asian economies. Data from the World Bank's World Development Indicators allow ready comparisons between Egypt and other countries. 40 other countries, in three groups, were considered:

Countries in Transition
- From Eastern Europe: Albania, Bulgaria, Croatia, Czech Republic, Hungary, Macedonia FYR, Poland, Romania, the Slovak Republic, and Slovenia
- From the former Soviet Union: Armenia, Azerbaijan, Belarus, Estonia,

Georgia, Kazakhstan, Kyrgyz Republic, Latvia, Lithuania, Moldova, Russia, Ukraine, Uzbekistan

Asian Countries
- Bangladesh, Cambodia, China, India, Indonesia, Lao PDR, Malaysia, Pakistan, Philippines, Sri Lanka, Thailand, Vietnam

MENA Countries
- Algeria, Jordan, Lebanon, Morocco, Tunisia

Korea and Singapore have been excluded on the grounds that their GDPs are significantly higher than the others, making comparisons more problematic. The countries cover a wide spectrum: from the poorest countries of Asia, such as Bangladesh and Laos, to the better-off countries of Eastern Europe, such as the Czech Republic and Slovenia. Egypt may well regard itself more as being in direct competition with the latter countries, but whether that is true bears questioning, as the graphs will show.

Before considering them, however, it is important to say that considerable care should be taken in reading too much into such broad statistics as those presented here, especially since the data sources may be doubtful in many cases. Nevertheless, the results are sufficiently clear for the exercise to reveal some disparities between the Egyptian economy and those of countries in transition in Europe. The following basic characteristics have been chosen to demonstrate this:

- Population growth rate. Population growth rates vary considerably; from declines in many former communist countries, to increases of 2% a year or more in some Asian countries. In Egypt, the growth rate is declining but was still just 2% for the period of 1990 to 1997. Population growth eventually feeds into the labor force and ultimately affects a country's GDP per capita.
- Labor force growth rates. There is a substantial time lag between achieving lower population growth and attaining lower labor force growth. For our countries as a whole, the labor force grew by about 1% per year from 1990 to 1997. Among the transition economies, eleven had zero or negative growth; but nine of the Asian economies had growth of at least 2%. Of these, only Pakistan has been growing faster than Egypt.
- Population aged 15 to 64 years. Most economic activity falls in this age group. For all countries in the group, 63% of the populations were in this age category. However, there is again a great difference between Asian and transition (especially European) economies. Egypt clearly has less capacity on which to base its economic, and consequently its social welfare, development.

Table 2.9. Overview of Active Labor Programs

Program	Appear to Help	Comments
1. Public Works Programs/Public Service Employment (13 evaluations)	Severely disadvantaged groups in providing temporary employment and a safety net.	Long-term employment prospects not helped: program participants are less likely to be employed in a normal job and earn less than do individuals in the control group. Not a cost-effective instrument if objective is to get people into gainful employment after program completion.
2. Job-search assistance/ Employment Services (18 evaluations)	Adult unemployed generally when economic conditions are improving; women may benefit more.	Relatively more cost-effective than other labor market interventions (e.g., training)—mainly due to the lower cost, youth do not benefit usually. Difficulty lies in deciding who needs help in order to minimize deadweight loss.
3. Training of long-term unemployed (23 evaluations)	Women and other disadvantaged groups generally when economy is improving.	These programs are no more effective than job-search assistance in increasing re-employ ment probabilities and post-intervention earnings and are 2–4 times more costly. However, job-search assistance may not be a direct substitute as it may cater to a different groups of the unemployed.
4. Retraining in the case of mass layoffs (11 evaluations)	Little positive impact— mainly when economy is doing better.	These programs are no more effective than job-search assistance and significantly more expensive. Rate of return on these programs usually negative. However, job search assistance may not be a direct substitute as it may cater to a different groups of the unemployed.
5. Training for youth (7 evaluations)	No positive impact.	Employment/earnings prospects not improved as a result of going through the training. Taking costs into account—the real rate of return of these programs both in the short as well as the long run is negative.
6. Micro-enterprise Development Programs (13 evaluations)	Relatively older groups, the more educated.	Very low take-up rate among unemployed. Significant failure rate of small businesses. High deadweight and displacement effects. High costs (cost-benefit analysis rarely conducted).
7. Employment/ Wage subsidies (15 evaluations)	Long-term unemployed in providing an entry into the labor force. However, no long-term impact.	Extremely high deadweight and substitution effects. Impact analysis shows treatment group does not do well as compared to control. Sometimes used by firms as a permanent subsidy program.

- Proportion of total population in the labor force. When looked at in terms of how many people are in the labor force, the position of Egypt seems even less advantageous. For the 36 countries in total, 48% of the *total* population are in the labor force. That is to say that for every person in the labor force there is almost one other dependent. For Egypt, the proportion is 37%, meaning that for every person in the labor force there are nearly two other dependents.   ·
- The proportion of the population living in urban areas. The total population of the 36 countries is split equally (50/50) between urban and non-urban areas. There is again a distinct difference between Asian and transition economies. Egypt is not greatly different from the average but it is still markedly more rural than all but a few transition economies. Its rural population makes up 55% of the country—compared to about 35% in countries like the Czech Republic, Hungary, and Poland.
- GDP per capita. In the end, all these figures lead to one dominant indicator, GDP per capita. The average for the 31 countries for which data are available was just under US$4250 in 1996. With the exception of Malaysia and Thailand, all the Asian countries are below the average, as is Egypt. The only transition economies that are poorer than Egypt on this measure are the countries of the former Soviet Union.

This juxtaposition of Egypt in a comparative context points in the direction that, in some respects, the country has some structural similarities which are more akin to the developing countries of Asia than to the majority of transition economies, especially those located in Eastern Europe. This observation is even more relevant in comparison to OECD countries. In short, this "distance" from OECD countries calls for a careful examination of active labor market policies vis-à-vis policies which aim at job creation in the informal sector (including agriculture), or even direct cash assistance to the poor.

Conclusions

This chapter has outlined the recent progress made in MENA towards the creation of a more flexible, private-sector driven and less government-dependent labor market and economy at large. It acknowledged the difficulty of reforms and the need to protect the vulnerable. And it went further than that by identifying the political economy considerations with respect to: first, reducing the size of public-sector employment, and second, the perceived need to spend public resources on those affected although they may not be the poorest.

Given that active labor market programs are always a possibility, the chapter proposes that these can be tried selectively in MENA—taking into account the structural and labor market characteristics of each individual country, as well as the international experience with each of these programs. For example, wage subsidies or training for youth seem unlikely to be cost-effective instruments in reducing unemployment while job-search assistance is more likely to have a positive impact.

Overall, the chapter proposes that MENA can adopt the following approach:

- If a country is going to institute labor market programs, a good practice is to start with modest programs.
- Sound impact evaluation techniques should be used to evaluate the instituted programs along the questions:
  (a) what is the impact of the program?;
  (b) are the impacts large and costs low enough to yield net social gains?; and
  (c) is this the best outcome that could have been achieved for the money spent?
- Based on these evaluations, the programs should be tightly targeted at those for whom they are found to be the most cost-effective, or, if the evaluations point towards these programs being ineffective, they should be amended or discarded.

Notes

1 This section draws from ongoing work in the Bank undertaken by Shantayanan Devarajan, Christian Petersen, and Vinaya Swaroop.
2 See Doh-Shin Jeon and Jean-Jacques Laffont, "The Efficient Mechanism for Downsizing the Public Sector." January 1999. *World Bank Economic Review* 13 (1): 67–88.

References

Amit, Dar, and Zafiris Tzannatos. 1999. *Active Labor Market Programs: A Review of the Evidence from Evaluations.* World Bank Social Protection Discussion Paper Series, No 9901.
OECD. 1994. *Jobs Study: Evidence and Explanations.*
OECD. 1997. *OECD Employment Outlook.*
Salvatore Schiavo-Campo, Giulio de Tommaso, and Amitabha Mukherjee. 1997. *An International Survey of Government Employment and Wages.* Policy Research Working Paper No. 1806. The World Bank.
Subbarao, K. 1997. "Public Works as an Anti-Poverty Program: An Overview of Cross-Country Experience." *American Journal of Agricultural Economics.*
Tzannatos, Z. 1995. "Labor Policies and Regulatory Regimes." In Claudio Frischtak, ed., *Regulatory Policies and Reform: A Comparative Perspective.* The World Bank.
Wilson, S., and A.V. Adams. 1994. *Self-Employment for the Unemployed: Experience in OECD and Transitional Economies.* World Bank Discussion Paper No. 263.
World Bank. MENA Region presentation library
World Bank. 1999. "The Employment Crisis in the MENA Region." MNSED mimeo/unprocessed.
World Bank. (Various issues). World Bank Development Indicators.

Figure A2.1. Annual Population Growth:
Variation from the Mean (0.8%)

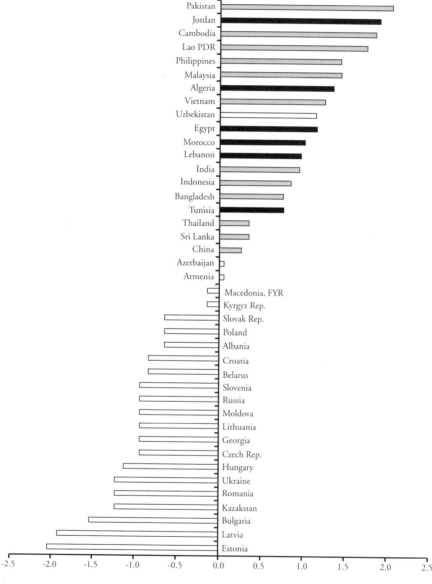

Source: The World Bank, *World Development Indicators.*
           Data refer to 1996.

Figure A2.2. Annual Labor Force Growth:
Variation from the Mean (1.1%)

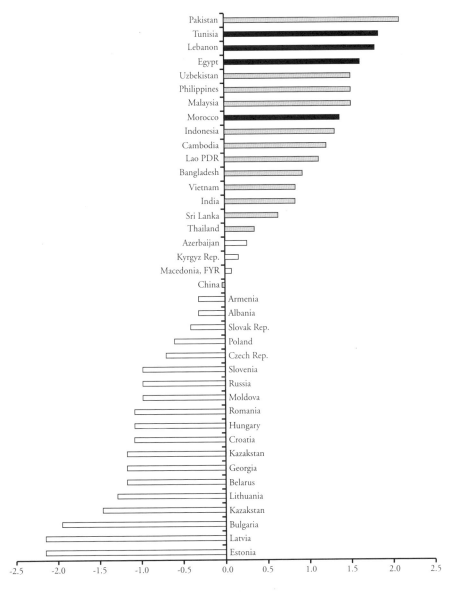

Source: The World Bank, *World Development Indicators.*
Data refer to 1996.

Figure A2.3. Proportion of Population in Labor Force:
Variation from the Mean (46%)

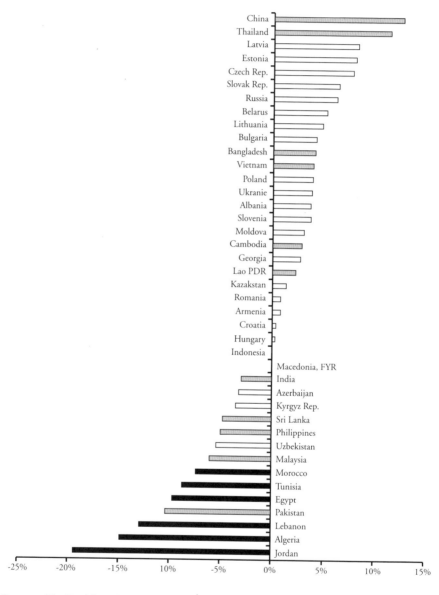

Source: The World Bank, *World Development Indicators*.
          Data refer to 1996.

3

Labor Representation in the Age of Globalization: Trends and Issues in Non-Oil-Based Arab Economies

Noha El-Mikawy
Marsha Pripstein Posusney

This is a chapter written by two political scientists specializing in the political economy of the Arab world. As such, it is not technical or statistical. Rather, our focus is on the institutions of labor/government and labor/business relations—the formal and informal mechanisms of, and regulations governing, workers' representation in policymaking bodies at either the national, industrial, or individual enterprise level. We explore both how labor may influence economic reforms through these mechanisms, on the one hand, and how the reform process may impact on the channels of labor representation, on the other.[1]

There is good reason to examine the issues of growth enhancement and poverty reduction at this time. It is readily acknowledged today that the standard package of orthodox (or, as they are sometimes called, "neoliberal") economic reforms, however well intentioned, typically has deleterious short-term consequences for vulnerable segments of the population. (*inter alia*, ILO 1997, 12–14) Urban workers, even if relatively privileged in relation to the rural poor, are likely to be among the first "losers" when price controls are removed, government budgets are cut, or public sectors are rationalized or privatized. At the same time, because they are concentrated in a single and often large workplace, and/or tend to live in close-knit communities with others of the same strata, workers are well positioned to either disrupt production or organize public manifestations of discontent in response to policies which harm their interests.[2] In addition, where workers are unionized, they may have recourse to organizational and financial resources that are unavailable to informal sector employees or rural laborers.

This situation poses a dilemma for reform-minded governments. If they seek to win the cooperation of labor, this may result in delays and/or modifications to the reform program that risk negative reviews from international creditors. However, the only alternative appears to be implementing the reforms over the objections of labor, while suppressing workers' ability to resist. This risks condemnation from international labor and human rights organizations, and alienating citizens from the government. Moreover, comparative studies of other developing regions suggest that it is precisely where labor feels insecure about its future position in the political system that it is most likely to mobilize defensively against reforms, thus making both the costs and the political risks of labor repression higher.[3]

At the same time, the process of reform itself, even if gradual and negotiated with unions, is apt to place pressures on existing labor laws and institutions for workers' representation. There are two inter-related reasons for this. First, throughout the developing and socialist world, where most policies affecting workers' livelihoods and employment conditions were made by the state, unions had a motivation to operate as highly centralized and non-competitive structures; such rigidities were often codified into law. As the state withdraws from the economy and privatization or public sector rationalization renders decisions made at individual plants more important to workers, both they and the expanding private sector entrepreneurial class may see a need for a more flexible and decentralized means of labor representation (ILO vi, 107).

Second, public sector jobs, which comprised a large segment of formal sector employment in many developing countries, typically carried with them more job security and better forms of social protection for workers. Governments often demanded labor quiescence in exchange for these benefits; prohibitions against work stoppages or other manifestations of labor discontent were written into labor laws and/or penal codes, and governments claimed the right to supervise union operations and elections. Now, with privatization and public sector reform threatening the accustomed privileges of public sector workers, such restrictions on labor militancy lose their rationale. However, especially in authoritarian countries, governments may be loath to sanction more democratic union practices, and/or to legalize any forms of popular protest; businessmen as well may prefer to maintain any pre-existing prohibitions against strikes.

This chapter examines how these issues are being handled in the non-oil-based states of the MDF region, with primary emphasis on Egypt, Morocco, Tunisia, and Jordan. These countries share a number of features that make them the most likely to experience the dilemmas highlighted above. The similarities among them include:

- None of these countries are major exporters of oil. Thus they must rely on merchandise exports, invisibles, and worker remittances for foreign-exchange earnings. All experienced serious balance of payments difficulties in the 1980s.
- In response to their external crises, all four countries turned to multilateral lending agencies, especially the IMF and the World Bank, in the 1980s and 1990s, and implemented stabilization and structural adjustment programs under their auspices. Because the stabilization programs brought macroeconomic stability to these countries, they have been considered "success stories" by the IMF. (Pfeifer 1999)
- Unlike some other MENA countries, all four permit trade unions to operate, albeit under varying degrees of restrictions. These unions maintain connections with international labor organizations.
- All four have experienced a degree of political liberalization along with economic liberalization. Egypt and Tunisia are former single-party states that now, within limits, permit opposition parties to contest elections and publish their own newspapers. Jordan and Morocco remain monarchies, but Jordan's late King Hussein revived a long-moribund parliament in 1989 and legalized opposition parties in 1992. The democratization process has gone furthest in Morocco, where elections have been contested since the 1960s, and where the leader of a former opposition party (the USFP) now heads the government.
- Finally, both political and economic liberalization in these countries has taken place in the context of the rise of militant political Islamic forces in the region. Fear of enhancing the popularity of such groups has made governments in these countries very cautious about implementing reforms that might increase poverty and thereby fuel discontent. At the same time, it has made governments wary of extending political freedoms, including those affecting the operation of labor organizations, too far or too quickly.

The next section of this chapter focuses on several aspects of unions in the non-oil-based Arab economies. The third section then offers a case study of how labor has interacted with government and the private sector in the process of privatization and public sector reform in Egypt and Morocco. Following this, the fourth section considers what the future of unionization is likely to be in all these countries, exploring how structural and institutional factors are likely to shape labor-state and labor-business relations. We conclude by summarizing the trade-offs faced by policymakers, businessmen, and labor leaders as non-oil-based Arab countries are further liberalized and integrated into the international economy.

Unions in Non-Oil-Based Arab Countries

In this section we discuss the relevance and necessity of autonomous labor unions, in light of the changing legal environment in the non-oil Arab countries under study.

Are Autonomous Labor Unions Necessary?
Some may doubt the economic and political wisdom of unionization. It is a view based on an often well-grounded fear lest unions drive up wages and other benefits, forcing businessmen into capital-intensive ventures or towards capital flight to cheaper labor markets. However, there is inconclusive knowledge of the negative impact of unions. Several recent studies found a positive relationship between unionization and productivity and between unionization and reasonable levels of profitability (admittedly not too high, but also not too low profit levels). (Hollister and Goldstein; G. Bosch 1999, 131–149; Freeman and Kleiner, 510–527)

Aside from the economic wisdom of unionization or lack thereof, the political reasoning on unions could go both ways. Since "unions can have a major influence on political strife particularly because they can be a mobilized force in otherwise weakly organized situations," the elite may find unions destabilizing, especially in times of liberalization and privatization (Hollister and Goldstein, 2)

But autonomous unions as such may not be destabilizing, for we know too little about transitional phases with autonomous unions. As Hollister has noted, "[W]eakening unions and dismantling labor laws has not been shown necessarily to be the best approach to labor market adjustment reform." (Hollister and Goldstein, 68) How destabilizing unions can be depends partly on society's reception of liberalization. Society's evaluation may be dependent on the following criteria:

- The size of gain/loss (actual and expected)
- The extent to which the change fits into the existing societal norm of justice (Rodrik, 30–32)

- Most importantly, the amount of information available to all on the labor market.

Liberalization and privatization measures often have a mixed effect on labor. Those who manage to hold on to their jobs in the public sector and those who manage to find stable jobs in the private sector are usually hopeful and supportive of economic reform. If they expect sustained benefit in the future, then their support is also guaranteed. The situation is reversed for those who lose jobs or remain unemployed and expect no improvement in the future. (Hollister and Goldstein, 68–71)

The organizational capacity of the winners and the losers is also quite relevant. If only winners are organized, then the ability of their organizations to prevent latent, anonymous street protest is still low. If only losers are organized, then the elite has no chance of relying on countervailing forces of positive supporters, which forces the elite to adopt authoritarian methods. The best possible scenario is for both winners and losers to be organized.

The potential of winners and losers to assess their gain/loss, to organize and to ally pragmatically or polemically is highly dependent on the availability of information about economic macro- and micro-trends and about the labor market. This is one major weakness of most Arab countries. In Egypt, one of the oldest bureaucracies and the most researched country in the region, one hears often enough the complaint that data is inconsistent, thin and unreliable (Hollister and Goldstein, 17). Increasing organizational levels together with availability of information to all could make a difference, reducing the threat of politically polemic stances.

Are Autonomous Labor Unions Relevant?

There are reasons to argue that labor unions are irrelevant in the Arab context. Firstly, the level of unionization among the working population is low, around 10% in Morocco, Jordan, and Tunisia. The highest rate of unionization that can be observed (25% of the work force) is in Egypt (Hollister and Goldstein, 67). Secondly, the unemployment rate—especially among new entrants to the labor market—is very high, keeping many out of reach for unions. Thirdly, the rate of newly created jobs in the informal sector surpasses that in the formal sector, depriving unions of membership. So why talk about unions in the Arab context?

Since the 1990s, it is in the Arab context in particular that one must pay attention to unions. Three reasons make that an imperative of institutional reform, to support sustainable economic growth. Firstly, a considerable portion of the work force are wage earners and thus could improve their lot in the labor market only if they aggregate their interests. Secondly, without clear institutions for the regulation of hiring, firing, rewards and incentive policies, among other labor conditions, the tendency of many businesses to evade the law will continue. At a time when the international competitiveness of nations is partly measured by the ability of businessmen to trust the laws of the country, widespread law evasion only proves weak governance. Competent unions could help come up with labor regulations that are acceptable and enforceable. Thirdly, the legislative trend since the 1990s in many Arab countries points towards a reduced role for the state in regulating labor conditions, leaving it to collective bargaining between businessmen and workers. That alone makes it imperative that there be labor representatives who are capable of engaging competently in collective bargaining. In a study of several cases of collective bargaining in Egypt, Magdi A. Shararah has shown the difficulty of engaging in collective bargaining in establishments whose workers are not unionized (M. Shararah).

Trends in Legal Reform of the Labor Institution
The Arab socialist period decreed several rights for workers, in effect hampering the freedom of businessmen and managers to make decisions about hiring, firing, and incentives within their enterprises. However, the guarantee of the rights to work, to holidays, to profit-sharing, to representation on executive boards, and to social security were coupled with the denial of the right to strike, and with strong state involvement in the affairs of labor unions through the co-optation of union leadership by the political elite. That was the story in the progressive republics of the Arab World. The conservative monarchies more or less followed suit, or prohibited unions altogether, in the case of the Gulf.

Since the beginning of the wave of privatization in the 1980s, private capital has improved its share of the market, and the need to create or amend labor laws has been put on the agenda of legal reform. In the 1990s, legislative change set the stage for institutional reform of labor relations, making them less state-dependent and more of an outcome of collective bargaining between businessmen and workers. In a way, the 1990s have been a watershed in labor relations.

Reforming the labor market to support the objectives of structural adjustment started in the early 1990s against a background of popular unrest. In Morocco unions came together to demand better social conditions, tried to organize a national strike in the 1990s that was only partially observed, but created a pretext for serious unrest in some cities. In Tunisia labor and student unrest took a good part of the 1980s, and in 1990 the government tried to bring representatives of labor and business together to discuss the reform of the labor code (Hollister and Goldstein, 67, 70). Although many voices were raised against that process, Tunisia issued Law 29/1994 to support its general liberalization program. After years of preparation, Jordan issued its own labor Law

8/1996, to reinforce its ability to attract extensive foreign investments. In Egypt, labor unrest increased in the late 1980s and early 1990s. Egypt's labor market has been regulated by a number of laws that correspond to the variety of existing business sectors: Law 47/1978 for civil servants, Law 48/1978 for public sector workers, Law 137/1981 for private sector workers, Law 159/1981 for workers in share holding companies, and Law 203/1991 for workers in the public enterprise sector. Since 1993, the government together with the ILO and representatives of labor and business have been discussing the unification of all these laws into one labor law. The suggested reform would introduce one new dimension to Egyptian labor relations, namely collective bargaining on labor relations, for the law would only set the minimum benefits, and labor representatives would be responsible for improving on them (Ilias, 16–17).

Similar developments occurred in other countries. Algeria started the reform process of labor relations in 1990. Law 2/1990, Law 4/1990, Law 11/1990 and Law 14/1990 deregulated labor relations away from guaranteed job security and wage levels, an orientation which characterized the rule of the FLN until then. Yemen also unified its labor laws after Yemeni unification. Though the ruling elite tried to harmonize labor laws of both Yemens into one, the resultant Law 5 of 1995 primarily deregulated labor relations (Ilias 1997, 15–16).

Future Tasks of Labor Unions
Two main features characterize the legal reform of labor relations in the Arab countries undergoing structural adjustment: labor relations have become an outcome of collective bargaining between businessmen and workers, who have been implicitly or explicitly given the right to strike. In other words, labor unions are supposed to become—almost overnight—competent and equal negotiators in collective bargaining with business on an expanding number of vital issues, such as work contracts, wages, and other work conditions.

Job Security
Unions can seek to provide job security by:

- Restricting the right to collective lay-off,
- Restricting temporary contracts,
- Guaranteeing jobs in case of a change of firm owner.

Restricting the Right to Collective Lay-off
Restricting the right to fire is usually done by abiding by international standards that do not allow employers to freely lay off workers without reason, regulating the process of workers' appeal and securing compensation for unfairly laid-off

workers. In that case, a considerable amount of administrative oversight by the state is required. The restriction of the right to lay off also could be guaranteed by laws that specify the reasons for which an employer can lay off a worker, allowing a worker who appeals and wins to return to work. In both cases, the "acceptable" reasons are confined to disciplinary firing of workers who demonstrate great negligence, or firing due to structural/economic reasons. In some cases, sanctioned by international standards, labor representatives are involved in single and collective cases of lay-off.

Pioneered by Tunisia, the trend since the 1990s has been for a more liberal lay-off policy. The Tunisian labor law of 1994 continued to put no limitation on the freedom to lay off. The Tunisian law involves a supervisory committee in the process, guaranteeing the worker financial compensation in the case of a successful appeal, though the appeal and compensation processes have not been explicitly regulated in the law (Ilias 1997, 29, 36). Also, the Jordanian law of 1996 does not limit the employer's freedom to lay off. Whereas the old law of 1960 allowed firing only during the probation period and allowed workers who won an appeal to return to work, the new law allowed firing in more cases. However, it involved a ministerial committee on which representatives of labor and business would sit. The job of that committee, according to the law, is to oversee the soundness of procedures, not to decide on the reasons of lay-off. The new law also clarified and retained the right of a worker who wins an appeal to return to work (Ilias, 38–39). Article 31, paragraph G, also allows workers to demand to return to work, when the economic reasons for lay-off have subsided (*Qanun al-Amal 8/1996 fi al-Mamlakah al-Orduniya al-Hashimiya* 1996, 25).

In Egypt, the existing Labor Law 137/1981 obliges the employer to submit a request for lay-off, in cases of partial suspension of operation or total shut-down, to a committee formed by the Prime Minister. In the suggested law amendment the committee would be formed by the Minister of Labor and would discuss the reasons for the lay-off, suspension of operation or shut-down. The committee would include representatives of labor. The law would prohibit the employer from laying off workers during the deliberation period with the committee, and encourage the employer to opt for solutions less damaging to workers (such as changing work contracts, reducing working hours, etc.). In the latter case, the law would allow workers not to accept the terms of change and resign without having to abide by any notice periods, nor having to suffer any reductions in their benefits (Ilias 1997, 40–45).

Similar trends are present in Algeria and Yemen. The Algerian law of 1990 kept the articles of the previous laws that allowed lay-offs for economic reasons. Decisions to lay off in the new law have to be discussed through collective bargaining. The law also encourages employers to use lay-off as a last resort, after trying out reduction of working hours or early retirement. The Yemeni unified law opted for a more liberal version. The right to lay off was given for economic or technical reasons without any procedural limitations. The unified law allows workers financial compensation, if they win an appeal (Ilias, 35–37).

Restricting Temporary Contracts
All trends in the 1990s point towards the acceptance of temporary working contracts. This is the case in the Tunisian and Jordanian labor laws that kept old features of previous laws, which considered any work contract a mutual agreement whose terms can only be determined by those who sign the contract. In the Egyptian amendment, this freedom would be extended. Not only would temporary work contracts be allowed; the proposed law amendment would allow several renewals of temporary contracts, without losing their temporary status. Only in the case of temporary contracts that end, while the work *de facto* continues, would the employer be obliged to accept the working relationship as permanent (Ilias, 31).

Compared to other cases, we observe how Tunisia, Jordan, and Egypt even more so have taken quite a liberal step. For in the case of Algeria, the right to sign temporary contracts is limited to cases specified by law. And in the Yemeni case, the unified law is very vague and badly written. On one hand, it assumes that work relations have to be permanent (Article 29), yet it says in another article that this could be changed if both parties (employer and employee) agree to something different (paragraph 2 of same article) (Ilias, 29–30).

Guaranteeing Jobs in Case of a Change of Firm Owner
The right to keep one's job even if the firm changes owners is an important component of job security. A firm can change owners if the owner dies, if the firm merges with another, or if it is privatized. Almost all laws under study retain one position: work contracts remain in force in cases of change of owner or firm identity. In the Egyptian case, the amendment does not add anything new (Ilias, 45–50).

This raises some difficulties for companies that privatize. However, the law on lay-off makes life easier for an employer in economic or technical trouble. For example, in the Jordanian case, Article 16 guarantees workers their jobs. Article 17, however, allows a change in job specification "if necessary," though Article 30 prohibits the reduction of a worker's wage (*Qanun al-Amal 8/1996,* 19, 24). Similarly, the Egyptian proposed amendment would secure workers their job in the case of privatization. However, the article on lay-offs would dilute this guarantee. The Egyptian amendment welcomes wage reduction as a less evil option than firing, if the employer wants to rationalize overhead costs.

Minimum Wages

In Tunisia minimum wages are set by a central committee. The Jordanian law did improve upon the previous one by specifying the representation of workers and businessmen in the minimum wage committee, which is to be formed by the Prime Minister. The Egyptian proposed amendment also adopted the national committee approach, for according to the existing law, minimum wages are determined by regional committees. According to the proposed amendment, a national council for wages would be set up by the Minister of Planning—including ministers, experts, and representatives of business and labor. The minimum wage would be reviewed every three years.

Algeria pioneered that trend in 1990 with the assertion that minimum wages are to be determined by law after consultation with representatives of labor and business. In contrast, the Yemeni unified law departs from that trend by setting the minimum wage in tandem with wages in the civil service, though one of the old labor laws had adopted the tripartite committee approach (Ilias, 51–61).[4]

One of the problems with the minimum wage process is that the last instance is not clear. Is it the Prime Minister or the Minister of Labor? The job of the council of wages in the Jordanian law is not clear: Article 52 says that such a committee meets "when needed" to determine the national minimum wage or the minimum wage for an industry or profession or region.[5] The word "or" in Arabic could signify inclusion or options (*Qanun al-Amal* 8/1996, 34). In the Egyptian case, the committee's opinion is advisory (a feature that characterized the work of the regional and sectorial committees in the old laws) and cannot enforce minimum wages nor is asked in cases of violation. Whereas a court looks into violations in the Egyptian case, the executive appoints a committee in the Jordanian case (Article 54). It is not clear whether this committee is ad hoc or permanent (*Qanun al-Amal* 8/1996, 35).

Collective Bargaining

It seems from the above comparison of five legal reforms that Arab laws are transforming populist, state-controlled labor/capital relationships, basing them instead on tripartite collective bargaining. This means that the state should reduce its regulatory role and allow collective negotiations between representatives of labor and business to decide on minimum wage, lay-off policies, duration of contracts, etc. While the Algerian law and the proposed Egyptian law make collective bargaining a fundamental right, other Arab laws are less forthcoming and assertive (Ilias, 67–68).

Unionization and Union Autonomy

However, a high level of unionization is not guaranteed by these laws. On one end of the spectrum stands the Tunisian law, which allows all enterprises with twenty or more workers to have a worker representative and every enterprise with 40 or more workers to have a labor committee (Ilias, 68). On the other end is the Jordanian law (8/1996, Articles 97–119). Collective bargaining is a guaranteed right, but the law requires 50 founders in the same industry/profession or related ones (private or public) to register a labor union, compared to 30 founders for a business association. In contrast, the proposed labor law in Egypt foresees collective bargaining in all enterprises. In enterprises employing 50 or more, negotiations take place between the union committee on the enterprise level, the general union on the industry level, and the employer. In smaller enterprises (less than 50), the general union represents the workers in negotiations with the employers' association (Article 148). Collective agreements last three years and should be ratified by majority vote of the executive board of the general union.

How autonomous are those unions? This is the most difficult dimension of labor/capital relations to assess. What ensures union autonomy? Union autonomy is a product of legal sanctions, hierarchical organization, and institutional traditions.

The Jordanian law made it an executive prerogative to determine the organizational structure of unions, saying little about the sanctity of union autonomy. Both the executive branch and the courts have final say if collective bargaining gets stuck. The law does not allow for a multiple-union structure, ordaining a unified hierarchy. The Minister of Labor specifies the industries that could have a union and the number of general unions in each industry. The internal operating procedures for unions are to be determined by the Federation of Unions, in consultation with the Ministry of Labor, according to Article 100. Unions do not exist until registered by the Ministry.[6] In case of any administrative or financial violation, the Ministry can sue the union, fortunately without the right to dissolve the union or assume leadership (Article 107). In cases of collective conflict, the minister assumes arbitration. Article 120 does not say when the executive should assume arbitration. The minister could form an arbitration committee comprised of an equal number of union members and employers' association members as well as a neutral arbiter. If it fails, a court composed of regular judges will give the solution.

The executive branch in Egypt for many years exerted control over the affairs of labor unions. It was able, for example, to exercise the right of exclusion by invoking Law 35/1976, which restricts the presence of workers who are also members of professional syndicates on the executive councils of labor unions. In 1993, however, the Constitutional Court ruled that such a restriction was unconstitutional, based on Egypt's international commitments and on the

Egyptian Constitution, both of which guarantee the freedom of labor unions, freedom of expression, and equal opportunities for participation (Egyptian Constitution Articles 47, 54, 55, and 56; *Dar al-Khadamat al-Ummaliya*).

Union leadership at the federation and confederation levels is nevertheless still open to manipulation by the state. The door has been left open to this possibility by Law 12/1995, which enables confederation leaders to remain in their positions past retirement age; additionally, federation and confederation leaders can remain in office even if promoted to senior management positions. Workers, for their part, cannot run for a federation office until they have served five years (full term) on a local executive board. They can achieve this status only with the support of federation leaders, who are given under this law enhanced powers to expel individuals from union membership.

Thanks to these opportunities for personal advancement, the union leadership has become comfortable and conservative. Some of these opportunities include serving on:

* Parliament and *Shura* Council,
* City councils representing the NDP,
* Board of General Council of the Holding Companies (according to Law 203/1991) which means profit share of 10%,
* Workers' institutions such as the Workers' Bank, Workers' University, North Coast Summer Resort.

This lack of clarity as to union autonomy further affects the right of workers to strike. This right had not been traditionally legalized in most of the Arab countries, under the assumption that workers had gained many benefits in the populist stage and should not harm the economy by going on strike. With the increasing withdrawal of the state from the economy and under pressure from the international community, the right to strike had to be sanctioned. There are two types of laws: one defines the right to strike negatively, and the other gives the right to strike with one hand while taking it away with the other.

In the Jordanian case (Articles 134 and 135) workers do not have the right to strike during arbitration, or during the implementation of the resolution of an arbitration, without notifying the employer fourteen days in advance (30 days in the case of public services). The right to strike is tacitly withdrawn by Article 116, according to which the Minister of Labor could submit a demand to the court asking a union to be dissolved because it was involved in a work stoppage, sit-in, or demonstration (*Qanun al-Amal* 8/1996, 57, 60, 66–67).

In the Egyptian case, the right to strike is slowly forcing itself onto the scene. Two court cases in 1987 and 1991 anchored that right in the Egyptian reality, ending the restrictive effect of Criminal Law Article 124 and Executive Decree 2/1977, which punished any civil servant who engaged with three colleagues or more in a strike, and anyone "who goes on strike to arrive at an interest, harming by their strike the national economy" (*Dar al-Khadamat*, 87–88).[7] In response to that, the proposed labor law would acknowledge the right to strike, but limit it to areas not considered "vital services." It is an executive prerogative to determine those services. Furthermore, workers have to obtain a two-thirds majority at the general union level and notify the employer and the concerned administrative agency two weeks before they go on strike (Articles 194–196).

Privatization and Labor in Egypt and Morocco

This section provides two case studies of how the dilemmas of labor and privatization discussed above have played out in practice, using Egypt and Morocco as examples. Separate overviews of each country begin with a review of its privatization program to date, noting specific policies aimed at winning labor support. We then summarize the structure of the country's labor movement and its relations to the government, followed by an analysis of how both union leaders, and rank and file workers, have responded to privatization and public sector reform. Finally, the overviews offer a more detailed look at the role of unions in shaping the legal framework for labor-state and labor-business relations in the context of structural reforms.

Morocco
Unlike its neighbors who more thoroughly embraced Arab socialism, Morocco has had an external orientation since independence.[8] The government has consistently offered incentives to attract private capital into export production. Nevertheless, a "Moroccanization" drive initiated in 1970 resulted in increasing the number of enterprises with direct or indirect state participation; these grew by roughly 75% in the following decade, and reached a total of about 620 companies by the end of 1985. (Payne, 149; World Bank 1996, 26–27; IMF 1995, 30) The monarchy began to express concerns about the size of the public sector towards the end of the 1970s. A stabilization plan implemented under IMF auspices in the early 1980s did include a freeze on civil service wages. However, the regime backed off of pursuing structural reforms when bureaucratic resistance became manifest. (IMF 1995, 8)

The call for privatization was renewed in 1988, with a ministry established in December, 1989. Law 39 of that year (officially promulgated in April, 1990), authorized privatization of 112 firms, to be completed by 1995. A program for public sector rationalization was initiated around the same time. Due to technical and political delays, however, the first sale did not occur until October, 1992. (Denoeux and Maghraoui, 60–61)

Through the summer of 1996, 25 companies and seventeen hotels were either completely or partially sold. At that point, Morocco led the Arab world in privatization proceeds. Nevertheless, the original privatization deadline had expired with less than half of the planned sales having been completed. The government extended it until 1998, adding two oil refineries to the original list. (World Bank 1996, 27; Khosrowshahi, 242–44)

With multilateral lenders urging a stepped-up pace, announcements of new tenders came rapidly in 1996 and 1997, including plans to privatize four of the largest state mines, the telephone service, and several sugar facilities. But the new government seated early in 1998, led by a former opposition leader, soon admitted that the process was hitting roadblocks, with only 52 companies having actually been sold. The first attempt at sugar privatization failed; the sale of the state development bank, BNDE, was aborted twice, with the intended sale of two other banks behind schedule; no buyer had been found for the fertilizer company (Fertimi); several hotel tenders had been launched without success; and telecommunications privatization was still in the planning stage. The government was faced with repaying privatization bonds issued in 1995, whose owners had been unable to trade them for shares of privatized firms.

In the spring of 1999, the parliament approved legislation proposed by new Privatization Minister Rachid Filali, to extend the program for selling the remainder until 2001. A law to this effect was passed in the spring of 1999, intended to expedite the sale of included firms. Plans to offer the state airline, Royal Air Maroc, were reportedly underway by the end of last year, with the government seeking international assistance in preparing for the sale of tobacco, phosphates, telecommunications, transport, energy, and other infrastructural concerns. However, the recent legislation also removed about 30 companies from the intended sale list, and the government is also expected to produce a "negative list" of firms that would be excluded from privatization.

Appeals for labor support

As in many developing countries, the public sector in Morocco provides not only a major source of employment for the lower strata, but also essential goods at subsidized prices. Accordingly, market reforms are a sensitive political issue. The country experienced food riots in 1981 and 1984 after attempted subsidy reduction, delaying price reform until 1985. Fearing that privatization would likewise engender social instability, the monarchy favored a gradual approach. Moreover, the regime delayed initiating privatization legislation until the late

1980s, after workers had begun to recover from the deleterious income effects of a public sector wage freeze in the early 1980s. Nevertheless, the original privatization law was the subject of sharp debate, even in a parliament dominated by pro-regime parties, and there were numerous modifications made to it. A wave of labor protest in 1989–90 reinforced the need for caution. (Payne, 55; Denoeux and Maghroui, 57–61; Khosrowshahi, 248–255; IMF, 9, 13)

The government therefore took steps to ensure that the program caused minimal social dislocation. One of the criteria for inclusion on the initial list of enterprises to be sold was lack of surplus labor, and all buyers were required to retain the inherited work force for at least five years. In addition, the regime sought to garner support for the program by using it to create opportunities for ordinary Moroccans to share in wealth generation. Although the ministry's preferred method of sale was to anchor investors, in many transactions a percentage of shares were reserved for employees and offered to them at a discount. In 1996, the government launched the sale of privatization bonds, which purchasers could exchange for shares in firms being privatized. (Khosrowshahi, 244–51; World Bank 1996, 27)

Various analyses suggest that the government was largely successful in these efforts to preempt or ameliorate popular opposition to privatization. According to Denoeux and Maghroui (65–66), the original 1995 deadline was not met in part because of resistance from entrenched financial, political, and bureaucratic interests. Nevertheless, they assert, privatization has not generated significant social disorder, and there has been a widespread acceptance among opposition forces regarding the need to diminish the role of state in the economy. Khosrowshahi (244) and the World Bank (1996, 26) concur that the sell-off program has popular support.

There was, however, uncertainty over the program's future after the success of the opposition bloc in the 1997 legislative elections. The government of USFP leader Aberrahmane Yousoufi, while proceeding with most of the intended sales, has removed some enterprises from the list. Moreover, the most recent privatization legislation passed in the upper chamber of parliament with a narrow 96–84 margin, with most opposition delegates casting negative votes. The new government is pushing, against some resistance from conservative forces, for increased social spending. A former privatization minister has suggested that future proceeds from privatization, previously earmarked for reducing the current budget deficit, should instead go towards social programs, including worker retraining. And the World Bank has suggested that, when the program moves from offering more successful firms to selling those with significant overemployment, there will be a need for some form of targeted compensation to redundant workers. Such measures may, however, conflict with IMF pressures on Morocco to quicken the reforms and reduce the burden of civil service wages on the treasury. (World Bank 1996, 27–28; IMF, 22; Layachi 1999, 17–18, 22)

Moroccan labor and privatization

Morocco maintains a system of competitive unionism. There are three main confederations: the UMT, the CDT, and the UGTM. The latter two are tied to political parties—the USFP and *Istiqlal*, respectively–which were until recently in opposition. Leaders of these confederations typically hold prominent party positions as well. (Alexander 1999, 2–3) Another fifteen smaller unions, including one recently launched by another former opposition party, the PPS, vie with these larger ones. Recently, six of the smaller unions formed a coalition in an effort to strengthen their position.

Historically, Moroccan unions have been closely supervised by the government. Their activities are monitored by the internal intelligence services, and the government has at times interfered in union leadership selection and union operations. At the local level, unionists have been subjected to police intimidation, and there is at least one recent case of a detained unionist being tortured. The International Labor Organization expressed concern earlier in this decade that the freedom to associate was not being respected in Morocco (U.S. Dept. of State 1994).

Morocco's main labor unions have been antagonistic towards the abandonment of the public sector. Unionists, in their own right and through the opposition parties they belong to, have joined other forces in charging that the structural adjustment program in general has contributed to a concentration of wealth in few hands. (Political Risk Service December, 1994; Khosrowshahi, 250–51) Supported by their affiliated unions, the opposition parties criticized the austerity budgets of the late 1980s as being "anti-social," and refused to join the government following the 1993 elections, when the monarchy made this offer conditional on their agreement to continue the IMF-mandated reforms and privatization. Thereafter, all the opposition parties represented in parliament voted against the bill extending the deadline of the sell-off program from the end of 1995 to the end of 1998. Likewise, there was a strong "nay" vote from opposition parties to last spring's legislation intended to speed up privatization.

Nevertheless, trade union leaders have to date not mobilized their membership behind any specific campaigns versus privatization. The political system provides one explanation for this. Given their links to political parties, unions have tended to feel that they need their party's support for any militancy, and thus to tailor their own organizing programs to the parties broader agenda. The opposition parties, in turn, have focused their energies on trying to end electoral irregularities, in order to increase their representation in parliament. (Alexander, 4–5, 13)

However, Morocco's partial use of indirect legislative elections, which enables union officials to select some of their ranks as MPs, does create incentives for unionists contesting local elections to champion workers' grievances. That privatization per se has not claimed greater attention in local union election campaigns seems due to the fact that, until very recently, the program has not directly threatened union members with job loss. In addition to the government-imposed requirement that buyers pledge to maintain the work force of the enterprises they purchase for at least five years, the sell-off list itself largely avoided large-scale employers and union strongholds—such as railways and phosphate mining and processing—in favor of smaller enterprises in such areas as tourism and food processing. With the government's efforts to control the budget deficit focused instead on holding down wages, slowing promotions, and cutting social expenditures, issues revolving around real wages and social protection have proven more central to workers than job protection. (Alexander, 4–5, 13) Strike waves in the late 1980s, and again in 1995–96, revolved around those issues.

Recent developments suggest that this dynamic is changing, however. With the opposition's agreement to form the government, the leadership of the main left-leaning parties has abandoned its opposition to privatization. This factor would tend to imply growing moderation on the part of the unions affiliated with these parties as well. However, the unaffiliated UMT may be using this situation to appeal to workers on the basis of non-complicity with the new government's reform program. The UMT was recently involved in strikes in the banking, postal, maritime, and pharmaceutical sectors, the latter incident related to the hiring of temporary workers. It expressed reservations about, and refused to sign some aspects of, a wage and benefits agreement negotiated between the government and the three large confederations in the summer of 1997. Unionists from the other two confederations may thus be feeling pressure to assert some independence from their affiliated parties. Just last December, a meeting between the unions and the government, initiated by the former, turned confrontational, and led to a union walkout. The UMT accused the authorities of consistently violating labor rights, and other union leaders called the new government's labor policy a failure.

At the same time, privatization is now moving into more strategic areas previously avoided, where there are more jobs at stake, and this could generate greater labor opposition. Thus far, the government and the unions have successfully negotiated compensation plans in those cases where job loss is anticipated. In the postal and telecommunications areas, a restructuring plan prior to privatization calls for most redundant workers to be reassigned, but some will be laid off with severance packages. A similar plan exists for compensating redundant miners. However, there are also indications that the progress of privatization is causing workers in general to feel more vulnerable, as evidenced by the fact that the first half of 1999 saw 32% more strikes than the same period in 1998, with a 44% increase in the number of workers involved, and a 102% increase in workdays lost.

Labor law and the private sector
• Job Security Provisions:
  A compendium of laws comprise the legal framework for employment in Morocco. These laws specify that workers must be hired by contract, which can be either temporary, for up to one year, or permanent. All hiring actions must be reported to the government, and dismissal or lay-off is considered a breach of contract. Workers may be dismissed without advance notice for serious fault, but the burden of proof rests on the employer. Employers are required to obtain official approval before individual or mass dismissals for economic reasons.[9] If such permission is obtained and the employer subsequently decides to expand operations again, s/he is required to rehire the laid-off workers before new applicants may be considered. Permanent workers who are laid off are also entitled to severance pay, based on their number of years in service. (World Bank 1997, vol. I, iii, and vol. II, Annex 5, 1–5)
  Workers maintain that outside of government employment, these provisions actually offer scant protection. Although private sector unionization rates are high in Morocco relative to its neighbors, the majority of private sector workers are nevertheless unorganized. Moreover, in areas such as textiles and handicrafts, as well as in the informal sector, labor laws and regulations are poorly enforced. Workers have charged that private sector employers routinely get around the labor laws by hiring them on temporary contracts and then asking them to resign after one year. They are given a small compensation and then rehired as newcomers. Employers thus avoid giving workers permanent status and the higher pay that would come with it. In addition, although the courts can order employers to rehire workers who were fired unjustly, workers complain that such cases can be expensive and drawn-out. (U.S. State Dept. 1994) All of this contributes to a preference on the part of employed laborers, as well as young job seekers, for government employment, and explains part of the reason for labor's reservations about privatization.
  Nevertheless, both domestic and foreign employers have complained that the labor laws are an impediment to successful business operations, and a disincentive to potential buyers of public sector firms. They and

Morocco's multilateral lenders have been pressing for revisions to the labor laws. A new labor code has been under discussion since 1994, but has yet to be passed. Unions have resisted attempts to diminish the existing laws' job security protections.

The proposed new legislation (as of the end of 1997) reflects a compromise that falls well short of investors' desires. On the one hand, it would lessen the time allotted to the government to respond to mass dismissal requests, from the current three months to one. At the same, however, it makes the requirements for submitting such applications more cumbersome. It also increases the severance pay for dismissed employees, more than doubling it for workers with more than five years of service (World Bank 1997, vol. I, vol. II).

• Collective Bargaining:

An implied right to organize and bargain collectively exists in the constitution, but institutions for the latter are not highly developed. Fewer than 5% of Moroccan workers are covered by collective bargaining agreements, and the vast majority of these are civil servants or parastatal employees. Unions complain that managers and employers refuse to negotiate seriously, even in the public enterprises. In addition, no specific law protects workers from anti-union discrimination, and unions charge that employers routinely fire workers for trade union activity. The ILO has criticized the Moroccan government for tolerating these practices. (U. S. Dept. of State 1994)

Formally, Moroccan workers enjoy the right to strike. However, work stoppages are expected to last 24 hours or less, and the penal code has provisions against "violating the sacred institutions of the state" and "interfering with the right to work." These stipulations are frequently invoked against strikers. (U.S. Dept. of State 1996)

Following a strike wave in 1995 that continued into 1996, representatives of various trade unions, the main businessmen's association, and the government entered into a "social dialogue" in June of 1996. They agreed to hold two meetings annually to examine issues of joint concern, and to establish a permanent tripartite committee to follow up on problems and implement joint decisions. In addition to a number of provisions intended to increases wages and pensions and improve social protection, employers and the government made a commitment to respect the right to organize and to strike, and to improve the climate for negotiation of collective bargaining agreements. The government also pledged to honor all international agreements that it had signed.

Yet despite the fanfare and optimism that accompanied the signing of this pact, unions charge that its terms were soon violated. In 1998, the CDT threatened a strike in the postal and telecom sectors, claiming that the stipulations of the 1996 agreement regarding working conditions and regular consultation had not been implemented. With the CDT's party affiliate heading the new government, the social dialogue resumed in the spring of 1999. However, although the government offered tax relief for the poor, increased social spending, including for youth job creation, and higher pensions, no agreement was reached. A new tripartite commission was established, but the end of 1999 saw the unions walk out of negotiations, suggesting that labor concerns have not yet been satisfactorily addressed.

Egypt
The first calls for privatization in Egypt were issued in 1973, but there was little progress during the 1970s and 1980s.[10] As late as 1988, President Hosni Mubarak repeated earlier vows that he would neither sell nor shrink the public sector. The government's new openness to privatization began in 1989, after the effective collapse of a standby agreement that Egypt had signed with the IMF in May, 1987. The IMF now insisted that many reforms be implemented *prior* to the signing of a new agreement.

The government began by selling off small enterprises owned by the governorates. Then, in June, 1991, Law 203, the "public enterprise legislation" necessary to proceed with privatization of larger industrial establishments, was passed. In addition to paving the way for full or partial privatization of parastatals, the law sought to make public sector firms operate more efficiently by grouping the 300-odd state-owned enterprises (SOEs) into several dozen holding companies whose members would be appointed by the government, and who were expected to manage their portfolios according to market principles. While the holding companies themselves would be wholly state-owned, their minimum share of equity in the subsidiary firms was set at 51%; the remaining 49% of the assets could be purchased by the private sector through subscriptions.[11] However, the holding companies could also decide to maintain only a minority share in a subsidiary, and in this case the firm would be considered a private sector joint venture subject to the terms of the private companies law. Finally, the holding companies were empowered to divest themselves of a subsidiary completely, or close it down.

The pace of the sell-offs in the early 1990s was nevertheless rather slow. There were delays in developing the capital market and in the identification and valuation of the candidates for privatization. Egypt's multilateral lenders complained publicly of government foot-dragging, and privately acknowledged that one reason for urging haste in the reform program was to deprive its opponents of sufficient time to mobilize resistance. Privatization rose to the forefront of new negotiations with the IMF in 1996. Accordingly, the government announced plans for more extensive and rapid privatization, marking a turning point in the sell-off program.

As of June, 2000, 137 out of 314 state-owned enterprises (SOEs) had been fully or partially sold.[12] These were mainly manufacturing ventures, but the government has now pledged to offer utilities, public sector banks and insurance companies, maritime and telecommunications firms, and prominent tourist hotels. In May, 1998, the IMF finally pronounced itself satisfied with the program's progress. Measured in terms of annual privatization receipts as a percentage of GDP, their report noted, Egypt's ranked fourth internationally, trailing only Hungary, Malaysia, and the Czech Republic.

Appeals for Labor Support
In the seventeen years from the first calls for privatization to the passage of Law 203, privatization was a highly controversial topic in Egypt. Labor unions and opposition parties spearheaded the campaign against it, but there was resistance from within the government and the ruling National Democratic Party (NDP) as well. Concerns revolved in part around the anticipated negative social consequences of a sell off for workers.

Social concerns arose from the fear that privatization would result in mass lay-offs, worsening an already severe problem with unemployment. As well, discrepancies in job security and social insurance between the public and private sectors have caused workers to fear that even if they are able to find private sector employment to replace a lost parastatal position, their futures will be more vulnerable. Private sector employees aspiring to government jobs in the future similarly fear the closing of that avenue to them.

As in Morocco, the Mubarak regime has taken several steps in an effort to assuage popular concerns about privatization. The government began the program in 1989 by selling off small enterprises outside of the large industrial areas where union membership was concentrated. After Law 203 was passed, the government proclaimed that its privatization program was geared towards protecting workers' jobs and livelihoods, and no lay-off clauses were specified in the agreements to sell SOEs.

In the early 1990s, the government supported a World Bank proposal for the creation of a "social fund," to which Egypt's creditors would contribute, to ease the burdens of structural reform on the poor. Part of the money is earmarked for retraining public sector workers who will be displaced by privatization. In addition, the government formally embraced the idea of employee share in ownership (ESOP) plans, which will give workers a stake in the financial success of privatized firms. Employee shareholder associations have been vigorously promoted, and some 10 facilities have been sold almost entirely to their employees.

Although mass lay-offs were thus avoided in the early 1990s, public sector managers were under pressure to make their firms more profitable, and their first line of attack was often workers. Numerous firms that had earlier resorted to hiring temporary workers now began to dismiss them. Other establishments simply declared that large numbers of their full-time, permanent employees were redundant, and therefore no longer entitled to the supplementary wages that often comprised about two-thirds of workers' take-home pay. Such actions provided a basis for continued popular opposition to structural adjustment.

Moreover, with the advance of the privatization program, the number of workers threatened with job loss has risen dramatically. Since the labor law still precludes mass lay-offs, prospective buyers must agree to maintain the existing workforce of their firms. As a consequence, the government is endeavoring to make the remaining SOEs more attractive to investors by streamlining the work force prior to sale. Early-retirement incentives are the vehicle for this.

Negotiated between the government and the trade union confederation, the program entitles workers accepting early retirement to receive a lump-sum payment, based on their years of service, and a monthly stipend. The agreed-upon package represents the minimum that workers can get; individual plant managers and local union leaders are in some cases free to negotiate more lucrative packages for workers.[13] The early retirement program is paid for by the Social Development Fund and by privatization proceeds.

While many workers have welcomed the early-retirement opportunity, others worry that the monthly stipend may be less than half the pension they would have received under the old system. Workers say it is insufficient to meet regular expenses, and that their prospects for finding new employment to supplement the stipend are bleak. In addition, retiring workers risk eviction from cheap company housing complexes.

The official rationale for the lump-sum approach is that recipients should invest in a small business, or in stocks, thus fostering economic growth. But many workers are instead tempted to spend the money on large-scale expenses, like those associated with marrying their children. Those who do spend their money rapidly, or whose investment schemes fail, face a dismal future.[14]

Reports in 1997 indicated that program enrollment was falling short of government targets, and labor activists charged that some workers were being pressured into enrolling under threat of wage cuts or transfer. By the end of 1998, however, the rate of acceptance had gone up to an unofficial estimate of 60,000 workers. Labor activists attributed this increase to workers' growing fear that once the new labor law was enacted they would risk being fired with no compensation whatsoever, in a country that lacks unemployment insurance. However, some Egyptian social scientists suggested at that time that the demand for early retirement had begun to exceed the funds available to the government for financing it, and that the regime itself was now seeking to slow down the program. More study is clearly needed before definitive conclusions can be drawn about the success of this program.

Trade Unions and Privatization

Trade unionism in Egypt

The trade union system in Egypt bears little resemblance to that in Morocco. Organized Egyptian workers—which means virtually all public sector employees but in the private sector only those in the largest establishments—all belong to a single trade union confederation, the Egyptian Trade Union Federation (hereafter ETUF).[15] The ETUF consists of 23 federations, each representing a different industry or service. It is hierarchically run and subject to government supervision, characteristics which, combined with the lack of union competition, comprise what political scientists typically associate with corporatism.

As in Morocco, but seemingly to a greater extent, the government also influences the union leadership selection process. During the single-party era, candidates for union office were required to be members of the Arab Socialist Union. Since the advent of partisan competition, senior union officials are expected to be members of the ruling NDP, and the ETUF president is typically pre-selected by NDP leaders prior to the ETUF's confirming vote. Recently, as previously mentioned, the government took steps to consolidate the position of the loyal unionists, further insulating them from rank and file pressures and tightening the control of the federations over the locals.

At the lower union levels, the government engaged in a purge of leftists during the late 1970s, and prevented dozens from contesting elections in the 1980s. These forms of intervention appear to have receded in the 1990s, but workers still complain of occasional electoral irregularities sponsored by management or local NDP officials.

Union leaders and privatization

Despite their NDP affiliations, senior unionists were staunch opponents of privatization in the late 1970s and 1980s, allied with some public sector managers in what some considered to be a "Nasserist wing" of the party. Indeed, with little effort by the ETUF to organize private sector workers, protecting the public sector came to be the organization's *raison d'être*, and a point of unity between it and both leftist and nationalist opposition movements. The ETUF's stance was a major factor in defeating several privatization initiatives prior to the 1990s.

It was a departure from past practice, then, that the ETUF did endorse Law 203. Union acquiescence was achieved in part through heightened levels of pressure, combined with a continuation of governmental co-optation techniques. Significant pressure was exerted on union MPs to win their votes, and some nevertheless refused to support the bill. However, the confederation's ongoing cooperation was also purchased through concessions to labor's concerns, which enabled senior unionists to claim that privatization would not harm the interests of their membership. One was that the prevailing requirement that 10% of company profits be distributed to workers remain intact; in fact a previously existing annual cap on the amount of profit shares workers could receive was removed. Secondly, the final version of Law 203 specified that existing national labor legislation, with its protections against arbitrary firing and mass lay-offs, and provisions for health and accident insurance and pensions, would continue to apply until overwritten by a new labor law.

Senior unionists nevertheless faced a contradiction between yielding to governmental pressures, and maintaining some semblance of credibility with a rank and file very fearful of privatization. In the 1991 trade union elections that followed the passage of Law 203, leftists opposed to privatization captured about 25% of the leadership positions in the public sector industrial locals, doubling their previous presence. The corporatist system protected senior union personnel from losing their posts in the elections—changes at the top occurred only due to retirements—but they appear to have been chastened by some significant NDP losses at the base.

Thereafter, the senior unionists did begin to draw more public and private battle lines around the maintenance of workers' customary rights and benefits. By the end of 1992 the confederation, despite having endorsed Law 203, was at odds with the government over its application. At its general assembly in December, the confederation passed a resolution condemning privatization and called for legalizing strikes if any workers did lose their jobs as a result of public sector diminution. Significantly, and for the first time in its history, the delegates refused to send the customary telegram of support to the government, and the decision rejecting this gesture was unanimous.

In an effort to mollify the ETUF, the government began adding federation officials to the boards of holding companies for firms whose workers the unionists represented. This enabled unionists so inclined to carry on the struggle against privatization in other venues. However, it also put them into the same social circles as the business elites comprising much of these boards'

membership, providing new avenues for unionists to identify with the entrepreneurial class.

Moreover, while ETUF leaders warned publicly that massive lay-offs due to
privatization could produce a "social explosion," they made no effort to mobilize
the membership behind these implicit threats. Their actions were confined to
public statements and behind-the-scenes lobbying of other governmental elites.
It also appears that, whatever their private motivations, the senior unionists
reached the conclusion that they had already lost the battle for preserving the
public sector and its work force, and now came to redefine their function as winning the best terms for workers who would be displaced or reclassified.
Discussions of trade-offs increasingly found their way into their public statements, as they negotiated these with the government in closed-door committees.

By 1994 ETUF opposition to privatization *per se* had receded. ETUF
President Sayyid Rashid declared in 1995 that Egyptian workers supported privatization in light of President Hosni Mubarak's promises that it would not hurt
them. Some senior unionists did prove more recalcitrant, trying to block sales
from their positions on the holding company boards, and/or fighting for better
terms for workers in the early-retirement program. However, these leaders were
removed by the government during the 1996 trade union elections.[16]

The rank and file

Lack of support from the union hierarchy is an obstacle to rank and file action,
but does not necessarily prevent it. Egyptian workers have a history of protest-
ing informally over their grievances when unions prove unresponsive. Such
actions often appear spontaneous, and tend to be short-lived. However, the vic-
tories of leftists in more local elections in the 1990s meant that more protests
have some support at the local level than in the past.

In the early 1990s, rank and file protest was largely focused on public sector
rationalization measures linked to impending privatization. Many of the actions,
as in earlier periods of rank and file insurgency, were symbolic—hunger strikes,
paycheck boycotts, or sit-ins—as opposed to actual work stoppages. In taking
such actions, workers communicated their belief that they were productive, and
that their labor contributed positively to Egypt's national development project.

Since the privatization program was accelerated in 1996, there has been an
upsurge of rank and file protests related to it. These incidents can be categorized
as follows:

1. Protests against sales and closures are precipitated by announcements
   from the holding companies of intended sales or closures of plants.
2. Protests against pre-sale take-aways may erupt following efforts by public

sector managers to improve the financial performance of their firms so that they will be more attractive for sale. Such measures have often resulted in diminutions of workers' pay and benefits, dismissals of temporary employees, and/or in harsh disciplinary actions intended to encourage workers to leave voluntarily.

3. Post-sale protests. There are numerous reports of setbacks for workers who initially remain employed after privatization. New owners have resorted to laying off temporary employees, subjecting permanent workers to forced transfers, cutting back on bonuses and incentive pay, forcing workers to sign new contracts with a lower basic wage, and increasing use of monetary penalties for lateness, absence, or poor job performance. In addition to the customary forms of symbolic protest, workers in such cases have also sought redress through the courts.

4. Unmet early retirement promises. There have been numerous cases of companies delaying early retirement payments to workers, or failing to pay them the promised amount. Also, some agricultural concerns have failed to deliver on promised parcels of land, rather than cash payments, as an incentive to retire.

5. Distributional norms. The desire for equal treatment of workers has also been in evidence. Some protests have been in response to perceived injustices in company decisions about which workers will be kept on, and which forced to retire or be transferred. Others have involved disparities between early-retirement packages offered to workers in different locations.

Although most of the above incidents continued to represent symbolic protests, recent years have included also a growing number of actual strikes. (LCHR Reports 1998, 1999) This appears to reflect a changing mentality among workers: if their labor is indeed unproductive, as the rationale for privatization suggests, then the basis for the government's legal prohibition against striking ceases to make sense. The government, in turn, appears to be changing its response to such incidents. Repression has not been eliminated. Several of the incidents reported here involved large numbers of arrests, and in numerous cases when state security was called upon to break up plant occupations, tear gas was employed. But in the most recent cases, and unlike previous labor incidents, there were no reports of either ordinance being used or of violence. It thus appears that the government is implicitly acknowledging that it cannot continue to repress labor protest sharply while giving state managers and private sector employers a freer hand in their treatment of workers.

Privatization and Labor Law
As previously explained, Egypt's current labor law (No. 37 of 1981) is very similar to Morocco's with regard to job security provisions. Also like in Morocco, many Egyptian private sector employers have systematically evaded the old protections against firing, through techniques such as using only temporary contracts and terminating workers briefly before renewing them, forcing workers to sign blank contracts, or undated resignation letters upon hiring. Nevertheless these employers, as well as multinational firms operating in Egypt, have pressed for an easing-up on anti-firing regulations, and multilateral agencies have joined the call for a more liberal labor code.

Debate over revising the labor law actually began several years earlier in Egypt than in Morocco. The government established a committee to begin drafting new legislation in October, 1991, but its progress was slow. Union leaders, under the spotlight of the opposition press, continued to resist the retraction of job security and other traditional benefits enjoyed by public sector workers. The various parties involved in the negotiations finally agreed on their sixteenth draft at the end of 1994, but the bill's submission to parliament was repeatedly delayed. A slightly modified version has now been scheduled for consideration at a later date.

As mentioned above, the proposed new legislation would retain the requirement for firms to obtain government approval for any mass work force reductions. But it signals a sea change by stating explicitly that it is an employer's right to adjust the work force according to economic conditions. The law does contain provisions for legalizing strikes, but would still render permissible work stoppages rare. Although these restrictions were endorsed, if not recommended, by the businessmen's representatives, some employers remain unenthusiastic about the proposed law. Indeed, because smaller domestic entrepreneurs have historically evaded the labor laws, they stand to gain little from the right to strike/right to fire exchange. It would increase their management prerogatives legally, but not actually, while they would lose some claim to government assistance in suppressing labor protest.[17] At the same time, the repeated delays in issuing the law suggest that the regime itself is not anxious to legalize labor protest in even this sharply limited manner. With rank and file workers, labor activists and leftist opposition parties opposing the law for different reasons, its main defenders appear to be the senior unionists whose control over the base would be further tightened by its provisions.

Nevertheless, the progress of privatization poses a challenge to the ETUF. Union centralization was beneficial to workers, and solicited by them, when the economy was largely centrally directed and the government was responsible for determining the wages, benefits, and working conditions of most formal sector workers. As the state's role in the economy recedes and workplace decision-making becomes more decentralized, the rationale for corporatist union systems is eroded. The more single agreements between workers and employers at individual plants come to define workers' wages and livelihoods, the more free they will want their locals to be. Thus, pressures for decentralized and competitive unionism, already evident in the 1980s and early 1990s, seem likely to increase with the anticipated passage of the new labor law.

The Future of Unions and the Potential for Autonomy

The populist deal that ensured workers their right to work and to a minimum wage is being dismantled. Instead, work relations are supposed to be negotiated by representatives who are not autonomous enough to be credible negotiators. That is an unsustainable position, in the long run. How can we explain/predict the future of unions? Which factors could help us understand the position of business and the ruling elite regarding more union autonomy? In the following section, we propose two approaches that could help us discern the structural and institutional factors contributing to unionization in the Arab non-oil economies.

The Factor Endowment Theory

The representation of labor is not just a political question. Labor is a factor of production that does not operate in isolation from other factors, namely land and capital. We focus our attention in this study on capital. The factor endowment theory[18] considers mobility of labor and capital crucial in explaining the building of a broad class alliance, for mobility would fragment both factors of production and make them focus on factory-level alliances/negotiations, rather than on class cleavages. For Ronald Rogowski, on the other hand, capital's willingness to cooperate with organized labor is strengthened if labor unions can limit disruptive strikes, and can impose uniform wage settlements, i.e., when labor is relatively immobile, which enhances the likelihood that unions are well organized and hence attractive partners to capital. (Garst, 23, 30–31; Rogowski) The same could be said of capital. If capital were mobile, it would have an exit option that could increase its intransigence in any negotiation with labor.

In other words, the endowment theory predicts fragmented factory-level alliances between business and labor when capital and labor are mobile. A capital-labor relationship based on strong unions requires, on the other hand, immobile capital (no exit option and no monopolistic mergers or cartels) and immobile labor (to allow unions captive membership).

Let us look at the position of capital and labor in the non-oil Arab economies:

Capital endowment

Capital endowment depends on the relative supply of capital, rates of savings, rates of growth, rates of inflow of FDI, credit policies, and domestic capital markets that facilitate investment (Hollister and Goldstein, 38).

Overall, the MENA region is capital-scarce, due to low rates of savings, low rates of growth, and capital flight. While earlier models of development had compensated for weak domestic capital endowment with foreign aid, development thought nowadays recommends FDI. FDI to all MENA countries constitutes only 2.01% of FDI flows to the emerging economies. That level of FDI constitutes only 0.5% of MENA GNP (similar for GDP), compared to 1.5% in developing countries. Capital scarcity is also not compensated for by funds raised in international capital markets, for the latter in the MENA region constitute only 2.3% of funds raised in international capital markets by emerging economies (ERF, 33, 41).[19]

If the non-oil Arab countries are economies with scarce capital, that should lead us to expect large-capital immobility. Moreover, given credit policies that are not yet able to mobilize savings or offer investment loans for medium- and small-level enterprises, and given the nascent to weak capital markets, one would expect medium- and small-sized capital to suffer from scarcity as well, and hence be immobile.

According to the capital endowment theory, immobile capital does not lead to fragmented alliances with workers on the factory level. The likelihood is that business will align itself with bigger unions, if the latter are capable of negotiating reliably. Therefore, one can see the relevance of labor representation, given the endowment position of capital.

Capital activity

There is yet another dimension to capital endowment, namely the activity of available capital. In the Arab context under study, the structure of capital is not yet diversified enough. There is a concentration of capital in public hands, despite liberalization and privatization. Moreover, private capital is concentrated in trade and services, with few ventures into value-added manufacturing. That could partly explain the weak business demand for autonomous labor unions. Business still is willing to depend on state control of unions, rather than bargaining collectively with autonomous labor unions.

For example, Jordan is a capital-poor country; local savings are relatively low, government debt service is high (al-Anani, 315), and FDI is limited (see

Table 3.1). But private capital is on the rise. The early 1990s witnessed an increase of 118% in private companies, whereas public corporations contracted from 31 to 25, and that of public share-holding companies declined from 115 to 112. Two features characterize Jordanian private capital, making it typical of most private capital in the MENA:

1. It "had essentially originated in the rent that accrued on the value of real estate properties as it enormously appreciated with the massive inflow of remittances of citizens working abroad, and... inflow of Arab and other external financial assistance" in 1970s and 1980s (Kanaan).
2. It is heavily concentrated in non-manufacturing activities such as finance, insurance, real estate, and business services.[20] Furthermore, although manufacturing exports have a high share of total Jordanian exports, their share of non-oil exports is quite moderate (see Table 3.2).

Compared to Jordan, Egypt's capital is starting to diversify, but is not yet strong enough in the manufacturing sector, not even in comparison to Morocco and Tunisia (Table 3.2). The public sector still possesses a dominant position in terms of investment, employment, and value added in the manufacturing sector. Where the private sector is strong, capital enterprises are small or medium-sized. The credit policy and the capital market are still not capable of increasing available capital for those firms. Big firms, on the other hand, tend to diversify their portfolios, and work in family business structures that rely heavily on strong government relations, a tendency that has characterized capital since the 1920s (Vitalis). A survey analysis of the business community in Egypt done in 1999 has proven that the ability of the business community to rely on the extensive network of business associations for collective bargaining still leaves a lot to be desired (El-Mikawy et al 2000).

Given capital activities in the non-oil countries, labor unions are mostly filled with public sector wage-earners or non-skilled workers in the private sector, workers who are anxious about unemployment and would not push for autonomous, strong unions.

Competitiveness

Ironically, globalization could give Arab businessmen in non-oil economies a reason to support state control of labor unions. Most countries of the region are engaged in the global market due to their dependence on international demand for their exports of primary products and their dependence on imports of essential goods and services. However, MENA's share of international trade is only 3.4% (in 1996) and dynamic manufactured products remain under-represented

Table 3.1. Net Foreign Direct Investment (FDI)
Inflows 1985–96 in $ mill.

Country	1985–90	1991	1992	1993	1994	1995	1996
Egypt	1086	253	459	493	1256	598	740
Jordan	25	-12	41	-34	16	15	20
Morocco	83	317	422	491	551	290	400
Tunisia	80	125	526	526	432	264	370
Turkey	340	810	844	636	608	885	1,116
Dev. Countries	24,736	41,696	49,625	73,045	90,462	96,330	128,741
Asia	13,492	23,129	29,632	50,924	57,507	65,249	84,283

Source: *Economic Trends in MENA Region 1998*, p. 34.

Table 3.2. Exports in Manufacturing and Services as % of Total
Exports

Country	Manufactured Exports as % of total Exports		Manufactured Exports as % of total non-oil Exports		Export of Services as % of total Exports	
	1980	1993	1985	1994	1993	1996
Egypt	11	33	41.5	63.7	69.1	66.0
Jordan	34	51	23.3	21.1	55.8	50.4
Morocco	24	57	21.7	35.5	40.4	25.5
Tunisia	36	75	47.8	71.2	35.0	32.3
Turkey	27	72	61.3	70.3	40.6	28.8

Source: *World Bank Development Report 1997*, p. 242–243 and
Economic Trends in MENA Region 1998, p. 61 & 71.

in the region's exports, with primary products constituting over 70% of total exports (ERF, 59–61). Though the share of manufacturing in total exports increased in the 1990s,[21] so that in 1994 the manufacturing of non-oil exports in countries like Egypt and Tunisia was in the same range as Eastern Europe (Table 3.2), most Arab non-oil economies still pale in comparison to Turkey, except for Tunisia. Furthermore, the service sector has the lion's share of value added as a percentage of GDP in all non-oil Arab economies, with manufacturing value added trailing behind (Table 3.3).

Pressed for competitive operating conditions, business could perceive unions that would ask for more wages and more management-sharing as a threat. What remains to be seen is how Arab capital will bargain politically to increase its competitiveness. Historically, big capital had to fight for resources by forming cartels, cultivating rent-seeking ties to the ruling elite, and welcoming state control of unions.

Labor endowment
Labor supply is an important factor determining the nature and strength of labor organization. Labor supply is influenced by the rate of population growth (and thus population structure), quality of education, rate of unemployment, and the type of labor market segmentation.

Population Growth Rates
The Arab world has some of the fastest-growing population rates in the world. Whereas the average population growth rate in lower middle- and middle-income countries in the 1980s and 1990s was 1.4%, Egypt's, Morocco's, and Tunisia's population growth rates grew by an average of 2.2%, and Jordan's by 4.1% (Table 3.4). Egypt and Morocco had almost 40% of their respective populations in the 0–14 age category in 1990, Jordan 45%, and Yemen 48% (Hollister and Goldstein, 18–19).

Growth Rate of the Labor Force
The non-oil Arab countries also share a high rate of annual growth of their labor force. Between 1980 and 1997, Jordan's labor force grew by 5.3%, Egypt's and Morocco's expanded by 2.6%, and Tunisia's grew by 2.9%. These are more than the average rates in low middle-income and middle-income countries (Table 3.5). Meanwhile, unemployment rates are also high—hovering between 12–18%. Most of the unemployed are young workers with no job experience.

Unskilled Labor Abundance
Unskilled labor is abundant, while skilled labor is scarce, despite all the effort and money spent on education in the past 25 years. The average number of years of formal education in the entire MENA region is far below that in Asia or Latin America (ERF, 126). Accordingly, most jobs are in the services and commerce, making the share of labor in value-added industries weak, compared with middle-income countries.

Manufacturing Sector Share of the Labor Force and of GDP
One common feature of labor markets in non-oil Arab economies is the predominance of the service sector's share of the labor force, compared to those of industry and manufacturing. On one hand, the distribution of the labor force

Table 3.3. Structure of the economy: production 1980 & 1995

Indicator	Egypt 1980	Egypt 1995	Jordan 1980	Jordan 1995	Morocco 1980	Morocco 1995	Tunisia 1980	Tunisia 1995
GDP in 000,000	22.91	47.34	—	6.10	18.82	32.41	8.74	18.03
Ag. VA as % GDP*	18	20	—	8	18	14	14	12
Ind. VA as % GDP**	37	21	—	27	31	33	31	29
Man. VA % GDP***	12	15	—	14	17	19	12	19
Ser. VA % GDP#	45	59	—	65	51	53	55	59

* = Agriculture value added
** = Industry value added
*** = Manufacturing value added as % of GDP
# = Services value added as % of GDP
Source: *World Development Report 1997*, p. 236–7

Table 3.4. GDP, Population, Population in Poverty in 1980–95

Country	GDP per capita in US$ 1987 & 1995	Annual Growth Rate 1980–95	Population in 000 & 1997	Annual Growth Rate 1980–97	Population in Poverty In % Urban 1980s & 1990s	Population in Poverty In % Rural 1980s & 1990s
Egypt	726	1.4	64,465	2.3	26 & 29	19 & 21
Jordan	—	—	5774	4.1	14	17
Morocco	871	0.7	27,518	2.1	28 & 14	45 & 17
Tunisia	1436	1.3	9326	2.2	22 & 10	42 & 7
Av. Lower-middle Income 1990–95		-1.5		1.4		
Av. Middle Income 1990–95		0.1		1.4		

Source: *World Employment Report 1998–99*, p. 213–14 and *World Development Report 1997*, p. 220 & 234.

by sector shows an increase in the share of industry in 1997, compared with 1980: Egypt (a ten-point increase), Morocco (7.5 points), and Tunisia (four points). On the other hand, the rise in the share of manufacturing in the labor force in those countries in 1997 was not as splendid when compared to 1980 levels: Egypt's labor force share in manufacturing rose by five points and Morocco's by almost 6 points, while Tunisia's rose by less than half a point. The services, on the other hand, experienced dramatic increases in their share of the labor force: Almost twenty points in Egypt, eleven points in Morocco, and nearly fourteen points in Tunisia (Table 3.6). There are considerable differences, however, in the rates of increase of the value-added share of those three sectors in the country's GDP. While the Egyptian service sector's value-added share in GDP increased from 45% in 1980 to 59% in 1997, compared to a modest increase of three percentage points in the value-added share of the manufacturing sector, the Moroccan manufacturing sector's share in GDP was comparable to that of the service sector, with an increase of three percentage points in each case. Only Tunisia had a manufacturing sector whose value-added share in GDP exceeded the share of the service sector (Table 3.3).

Labor Flexibility
Labor flexibility is characteristic of many Arab non-oil countries. This manifests itself in three forms. Geographically, labor moves across regions and sectors. Structurally, there is a large share of labor in the informal sector, a sector of flexible working conditions. Arab labor also experienced "a high degree of real wage flexibility during the past decade and a half, compared to some of the Latin American countries" (ERF, 122). Wage rate performance in the manufacturing sector is particularly telling of the story of labor flexibility, revealing rising productivity but declining wages and wage share in value added.[22] Notice that the performances of Tunisia and Morocco are better than those of Egypt and Jordan (Table 3.7).

Labor Market Segmentation

Labor flexibility in Arab markets is limited, however, by noticeable market segmentation along a public/private sector divide, a male/female divide, and a rural/urban divide. In countries with a diverse private sector in which labor relations are differently regulated, a further labor market segmentation due to different labor regulations occurs. For instance, in Egypt there are various types of sectors with different labor regulations: public sector, public enterprise sector, share holding companies, investment sector. Various labor relations in countries with free zones create another layer of labor market segmentation. In some

Table 3.5. Labor Force in the MENA Countries 1980–95

Country	Labor Force	
	Absolute in 000 In 1997	*Av. Ann. Growth Rate 1980–1997*
Egypt	23.817	2.6
Jordan	1.671	5.3
Morocco	10.748	2.6
Tunisia	3.562	2.9
Av. Low Income 1990–95		1.7
Av. Middle Income 1990–95		1.8

Source: *World Employment Report 1998–99*, p. 217 & 218; *World Bank Development Report 1997*, p. 220–221.

Table 3.6: Distribution of labor force by sector (%)

Country	Agriculture		Industry		Manufacturing		Services	
	1980	*1997*	*1980*	*1997*	*1980*	*1997*	*1980*	*1997*
Egypt	57.1	29.5	15.7	25.2	10.6	15.7	27.2	45.3
Jordan	17.8	14.2	23.7	23.4	7.3	7.4	58.5	62.6
Morocco	56.0	37.5	20.2	27.7	12.9	18.7	23.8	34.8
Tunisia	38.9	21.4	30.3	34.4	16.3	16.6	30.8	44.2

Source: *World Employment Report 1998–99*, p. 221–222.

Table 3.7: Productivity, Unit Labor Cost & Wage Rate 1970–95

Country	Productivity In US$ 1970			Unit Labor Cost In US$ 1970			Wage Rate Over Time %			Share of Wage in VA
	1970	*1995*	*ACGR*	*1970*	*1995*	*ACGR*	*1970*	*1995*	*ACGR*	*ACGR*
Egypt	4,35	5,21	0.7	14	9	-1.8	626	451	-1.3	-2.5
Tunisia	9,35	13,92	1.6	11	10	-0.4	1,044	1,441	1.3	-1.2
Morocco	8,62	8,55	0.0	15	12	-0.9	1,313	1,055	-0.9	-0.8
Jordan	7,79	11,23	1.5	12	7	-2.1	961	766	-0.9	-1.5

ACGR = average compound growth rate

cases, workers combine jobs in different sectors, with one mostly in the public sector, making the issue of labor flexibility and market segmentation complex and in need of further analysis, especially with regard to unionization.

Labor features four weaknesses: First, the population is growing very rapidly; secondly, the labor force is also growing rapidly in a context of high unemployment; thirdly, most workers are non-skilled and semi-skilled labor; fourthly, there is noticeable geographical and wage mobility. In an opinion survey conducted in early 1990s in Jordan, 70% of a sample of more than 2000 unemployed said they would accept lower wages and jobs below their qualifications (Amerah, 55). This is a bad starting point for strong unionization.[23]

As another example, unionization is relatively high in Egypt (3,313,000 workers or 25% of the labor force). Union membership is biased towards service sector workers and civil servants, with only 25% of unionized labor in the manufacturing public sector.[24] Of all the members, only 25% work in the private sector, despite high numbers of workers privately employed in tourism, transportation, and agriculture (Barakat, 280–81).

To sum up, the structural endowment of capital and labor is unfavorable to strong labor unionization. To deal with weak endowment conditions, the business community resorts to lobbying strategies that show a number of features unfavorable to strong unions.

- Small-sized capital avoids collective bargaining and prefers individual or informal work arrangements.
- Large manufacturing capital has a historic tendency towards cartelization in family groups that function in monopoly markets or in diverse sectors. It also prefers individual, not collective, action—to lobby government and depend on it to keep labor under control.
- Lack of information transparency and fear of hard global competition do not allow large- sized capital to see the fact, proven by various recent studies, that more unionization does not harm profit-making, but rather helps productivity in the firm.[25]

Despite these structural impediments, there are some bright cases of collective bargaining between business and labor, in which compensation for shut-down, profit-sharing, and wages have been successfully negotiated. In those cases business was willing to sit, talk, negotiate, and compromise. Equally important, in those cases labor representatives manifested a considerable level of awareness, pragmatism, and willingness to grant concessions. Hence, structural factors, though adverse in general, are only formative, not determinative, of strategies and decisions.

The Institutional Approach
One of the main assumptions of the institutional approach is that countries under pressure of globalization tend to experience institutional reform more rapidly (Maxfield; Frieden and Rogowski). The other assumption doubts the potential of convergence. Globalization may produce international imitation. However, imitation affects the form, not the content of institutions. The latter is more a result of domestic legacies than of international examples (Powell and Dimaggio; Stark).

For example, an issue such as the institutional reform of collective bargaining is value-laden, easier to link to social justice or to primordial fear of business freedom. The pace and content of a reform of labor relations towards collective bargaining will depend on perceptions of justice, informal networks of civic groups, attitudes towards capital, and capital accountability (Evans; Silva; Putnam).

Perceptions of justice

There are two perceptions of justice that impact the relationship of labor and capital. *Contractual justice* is a matter of agreement between two equal actors, who sanction their agreement with a contract. Contractual justice is respecting agreed-upon procedures, without predetermining results (Von Hayek *The Constitution of Liberty* 1960; James Buchanan *Constitutional Liberalism*). *Collective justice* is a matter of collective responsibility. The best way to achieve a level of collective awareness of one's social responsibilities is to organize and create associations that collectively represent interests. Collective justice is often about socially acceptable results.

Those perceptions of justice correspond to two types of labor laws—those regulating an individual labor relation between employer and employee, and those regulating a social relationship between labor and capital as two collective actors equally responsible for the general good of society. In the former case, the language of the law is similar to civil law; the main concern of the law is to sanction an individual agreement between two free agents. In the case of social labor laws, the language of the law and its concerns are oriented towards collective goals of social justice for which both capital and labor bear some general societal and economic responsibility (Ilias, 8). Social labor laws are negotiated and reinforced by autonomous collective representatives of capital and labor, or by a state that claims to represent the general, collective good.

Two Arab traditions make the Arab perception of justice collective, but organizationally weak. One is the Islamic tradition, which sanctions private contractual relations, but also sees capital as having a collective social function. It is silent on the issue of labor organization, for social responsibility is an outcome of moral commitment (al-Fangari; al-Qaradawi; Mashhur; Siddiq; Imara; Ghanem). The other is the populist, corporatist tradition in which the state is the guarantor of social justice, defined in terms of full employment at low levels of labor-independent organization.

What the non-oil Arab economies have done is transform the legal language and judicial notion of labor relations from the collective one to the contractual. However, the tradition of weak organization, whether based on the moral Islamic or the state populist legacies, will linger much longer and impede the transition to contractual labor relations.

Societal networks

While the rise of the middle class and its populist policies supported a collective but organizationally weak perception of justice in the 1950s–1970s, more recently NGOs have been contributing to an organizationally stronger society. How that could help strengthen labor unions is not certain. The populist middle classes of the state capitalist regimes claimed to have forged an alliance with the working classes, but this alliance lasted only ten to fifteen years and has started to fall apart during the liberalization phase (Ibrahim, Salama et al, 269–78). Current thought on the middle class sheds doubt on its ability to stand by workers in their call for stronger unions.[26]

The average constitution of an Arab middle class manifests conservative potential. The middle stratum constitute 8% of the middle class, with more than half in commercial activities and one quarter in manufacturing, whereas the lower stratum of the self-employed middle class constitute a majority, with a concentration in agriculture, followed by trade and manufacturing (Abdel Baset Abdel Mo'ti cited in Ibrahim, Salama et al, 276). This stratum either follows Islamic ideas or is afraid of radical Islamization and supports the status quo if they individually can improve their lot. Therein lies the weakness of the Left (Shukr, 270–71).

The segment of the middle class most frustrated with liberalization is civil servants whose wages have declined in absolute and relative terms due to government austerity measures. Though most unhappy with change and potentially supportive of anti-liberalization labor unions, civil servants are busy making ends meet, obtaining second jobs in the private or informal sector (al-Hermasi, 66).

Capital accountability

Big industrial business historically has resorted to two main strategies—oligarchic concentration through the establishment of business groups, and personalized ties to the executive branch (Vitalis 1995). Indeed, business associations have become a fundamental part of civil society. However, big business still relies on business groups (a constellation of family members representing a diversity of firms across economic sectors) to avoid improving on the institutions of collective bargaining. This leaves them with better access to power circles at lower cost, in the process marginalizing the business associations that could present a forum for discussion with labor representatives.

Lack of organizational capacity on the part of capital would mean leaving the rent-seeking behavior of a handful of businessmen to speak for all business activities. That would play into the hands of those suspicious of business. There are enough sociological observations which point towards widespread frustration with the conspicuous consumption of the rich and a belief that success doesn't require work or skills, only relationships and corruption (al-Hermasi, 72–75).

Conclusions

The 1990s were a threshold for legal reform of labor relations, introducing a contractual dimension and sanctifying collective bargaining instead of state regulation. This is a fundamental change in the political regime of many of the Arab non-oil based economies. Our study has shown the tremendous collective bargaining tasks awaiting labor unions in those countries, based on labor laws already in operation. However, structural, political, and institutional factors impede a quick transformation of labor unions into competent and autonomous negotiators. This is a good example of how legal reform alone would not do the trick of catching up with the race of globalization.

At the same time, the shape of economic reform in these countries clearly shows the importance of workers' representation. Our comparison of Egypt and Morocco has shown that labor, broadly conceived, has played an important role in shaping the new labor legislation and the economic reforms more generally. Whether union leaders have endorsed privatization (Egypt) or resisted it (Morocco), governments have adopted a gradual approach to reform, initiating programs designed to win workers' support and minimize social dislocation. Nevertheless, recent developments in both countries indicate that labor discontent at the local level is on the rise, suggesting the need for more capable, autonomous, and representative labor organizations.

A lot of thinking needs to be done in order to figure out the best way of improving the autonomy and negotiating capacity of labor unions. We need to address the following questions:

- What is the ideal level of unionization, given the mix of structural, political, and institutional factors in the non-oil Arab cases aforementioned?

Egypt and Morocco attest to the variety of options available in Arab countries for pluralist, non-hierarchical union structures. Should labor autonomy be guaranteed to all levels of organization, only to the federation level, or mostly to the factory level?
• How could we provide labor with information and improve its information-management skills?
• How could we improve the organizational capacity of businessmen, so that they too will be compatible negotiating partners?

Notes

1 In this chapter we use the term "labor" in two different senses. Here it refers to blue-collar workers in industry, construction, and services, regardless of union membership. At other times, however, it will be used to refer to a country's trade union apparatus, which may include members who fall outside of this definition of workers (e.g., white-collar civil servants, or teachers). The context should clarify which meaning is intended.

2 The suggestion that workers will protest negative changes to their wages, benefits, or working conditions rests on a "moral economy" interpretation of workers' behavior. For a detailed discussion contrasting this approach with other theories of labor protest, see Posusney, esp. Introduction and ch. 4.

3 See Haggard and Kaufman, 269. Przeworski, citing this work while extending the analysis to post-socialist countries as well, puts the choice even more starkly: "To put it bluntly, reform-oriented governments face a choice of either cooperating with opposition parties and unions, as did the Spanish Socialist government, or destroying them, as did the Bolivian government of Paz Estenssoro with regard to unions." (181).

4 The Algerian law urged policy-makers to consider both productivity and price indexes, whereas the Yemeni law included an innovation on that theme, necessitating that the minimum wage be linked to the minimum wage in the civil service.

5 This is a very weak position given the reality of the wages in Jordan. Apart from state employees and bankers, other employees are paid the minimum wage or just above. By higher positions, wages are freely negotiated but often due to fear of unemployment, they are low. This is the situation of two thirds of the work force, according to the German Federal Work Bulletin April 1994, p. 19.

6 The Ministry has to decide within 30 days of submission, and, if refused, the union must appeal to court within 30 days of refusal (Article 102).

7 In 1987, the State Security Court ruled that the workers of the national railroad company did not violate any law of the land when they went on strike to demand better working conditions and higher wages. The court reaffirmed this in 1991, in a case against workers of a carpet factory in al-Mahalah al-Kobra.

8 In addition to the cited references, this section draws on coverage from the follow-ing news services: *MEED, Mining Journal, Business International, Financial Times, Middle East Newsfile, Africa News Service, Middle East Business Intelligence, Info-Prod, BBC, Inter-Press Service,* and *Middle East Economic Review.* In the interest of saving space, individual citations for these are not provided.

9 Employers must also get government approval to operate back shifts.

10 Material on labor and privatization in Egypt through the spring of 1996 is drawn from Posusney, 1997, and referenced in full there. Only material on the past three years is referenced below.

11 The resulting joint ventures would still be considered part of the public enterprise sector.

12 Unless otherwise noted, information on Egyptian privatization since 1996 is drawn from *Al-Ahram Weekly* and *Business Monthly.*

13 Interview with Niyazi 'Abd al-'Aziz, Cairo, January 4, 1999. The ETUF/govern-ment negotiations were also covered in the Egyptian Arabic press.

14 This discussion is based on interviews with numerous labor activists and social sci-entists conducted in Cairo in January, 1999.

15 For further details on this system and its evolution, see chapters one through three of Posusney, *Labor and the State.*

16 Interview with Niyazi 'Abd al-'Aziz, former president of the EEMWF. Cairo, January, 1999.

17 We are grateful to Ragui Assaad for calling this to our attention. On employers' objections to the strike/lay-off trade-off, see *Al-'Alim al-Yawm,* June 5, 1993.

18 Heckscher-Ohlin, Stolper-Samuelson, and Ricardo-Viner.

19 Several reasons account for the unattractiveness of MENA as an FDI-absorbing region: (a) weak social acceptance of foreign direct investment; (b) weak govern-ments that are not capable of reaching a consensus on liberalization policies; (c) underdeveloped physical and legal infrastructure, though improvements have been recorded in the 1990s; (d) weak capital—promoting credit markets, though reform is on the way; and (e) insufficient highly skilled labor (ERF 1998, 41).

20 If one examines private capital formation in construction and machinery from the mid-1980s to the beginning of the 1990s, a similar trend appears. Although capital formation in machinery almost doubled between 1985 and 1990, it increased almost three times in construction (Ministry of Planning cited in Kanaan, 1995).

21 From 10.7% in 1990 to 16.4% in 1995 with an average annual growth rate in man-ufacturing of 12.6%, which is higher than the growth rate of total exports (*ERF* 1998, p. 60–61).

22 The wage rate of total manufacturing, in constant 1970 US$-terms, has been grow-ing at a modest compound rate of 0.2% between 1970 and 1995, while food, inter-mediate, and capital goods industries experienced a positive growth rate of 1.3, 1.1, and 0.5, respectively. The share of wages in manufacturing value added declined for all sectors during the same period, with the food sector—which had the relatively

higher growth rate—registering the lowest share of wages in value added: 19% in 1996, reflecting a high profit share of 81% (ERF, 87).

23 Union membership in the manufacturing sectors (fabric, weaving, and food) amounted to 3720 members, or 2.6%. Adding mining and electricity the number comes up to 11,832 or 8% (Report of the General Federation of Trade Unions in Jordan 1992). The biggest union in 1992 was the union of land transportation workers (99,700 or almost 70% of total union membership). This is a non-manufacturing sector.

24 Of all the unions (23), only six are industrial. Of all the factory-level committees, only 25% are in public enterprises. The biggest three unions are in the non-manufacturing sector (construction: 500,000 members, half of whom are privately employed; surface transport: 370,000 members; educational services: 287,000 members, all of whom are government-employed).

25 A study for the ILO showed that stronger unions and more centralized collective bargaining leads to less inequality together with higher social security payments, and increased working hours and productivity (Bosch 131–49). Also Kleiner and Freeman, studying the impact of unionization on closures of firms, business lines and establishments, concluded that unionization makes firm profit expand less rapidly, but not to the point where a firm or production line would close. (510–27).

26 The upper stratum of the middle class is oriented towards financial profit and conspicuous consumption. Managers, according to C. Wright Mills, are a "power elite." They respect technocratic expertise, are submissive to their institutions because they are dependent on organizational resources, and they are suspicious of popular accountability. The millions of civil servants could go either way, supporting workers' rights or elite privileges. The same is true of the traditional middle class of self-employed; they have historically supported democracy as well as fascism (Glassman 1997).

References

Al-Anani, Jawad. 1998. "Requirements for Restructuring the Jordanian Economy" *The Jordanian Economy.* Amman: Al-Urdun al-Jadid, 299–318.

Al-Fangari, Mohamad Shawqi. 1994. *Al-Wajiz fi al-Iqtisad al-Islami.* Cairo: Dar al-Shuruq.

Al-Hermasi, Mohamad. 1992. *Al-Mujtama wa al-Dawla fi al-Maghreb al-Arabi* (Society and State in the Maghreb). Beirut: Merkez Dirasat al-Wahda al-Arabiya.

Al-Qaradawi, Yussef. 1995. *Dor al-Qiyam wa al-Akhlaq fi al-Iqtisad al-Islami.* Cairo: Maktabit Wahba.

Al-Sayyid, Mostapha. 1996. "Privatization and the Issue of Privatization." In Wadouda Badran and Azza Wahby, eds., *Privatization in Egypt: The Debate in the People's Assembly.* Cairo University: Center for Pol. Studies, 301–27.

Alexander, Christopher. 1999. "Trade Unions and Economic Reform in the Maghreb," Paper presented at the 1999 meeting of the American Political Science Association, September 3–6. Atlanta.

Amerah, Mohamad. 1993. *Unemployment in Jordan.* Amman: Center for International Affairs.

Arab Labor Organization. 1998. *Al-Kitab al-Dawri Li Ihsa'at al-Amal Fi al-Buldan al-Arabiya* (Arab Periodical of Labor Statistics). Cairo: Arab Labor Organization.

Baldwin, Richard. 1984. "Rent-seeking and trade policy: An industry approach." *Weltwirtschaftliches Archiv* 120.

Barakat, Saber. 1994. *Al-Haraka al-Umaliya fi Marhalat al-Tahawul* (The Labor Movement in Transition). Cairo: Dar al-Khadamat al-Umaliya.

Bosch, Gerhard. 1999. "Working Time: Tendencies and Emerging Issues" *International Labor Review* 138 (2):131–49.

Chilcote, Ronard. 1994. *Theories of Comparative Politics.* Boulder: Westview Press.

Dar al-Khadamat al-Umaliya. 1996. *Al-Idhrab wa al-Hurriya al-Niqabiya: Ahkam wa Watha'iq* (Strike and Freedom of Unions: Court Cases). Cairo: Dar al-Khadamat al-Umaliya.

Denoeux, Guilain P., and Abdeslam Maghraoui. 1998. "The Political Economy of Structural Adjustment in Morocco." In Azzedine Layachi, ed., *Economic Crisis and Political Change in North Africa.* Westport: Praeger.

Dieterich, Renate. April 1998. "Ein Schritt vor und zwei Schritte zurück: Die jordanischen Parlamentswahlen vom November 1997 und der Demokratisierungsprozeß." *Orient* 39: 583–604.

Economic Research Forum. 1997. *Economic Trends in MENA Region.* Cairo: Economic Research Forum.

El-Mikawy et al 2000 "Institutional Reform of Economic Legislation: the case of Egypt" Discussion Paper # 30. Bonn: Center for Development Research.

El-Mikawy, Noha. 1999. *Building Consensus in Egypt's Transition Process.* Cairo: AUC Press.

Evans, P. 1995. *Embedded Autonomy: States and Industrial Transformation.* Princeton: Princeton University Press.

Freeman, Richard, and Moris Kleiner. July, 1999. "Do Unions Make Enterprises Insolvent?" *Industrial & Labor Relations Review* 52 (4): 510–27.

Frieden, J., and R. Rogowski. 1996. "The Impact of the International Economy on National Policies: An Analytical Overview." In Robert Keohane and Helen Milner, eds. *Internationalization and Domestic Politics.* Cambridge: Cambridge Unversity Press.

Garst, W. Daniel. 1998. "From Factor Endowment to Class Struggle." *Comparative Political Studies* 31 (1).

Geddes, Barbara. 1994. *Politician's Dilemma: Building State Capacity in Latin America.* Berkeley: University of California Press.

Ghanem, Ibrahim al-Bayumi. 1998. *Al-Awqaf wa al-Siyasa fi Misr.* Cairo: Dar al-Shuruq.

Glassman, Ronald. 1997. *The New Middle Class and Democracy in Global Perspective.* London: Macmillan.

Haggard, Stephan, and Robert Kaufman. 1989. "The Politics of Stabilization and Structural Adjustment." In Jeffrey D. Sachs, ed., *Developing Country Debt and the World Economy.* Chicago: University of Chicago Press.

Hollister, Robinson, and Markus Goldstein. 1994. *Reforming Labor Markets in the Near East.* San Francisco: International Center for Economic Growth Publication.

Ibrahim, Saad Eddin, and Ghassan Salama et al. 1996. *Al-Mujtama' wa al-Dawla fi al-Watan al-Arabi (Society and State in the Arab World).* Beirut: Markaz Dirasat al-Wahda al-Arabiya.

Ilias, Youssef. 1997. *Al-Itijahat al-Tashri'iya Liqawanin al-Amal al-Arabiya fi al-Tis'inat.* Cairo: Arab Labor Organization.

Imara, Mohamad. 1998. *Al-Islam wa al-Amn al-Ijtima'i.* Cairo: Dar al-Shuruq.

International Labor Office. 1997. *World Labor Report 1997–98: Industrial Relations, Democracy, and Social Stability.* Geneva: ILO.

International Monetary Fund. 1995. *Resilience and Growth through Sustained Adjustment: The Moroccan Experience.* Washington, DC: IMF.

Kanaan, Taher. 1995. "The State and the Private Sector in Jordan." ERF working paper submitted to the Workshop on Strategic Visions for the Middle East and North Africa. June 9,1995.

Karmoul, Akram. 1998. "Jordanian Industry in its Encounter with Challenges and Changes." In Hani Hourani et al, eds., *The Jordanian Economy.* Amman: al-Urdun al-Jadid.

Khosrowshahi, Cameron. Spring1997. "Privatization in Morocco." *Middle East Journal* 51 (2): 242–44.

Kienle, Eberhard. Spring 1998. "More than a Response to Islamism: the political deliberalization of Egypt in the 1990s."*Middle East Journal* 52 (2).

Korany, Bahgat. 1991. "The Maghreb." In Tareq Ismael et al, eds., *Politics and Government in the Middle East and North Africa.* Miami: Florida University Press.

Land Center for Human Rights, 1998, 1999. "Labor conditions in Egypt in 1998," and "Labor conditions in Egypt in the First Half of 1999," Cairo.

Layachi, Azzedine. November 1999. "Reform and the Politics of inclusion in the Maghreb." Paper presented at the 1999 annual meeting of the Middle East Studies Association. Washington, DC.

Lynch, Marc. Spring 1999. "Review Article: Privatization and State Intervention." *Journal of Palestine Studies* 28 (3): 104–05.

Magee, Stephan. 1980. "Three simple tests of the Stolper-Samuelson Theorem." *Issues in International Economics.*

Mashhur, Nimat Abdel Latif. 1996. *Al-Nashat al-Ijtimai wa al-Takafuli lil Bunuk al-Islamiya.* Cairo: al-Ma'had al-'alami lil Fikr al-Islami.

Maxfield, Sylvia. 1997. *Gatekeepers of Growth: The International Political Economy of Central Banking in Developing Countries.* Princeton: Princeton University Press.

Mufti, Malik. February 1999. "Elite Bargains and the Onset of Political Liberalization in Jordan" *Comparative Political Studies* 32 (1): 100–129.

Mussa, Michael. 1982. "Imperfect factor mobility and the distribution of income." *Journal of International Economics* 12.

Pawelka, Peter. 1997. "Wirtschaftliche Liberalisierung und Regimewandel in Ägypten." *WeltTrends* 16. Herbst.

Pfeifer, Karen. Spring 1999. "How Tunisia, Morocco, Jordan and even Egypt became IMF Success Stories in the 1990s." *Middle East Report* 210: 23–27.

Pfeifer, Karen, Marsha P. Posusney, and Djavad Salehi Isfahani. Spring 1999. "Reform or Reaction?" *Middle East Report* 210: 14–17.

Piro, Timothy. 1998. *The Political Economy of Market Reform in Jordan.* Lanham: Rowman & Littlefield.

Posusney, Marsha Pripstein. 1997. *Labor and the State in Egypt: Workers, Unions, and Economic Restructuring.* New York: Columbia University Press.

Powell, W., and P. Dimaggio, eds. 1991. *The New Institutionalism in Organizational Analysis.* Chicago: University of Chicago Press.

Przeworski, Adam. 1991. *Democracy and the Market.* Cambridge: Cambridge University Press.

Putnam, R. 1993. *Making Democracy Work: Civic Traditions in Modern Italy.* Princeton: Princeton University Press.

1996. "Qanun al-Amal 8/1996 fi al-Mamlakah al-Orduniya al-Hashimiya." *Al-Nashra al-Tashri'iya* 32.

Rhys Payne, Rhys. 1993. "Economic Crisis and Policy Reform in the 1980s." In I. William Zartman and William Mark Habeeb, eds., *Polity and Society in Contemporary North Africa.* Boulder: Westview Press.

Rodrik, Dani. 1997. *Has Globalization Gone Too Far?* Washington, DC: Institute for International Economics.

Rogowski, Ronald. 1989. *Commerce and Coalitions.* Princeton: Princeton University Press.

Salama, Ghassan. 1987. *Al-Mujtama wa al-Dawla fi al-Mashreq al-Arabi* (Society and State in Mashreq Countries). Beirut: Merkez Dirasat al-Wahda al-Arabiya.

Shararah, Magdi A. 1999. *Al-Tafawudh: Namathij Amaliya* (Negotiations: Practical Examples) Cairo: Friedrich-Ebert-Stiftung.

Shukr, Abdel Ghaffar. 1994. *Al-Haraka al-Umaliya fi Marhalat al-Tahawul* (The Labor Movement in Transition). Cairo: Dar al-Khadamat al-Umaliya.

Siddik, Mohamad Jalal Soleiman. 1996. *Dor al-Qiyam fi Najah al-Bunuk al-Islamiyya.* Cairo: Al-Ma'had al-'alami lil Fikr al-Islami.

Silva, E. 1996. *The State and Capital in Chile: Business Elites, Technocrats and Market Economics.* Boulder: Westview Press.

Stark, David. Winter 1992. "Path Dependence and Privatization Strategies in East Central Europe." *East European Politics and Societies* 6.

U.S. Dept. of State. 1994. *Moroccan Human Rights Practices, 1993.*

U.S. Dept. of State. 1996. *Moroccan Human Rights Practices, 1995.*

Veltmeyer, Henry. November 1997. "Challenging the World Bank's Agenda to Restructure Labor in Latin America." *Labor Capital & Society* 30 (2): 226–259.

Vitalis, Robert. 1995. *When Capitalists Collide.* Berkeley: University of California Press.

Weeks, John. 1999. "Wages, employment and workers' rights in Latin America 1970–1998." *International Labour Review* 138 (2): 151–169.

World Bank. 1996. *Growing Faster, Finding Jobs: Choices for Morocco.* Washington, DC: Oxford University Press.

World Bank. 1997. *Kingdom of Morocco, Growth and Labor markets: An Agenda for Job Creation.* Washington, DC: Oxford University Press. Vol. I, and II, Annex 5.

World Bank. 1997a. *World Bank Development Report 1997.* Washington, DC: World Bank Publications.

4

National Versus Migrant Workers in the GCC: Coping with Change

Maurice Girgis*

Introduction

Labor markets in the Gulf Cooperation Council (GCC) countries appear to have functioned smoothly until the mid-1980s as the demand for labor, fueled by an ever increasing level of government outlays, generated plentiful job opportunities.[1] GCC nationals were able to pick and choose jobs as they pleased. Expatriate workers from Arab and Asian countries took up jobs that could not be filled by nationals.

The growth in the demand for labor began to taper off, as a result of the decline in government spending precipitated primarily by declining and generally unstable oil revenues. Meanwhile, the number of national secondary school and university graduates continued to rise, most of whom did not possess the skills much in-demand by the private sector. This situation created an unprecedented and unexpected phenomenon, namely, the emergence of open unemployment among GCC nationals in the midst of a substantial number of foreign workers who are gainfully employed in all sectors of the economy. The open unemployment compounded a long-recognized disguised unemployment problem among nationals employed in the government sector.

---

* This chapter draws on a larger study prepared by the author in collaboration with Robert Fearn for the World Bank in 1997, titled "Unemployment-Reduction Measures in the GCC." The views expressed are those of the author and do not necessarily reflect those of the World Bank or of LTC.

GCC governments are justifiably concerned about this phenomenon for many reasons. First, there is an unwritten rule that the public sector is responsible for creating job opportunities for *all* national workers. Second, most of the unemployed are young secondary school graduates whose qualifications do not match the needs of the private sector. And even if they did, private-sector employers still prefer to hire foreign workers for reasons that will be delineated shortly. Third, government budgets can ill afford to create additional public jobs for nationals since the current wage bill already exhausts more than half and, in some countries, more than the entire oil revenue.

The primary objective of this chapter is to clearly understand this phenomenon as a basis for developing a long-term, comprehensive strategy to eliminate its recurrence.

Section 1: Magnitude, Causes, and Diagnosis of the Nationals' Unemployment Problem

Magnitude

The GCC economies are currently faced with both *structural* and *cyclical* unemployment. The former occurs when the demand and the supply of labor are not in step with each other due to changes in the structure of the economy. This kind of mismatch is evident as national workers cannot find jobs that match their skills at the reservation wage rate, which is determined largely by the opportunity wage rate in the government sector—the traditional job heaven for national workers.[2] Cyclical unemployment occurs due to economic slowdowns resulting from the instability of the oil market. The decline in government spending and its effects on the private sector had caused the public sector to seriously slow down hiring at past rates while the private sector sought to consolidate, streamline and, otherwise, downsize as a means of coping with the ongoing economic downslide (1984–95). As these two forces were set in motion, nationals largely felt their combined effect.

The number of new national job-seekers in Kuwait, based on published data about the size of the national labor force during the last six years, is estimated at about 6500 annually. In Saudi Arabia, the comparable figure is about 74,000, most of whom (63%) are secondary school graduates. In Bahrain, the number is estimated at about 8000. This group of individuals and those like them in Oman, Qatar, and the UAE, who represent the annual additions to the national labor force exemplify the core of structural unemployment in the GCC.

With the exception of Bahrain, data on unemployment in the GCC are not made available. Population census data include statistics on frictional unemployment, which is part of natural unemployment.[3] However, given the recent information on new national entrants to the labor force in each GCC country, the economic growth record and, hence, the extent of new jobs created annually and the degree to which nationals have been replacing expatriates in different skills, we estimate that the current structural unemployment is somewhere between 420,000 to 475,000 national workers in the GCC as a whole. This represents only 6.4% of the total expatriate labor force and 4.7% of total manpower. Yet, it constitutes a sizable 17.8% of the total national labor force. See Table 4.1.

The following features provide a rough characterization of the pool of unemployed nationals in the GCC:[4]

They are less educated than the overall average of the national work force.

Unemployed women are mostly secondary school graduates, while unemployed men are mostly primary school graduates or lower.

Their profile is likely to be somewhat consistent with the following:[5]
- 97.3% are graduates of secondary schools or lower levels of education, 50.9% are high school graduates, and 40.7% are intermediate level or lower.
- Those that are concentrated in the lower end of the educational scale (illiterates, read-and-write, and elementary school graduates) are 40 to 50 years old. As one moves up the educational ladder, the average age declines.
- The overall level of education is higher among females than males.
- Most of the job-seekers are in the labor market for less than three years.

Contributing Factors
Labor markets in the GCC have undergone three major transitions. The first, the "massive influx," occurred between the early and mid-1970s due to the substantial increase in oil revenues. The inflow was such that it caused the size of the indigenous population to more than double by 1975, as shown in Table 4.2. The second transition—the "dominant Asian presence"—began a decade later, due in part to declining oil revenues from 1982 to 1986; the shift in skill requirements to maintenance of established infrastructure rather than building new projects; and the expansion of the services sector and import substitution industries that are typically intensive in the use of low-skill labor.[6] Given the lower wages accepted by Asian workers, a substitution of less-skilled Asian workers for European and Arab workers started to take place. The third transition, the "open unemployment of nationals," is going on at the present time and its outcome is yet to be seen.

Table 4.1. National and Expatriate Manpower Growth in the GCC,
1975–1995

(000)

	Bahrain*	Kuwait	Oman	Qatar	Saudi Arabia	UAE	Total
1975							
Nationals	38.0	55.4	155.0	11.7	1,438.9	44.6	1,743.7
Expatriates	22.0	249.2	70.0	57.0	484.8	234.2	1,117.1
Total	60.0	304.6	225.0	68.7	1,923.7	278.8	2,860.8
Percent of							
Nationals/Total	18.2%	18.2%	68.9%	17.0%	74.8%	16.0%	61.0%
1980							
Nationals	61.2	74.2	168.0	16.6	1,519.6	53.9	1893.6
Expatriates	81.2	417.3	112.0	79.0	1,693.1	470.8	2853.3
Total	142.4	491.5	280.0	95.6	3212.7	524.7	4746.9
Percent of							
Nationals/Total	43.0%	15.1%	60.0%	17.4%	47.3%	10.3%	39.9%
1985							
Nationals	71.8	95.9	177.9	23.5	1,619.6	65.1	2,053.8
Expatriates	98.8	574.5	191.1	76.7	2,722.5	460.2	4,123.8
Total	170.6	670.4	369.0	100.2	4,342.1	525.3	6,177.6
Percent of							
Nationals/Total	42.1%	14.3%	48.2%	23.5%	37.3%	12.4%	33.2%
1995							
Nationals	90.7	174.9	240.0	39.0	1,869.0	111.2	2,524.8
Expatriates	135.8	876.6	430.3	179.0	4,581.0	843.9	7,046.6
Total	226.5	1,051.5	670.3	218.0	6,450.0	955.1	9,571.4
Percent of							
Nationals/Total	40.0%	16.6%	35.8%	17.9%	36.5%	11.6%	26.4%
Annual Rates of Growth							
Nationals							
1975–1985	6.6%	5.6%	1.4%	7.3%	1.2%	3.9%	1.7%
1985–1995	2.4%	6.2%	3.0%	5.2%	1.4%	5.5%	2.1%
1975–1995	4.4%	5.9%	2.2%	6.2%	1.3%	4.7%	1.9%
Expatriates							
1975–1985	11.0%	8.2%	5.1%	3.8%	8.5%	6.5%	8.0%
1985–1995	2.9%	4.6%	6.2%	8.1%	4.0%	6.2%	4.5%
1975–1995	6.9%	6.4%	5.6%	5.9%	6.2%	6.4%	6.2%

Notes: * Bahrain data are for census years 1971, 1981, 1985 (estimate), and 1991.

Sources: Bahrain data from the *1994 Statistical Abstract*; Kuwait data from CSO,*1994 Annual Statistics Abstract* and the Public Org. for Civil Information, Population and manpower in 1996; Data for Oman, Saudi Arabia, and United Arab Emirates for 1975, 1980, and 1985 are estimates made by ESCWA, *National Manpower in the GCC*, 1985 and for 1995 Gulf Business Books, The *GCC Economic Data Book*, 1996; 1995 United Arab Emirates data are from the Ministry of Planning, *Annual Economic Report*, 1995;1995 Oman data: Central Bank of Oman, *1995 Annual Report*; and for Qatar: Data pertain to 1994 and are estimated from the *1995 Annual Statistical Abstract* and the *1994 Industrial Survey*.

Table 4.2. National and Expatriate Population Growth in the GCC,
1975–1995

(000)

	Bahrain	Kuwait	Oman	Qatar	Saudi Arabia	UAE	Total
1975							
Nationals	201.6	307.8	666.0	63.7	6,089.3	194.3	7,522.7
Expatriates	60.0	687.1	100.0	84.0	937.0	330.8	2,198.9
Total	261.6	994.9	766.0	147.7	7,026.3	525.1	9,721.6
Percent of Expats/Total	22.9%	69.1%	13.1%	56.9%	13.3%	63.0%	22.6%
1980							
Nationals	233.3	386.7	805.0	84.6	7,306.0	280.1	9,095.7
Expatriates	103.4	971.3	179.0	122.0	2,382.0	697.3	4,455.0
Total	336.7	1,358.0	984.0	206.6	9,688.0	977.4	13,550.7
Percent of Expats/Total	30.7%	71.5%	18.2%	59.1%	24.6%	71.3%	32.9%
1985							
Nationals	276.1	470.5	973.0	115.0	8,764.2	403.8	11,002.6
Expatriates	158.6	1,226.8	220.0	126.0	3,878.0	713.0	6,322.4
Total	434.7	1,697.3	1,193.0	241.0	12,642.2	1,116.8	17,325.0
Percent of Expats/Total	36.5%	72.3%	18.4%	52.3%	30.7%	63.8%	36.5%
1995							
Nationals	362.2	708.1	1,563.0	162.0	13,272.0	597.0	16,664.3
Expatriates	223.9	1,250.7	586.0	385.0	5,475.0	1,781.0	9,701.6
Total	586.1	1,958.8	2,149.0	547.0	18,747.0	2,378.0	26,365.9
Percent of Expats/Total	38.2%	63.9%	27.3%	70.4%	29.2%	74.9%	36.8%
1999 (Estimates)							
Nationals	401.3	772.0	1,793.5	186.8	16,182.7	644.8	19,981.1
Expatriates	227.8	1,466.0	653.1	443.8	5,321.9	1,576.6	9,689.2
Total	629.1	2,238.0	2,446.6	630.6	21,504.6	2,344.4	29,670.3
Percent of Expats/Total	36.2%	65.5%	26.7%	70.4%	24.7%	67.2%	32.7%
Annual Rates of Growth							
Nationals							
1975–1985	3.2%	4.3%	3.9%	6.1%	3.7%	7.6%	3.9%
1985–1995	2.8%	4.2%	4.9%	3.5%	4.2%	4.0%	4.2%
Expatriates							
1975–1985	10.2%	6.0%	8.2%	4.1%	15.3%	8.0%	11.1%
1985–1995	3.5%	0.2%	10.3%	11.8%	3.5%	9.6%	4.4%

Sources: Bahrain data from the *1994 Statistical Abstract*; Kuwait data from the *1994 Annual Stat. Abstract* and the Public Org. for Civil Information, Population and Manpower in 1996; Data for Oman, Saudi Arabia, and the United Arab Emirates for 1975 to 1985 are estimates made by ESCWA in *National Manpower in the GCC*, 1985 and data for 1995 from *Gulf Business Books*, The *GCC Economic Data Book*, 1996; 1999 estimates: *World Factbook*, Department of State, USA (www.odci.gov/cia/publications), Kuwait: NBK, *Econ and Fin Quarterly*, ii/99.

Empirical evidence found in numerous studies in the GCC point to the following contributing factors as grounds for not hiring sufficient numbers of nationals in the private sector:

• Nationals do not possess the requisite skills.
• Nationals' reservation wages are significantly higher than their foreign counterparts; i.e., their wage expectations are too high.
• Nationals' productivity levels are low.
• A welfare state allegedly encourages idleness, reduces work incentives, and lowers labor participation among nationals.
• Expatriates command low wages, partly because of their low share in the national dividends; i.e., in terms of subsidized public utilities, health care, etc.
• The mechanics of the labor market are underdeveloped, where supply and demand information is segmented and often unavailable to nationals.
• There is a lower pay scale and longer working hours in the private compared to the public sector.
• Typically, nationals are paid higher wages than expatriates for the same job.
• In contrast with the public sector, the private sector offers limited fringe benefits.
• Private sector employers can terminate the employment of expatriates more easily than that of nationals.
• Past government 'quick fixes' have failed to produce their intended results.
• Government interference in the labor market has and will continue to lead either to excess demand or an excess supply of labor. Market forces have not been allowed to operate freely. Private sector employers are constantly trying to cope with and adjust to new labor regulations.

Rigid Institutional Labor Policies
An historical review and assessment of past labor policies lie outside the scope of this study, for the emphasis is placed on future remedial policy recommendations rather than on an evaluative review of previous policies. It is interesting, however, to highlight the major policy tools employed in the GCC during the last decade to stem the tide of foreign workers to the region.

Work permits
Except in free zone areas (e.g., *Jabal Ali*), employers must obtain government approvals (work permits) for each foreign worker prior to their arrival.

Sponsorship permits

For an individual employee, a 'no-objection' permit is required—known as *kafala*.

Quotas

Some GCC countries restrict the number of work permits to potential business employers. These are firm-specific quotas.

Bans

Most GCC countries publish lists of jobs/skills that are banned on the premise that they are available at home from among the ranks of national labor or expatriate workers already working in the local economy. The lists are usually expanded and updated periodically. The degree to which these bans are adhered varies from one country to another.

Employment fees

There are several types of fees: (a) a work permit fee, which is paid at the time the application for hiring a foreign worker is submitted; (b) a residency fee, paid annually; (c) insurance fees, and (d) training fees, among others.

Job nationalization

This policy aims at substituting nationals for foreign workers. The civil service sector was the first to apply this policy, followed by SOEs, especially in the oil sector. The private sector has been under pressure to do likewise.

Employment subsidies

There are a few programs designed to subsidize the cost of hiring nationals in the private sector as a means of replacing expatriate workers and minimizing the wage gap between the two groups.

Active persuasion

Some GCC governments have made access to industrial incentives (e.g., soft industrial loans, import duty exemptions, tariff protection, etc.) subject to private sector industries maintaining certain minimal levels of national manpower participation in total employment. Countries differ greatly in the methods applied to coerce the private sector to adhere to these ratios.

Job transfers

All GCC countries prohibit the unrestricted transfer of expatriate workers between jobs. Some require approval from employers or a minimum stay, etc.

Where it is prohibited outright, expatriates usually resort to leaving the country and returning back. Adherence to the restrictions varies among the GCC countries, across job classifications and among individuals within the same country.

Residency permit for families
The issuance of such permits is normally limited to highly skilled/highly paid expatriates.

Section 2: A Strategy for Eliminating Unemployment

Fundamentals of the Strategy
While the unemployment problem is indeed a serious concern, the GCC, luckily, appears to have sufficient time to effectuate the envisioned transition. The number of foreigners is so large relative to that of nationals in the labor force that the latter easily could replace foreigners if they had the requisite skills. Equally important, oil revenues will continue to flow for some time into the future although they have been declining in real terms. Thus, national governments have time to implement a strategy that would reduce unemployment and raise labor force participation among nationals, eventually erasing the dual labor market in these nations.

Our strategy consists of a three-pronged plan of action, which we call the *National Renewal Plan*. The first stage, *Human Resource Development,* suggests policy actions in the immediate term. It calls for the establishment of special one-to two-year programs and special training and retooling activities that will immediately upgrade the skills of unemployed national workers. The key here is to raise the skills of nationals so that they can compete on equal terms with highly skilled foreigners. Without that investment in human capital, the high reservation wages will continue to induce nationals to opt out of the production process in whole or part. This would doom them to unemployment, or place them in direct competition with the lesser-skilled members of the foreign work force.

Stage II, the *Substitution of Nationals for Expatriates* represents an intermediate-run adjustment and is centered on a gradual reduction in social benefits provided to both nationals and foreigners. Although it has been difficult to determine the full extent of the social benefits per person or per family, it is obvious that such levels will be difficult to sustain in the future. A number of complementary policies will also be offered to close the wage gap between the private and the public sector, and between nationals and expatriates. Reforms of the labor market infrastructure will also be addressed. Stage III, the *Job Creation*

Phase, focuses on long-term policy options whose primary objective is to create new jobs through economic deregulation, elimination of price distortions, and the acceleration of the pace of development.

We should draw attention to an inherent danger in this strategy; namely, unless discernible progress is made in Stage I, the gradual privatization of the SOEs and the envisioned economic expansion in Stage III would make the plight of nationals worse off. If nationals cannot hold their own in the labor market, profit-maximizing firms (public, private, or joint) would find it in their interest to employ foreigners for most positions; just as they do now.

In its totality, the proposed three-stage National Renewal Program would gradually move each of the Gulf states away from the dual labor markets and the undue dependency on governmental largesse, toward the efficiencies produced by a market-oriented system as distinct from one in which the government dominates economic decisions. Stage I stands on its own feet as a viable course of action even in the absence of the other two stages. Yet, it is clear that the implementation of the *whole* package, through its multifaceted influences on the numerous components affecting this problem, will channel the investment of some of the remaining oil revenues in ways that will permit nationals to earn much of what they consume rather than rely on the social dividend to maintain their consumption levels.

Recognizing that the usual partial microeconomic analysis of a positive cost-benefit ratio may indicate direction, it rarely helps in assessing the degree to which maximum productivity and growth will be achieved. Nor does it contribute to a precise assessment of economic balance or equity. The best one can do, it would appear, is to create the conditions under which incentives will be strong enough to encourage productive use of the labor force and other assets in the economy. Note that the suggested long-term strategies should be subjected to the following two constraints:

- Gradualism: Radical changes that are politically or economically destabilizing must be avoided. The GCC States also must avoid being "high-handed" towards expatriates.
- New programs or policies should not add fiscal burdens to already-strained public budgets. It maybe advisable to request that each new policy or program should have its own source(s) of funds in order to gauge cost-effectiveness and ensure transparency.

No Quick Fixes

A number of policies to improve labor markets and forestall future unemployment of nationals readily suggest themselves. We call these policies 'quick fixes.' While there may be some merit to them, none will address satisfactorily the longer-range labor market problems. Among the 'quick fixes' are:

1. A ban on, or a precipitous reduction in, foreign worker permits.
2. A lucrative system of unemployment compensation.
3. Reduction in the length of the workday or workweek.
4. A system of required preferential hiring of nationals in all sectors.
5. An attitudinal adjustment program designed to convince young people that their attitudes towards employment and their wage expectations are unrealistic.
6. Creation of more government jobs.

These policies are ineffective and, in fact, may reduce productivity or increase costs wherever major skill differences exist between foreign and national workers (likely in 1, 3, and 4). Moreover, policy option 1 will have some regional foreign policy implications that ought to be considered carefully. Option 2 would simply exacerbate the incentive problems already produced by current levels of social benefits and, furthermore, it is not intended to address structural problems. It is unlikely that 5 would have any substantial effect on labor market decisions unless it were accompanied by changes in employment and social welfare policy. We would expect attitudinal adjustments to lag behind, not lead, social and economic changes.

'Quick fix' 6—one used heavily to date—appears to be the simplest solution. One simply creates government jobs, offers some salary, and pays little attention to the skills required or service rendered to society. One example of this is the creation of lucrative employment in security forces or the army. While these forces are important to the maintenance of the society, they represent just that: maintenance expense rather than using resources to generate higher standards of living for the nation. Similarly, one might enforce national employment quotas on private companies and/or coerce SOEs to increase employment of nationals (option 5). That, too, appears to be a straightforward way of dealing with the employment and income aspirations of nationals. However, if nationals are less skilled than the foreigners they replace or, alternatively, they command higher wages, the national economy will be imposing opportunity costs on itself in the form of foregone productivity and lower economic growth.

We urge the rejection of all 'quick fixes.' Reliance should be based on policies intended to enhance productivity and replace foreigners without reductions in actual or potential economic growth.

Specific Policy Recommendations

Stage I—Immediate Term: Human Resource Development

We propose the immediate implementation of a set of special schools for high school graduates, which are intended to generate in these young men (and perhaps women) the skills necessary to replace foreigners in key positions in both private and public employment. In the very short run, the schools will provide direction for youth searching for a useful role in their own nation, including those currently unemployed or out of the labor market. The training should be in particular occupational specialties, with required core courses emphasizing analytical disciplines such as mathematics and statistics, the English language, computer applications and Internet operations, and supervisory or management skills, where appropriate. To begin this process, each nation must assess the areas in which it is especially dependent on high-paid foreigners and/or areas where the highest rate of natural replacement has taken place during the last decade. Training programs should emphasize those two areas where nationals have a "natural comparative advantage."

Students will continue to be supported by the government, but at different support levels, which depend upon superior performance in their studies. If successful, the rigorous schooling experience will provide those same young men (and women, where desired) with a strong sense of pride and accomplishment—in much the way rigorous military training does for new recruits. Moreover, mastery of a rigorous curriculum will go a long way towards assuring them of high-paying employment in the future. It will also reinforce job security in the private sector. It is essential that such schools represent a meritocracy, and that family position and circumstances not pay any role in the success or grades of the students. That means, first and foremost, that the faculty is charged with creating the appropriate climate—tough, but fair—and that the national governments support them in that endeavor.

We also propose that on-the-job training programs be established for nationals in selected firms and government ministries. Entry to such programs should be on a competitive basis with the expectation that the young men and women will move up in responsibility and pay as they complete various aspects of the training.[7] It is important that the incentive structure of each program meets the needs of the participants and potential employer. For the individual student, he or she must bear some of the costs of the training, perhaps by accepting training wages that are lower than those of an alternative full-time job. Moreover, the promise of future higher earnings and recognition must be realized for successful participants. Hence, firms establishing such on-the-job training programs must envision and establish job ladders for successful trainees. The firm must also pay some part of the cost and must be able to establish part of the curriculum so as to meet its own needs. In general, profit-maximizing firms will lean toward firm-specific training—training that will raise productivity within the firm, but not raise the value of transferable skills.

If this first stage in the action program is successful in developing a cadre of skilled nationals in areas formerly dependent upon foreigners, a gradual replacement of foreigners can begin. If the programs in fact "deliver" the requisite skills, private sector firms will be much more willing to replace foreigners with nationals in these areas. The savings to the state are obvious. We would not anticipate any reductions in consumption subsidies for nationals until necessitated by future budgetary shortfalls, but each time a GCC national substitutes for a foreigner, the nation saves the social dividends which have traditionally been provided to the foreigner. In addition, by training nationals so that they are the productive equivalent of skilled foreigners, their productive potential will better match or exceed their wage expectations. Many young nationals have unrealistic expectations of what they are worth in the market. Those unrealistic expectations are not apt to change in the short run, given the existing welfare state and prevailing attitudes. Wrestling with what it takes to be an effective worker or manager is good therapy for such expectations.

The envisioned training programs should be offered through the private sector. Not only would this generate better and less costly programs through competition, it would also help diversify the economy, energize the private sector, and avoid any further expansion of the public sector. The cost of the programs should be borne primarily by the government and, to a much lesser extent, by trainees as well as potential employers. Its cost should be covered by tax revenue levied on expatriate workers, as we shall explain below.

Stage II—Intermediate Term: Substitution of National Manpower for Expatriates

In order for the proposed substitution to be economical, nationals must be as well trained as the foreign workers they replace. Our approach sees little sense in trying to substitute nationals for low-skilled expatriates—now largely Asians. The high levels of social dividends among nationals make that type of a substitution highly unlikely from the supply side. And, as discussed above, the low wage levels for service and other low-skilled foreign workers make them the preferred workers among profit-maximizing and cost-minimizing enterprises. Unless one wishes to lower social dividends substantially for nationals, replacement of foreigners with nationals must occur at higher levels of skill.

The program for replacement of foreigners with nationals—while maintaining current efficiency levels—is not simple. The difficult challenge facing the

GCC in this stage is that with reductions in real revenues from oil, budgetary deficits, and the ensuing drawdowns in international reserves, it is essential that labor force participation be increased and unemployment be lowered while *maintaining efficiency and the social dividend policy in the long run.* This calls for specific policy tradeoffs.

One reasonably might select the reduction in social dividends—to nationals and non-nationals—as the one policy variable that can be sacrificed to reach the other objectives. In general, lower social dividends will reduce reservation wages among nationals, thus increasing their work incentives. Coupled with higher productivity among nationals by virtue of the proposed training program, some of the current dependence on foreign labor can be reduced. Lower dividends for foreigners will reduce the cost-benefit ratios upon which they base their decisions to migrate to the Gulf states. The safest adjustment we can see is to *lower social dividends somewhat more for foreigners than for nationals,* presuming that nationals are sufficiently well trained to make up for any shortfall in the availability of foreigners. However, given the great difference between earning levels in the Gulf states and the Asian nations that now send low-skilled workers to that area, we would not expect lower dividends to lessen that flow in the near future.

Policy timing and sequencing in this intermediate period will be crucial. The logic of our approach is that the training of nationals must come first, before adjustments in social dividends and even salaries reduce the availability of foreign workers. Other complementary policies should be pursued simultaneously, the most important of which are discussed below.

Removal of the Gap Between Social and Private Wages of Expatriate Workers
Foreign workers accept low wage rates partly because of the absence of any form of taxation on income or consumption and, in most cases, because the employer provides free housing, paid-up home leaves and, possibly, food and education allowances. The employer, on the other hand, can readily afford to defray these expenses because they are highly subsidized by the state. Thus, a portion of the foreign worker's earnings and/or remittances is borne by the government sector.

On the other hand, GCC nationals receive greater subsidies by virtue of their nationality (there are several citizen-specific subsidies) and because most of them are employed in government offices and SOEs where the average wage and benefits package is considerably superior to what the private sector is willing to offer. Such high reservation wages of GCC nationals have long created a wedge between the wages of foreign and national labor. In order to address the unemployment problem and effect a better allocation of resources, *it is recommended that a fee be levied on expatriates' wage rates to close the gap between their social and private wages (i.e., the "dividend")*. By so doing, the decision-making process of private sector employers will take into account the real cost of labor, thus eliminating this source of distortion. The idea of eliminating the subsidy from foreign workers' wages is not new. In fact, almost all GCC countries have already put this policy into effect by levying a variety of fees.[8]

In this context, it is important that the *full* subsidy be collected, for if the tax is too small, its intended objective will be lost. Moreover, depending on its magnitude, it is advisable to implement this policy gradually to allow private sector employers sufficient time to make the necessary adjustments.

Should the foreign labor 'subsidy-removal fee' be applied to *all* foreign workers? The answer is yes. One may argue, however, that it may be politically palatable to exclude the fee on jobs or skills that are not likely to be filled by nationals, such as house maids, cooks, drivers, office boys, building caretakers and the like. If so, this would imply resource misallocation. For in principal, the policy prescription is to eliminate implied wage subsidies in expatriate wages across the board. In Kuwait, this group alone represents 25% of the foreign labor force, or about 218,000 jobs out of 871,000 in 1996. Recognizing the substantial pressure that is quite likely to be placed on politicians to exclude this group, perhaps further consideration is needed to determine how best this group can be handled.

Should the foreign labor 'subsidy-removal fee' be applied to *all* foreign workers equally? Unless there is evidence that social dividends vary among subgroups of foreign workers, the fee should be the same. It should also be sector-neutral, skill-neutral, and nationality-neutral. Moreover, the proposed fee should not discourage highly skilled expatriates because their productivity level and their role in on-the-job training for nationals are much higher than may be suggested by their money wages. Also, many are not substitutable by nationals at the present time.

There is little research in the GCC countries that measures the extent of the social subsidy received indirectly by foreign workers. An attempt is made here to do just that, using published data from Kuwait. Due to data unavailability, we had to rely on macro data; e.g., budgets and national income accounts. Our findings, to be sure, are underestimated to the extent that, in the case of power and water subsidies, the public sector's cost estimates do not take into account the implicit subsidy in fuel prices, nor do they include capital depreciation and interest charges. The social dividend is assumed to consist of only three parts: subsidization of public utilities (electricity and water), health care, and public transportation.[9] Based on actual government spending for FY 1993/94, the average annual subsidy per worker is estimated at KD 445 or KD 37 per month.

Foreign workers at the present time are charged annual government fees of about KD 120 on average. Consequently, the suggested fee is estimated at KD 325 annually, or KD 27 per month. In relation to salaries of clerical private sector expatriates in the 25–35 age group during 1997, this amounts to an increase of 16.8%, 12.7%, and 11.5% of the following educational levels, respectively— preparatory, secondary, and higher education. The higher the educational, skill or age brackets, the smaller the incidence of the fee. The fee, contrary to common belief, is not expected to materially raise costs and threaten the GCC's competitiveness.[10] Eventually, the expected revenue from the subsidy-removal fee would reach about KD 240 million annually, even after excluding household labor. This revenue may be used to finance the policies suggested herein.

Transferability of Non-Wage Benefits
It is recommended that nationals who are presently employed in the government sector and who wish to shift employment to the private sector can transfer their non-wage benefits (e.g., children, social, family, and/or skill allowances) to their new jobs. Nationals who are entering the labor force for the first time, or who are currently unemployed, may be paid the same non-wage benefits as an incentive to compete for jobs in the private sector. Such a policy will help reduce the size of the public sector, minimize the extent to which it is over-staffed, lower the government wage bill and, most importantly, address the observed imbalance in the national labor market between public and private employment. The transferability policy is already in place in several developed countries. It applies to shifts within the private sector as well. Another alternative would be to transfer years of service in the public sector in terms of specific credit points, each of which is equivalent to certain cash payment, when government employees move to the private sector.

Employment Subsidy to Hire Nationals
Even after the subsidy-removal fee is levied, there will still remain wage differentials between nationals and expatriates due to disparities in experience, educational background and track records. In order to encourage employers to hire nationals, it is suggested that a subsidy be granted in an amount near or equal to the remaining difference between the wage rate in the private sector and its counterpart in the government sector. This is not intended as a subsidy to the employer; rather, it is a subsidy that will be passed, at the margin, to the new national employees. This is also necessary to minimize the impact on the cost of production.[11]

The proposed subsidy should be transitory, e.g., limited to three to five years. It should apply to all economic activities, and to employers of all sizes. Some yardstick such as national content or value added may be employed to determine qualified firms.[12]

Gradual Reduction in Labor Market Duality
One of the major obstacles facing young GCC nationals in finding suitable job opportunities in the private sector is the unreasonable disparity that exists between the total compensation package received in the public sector compared with the private sector for the same skill/occupation. In comparison, employment in the government sector normally provides the following superior conditions:

- A higher salary at the entry level;
- A larger fringe benefits package;
- Shorter working hours;
- The possibility of owning another private business;
- A faster promotion track;
- Social acceptability;
- An unstressful job environment;
- Job security that resembles permanent tenure;
- The security of an established network of colleagues with whom to swap favors;
- Attractive training opportunities.

Nationals, hence, are constantly seeking job opportunities in the government sector. In fact, some may wait for a year or two until such an opportunity materializes. Though the wage gap between the public and private sectors was caused by the government's intent to improve its nationals' standard of living, it has contributed to the misallocation of one of the GCC's most valuable resources, its manpower. In order to narrow the gap, we suggest the following remedies:

- New entrants in the government sector should start at lower salaries.
- Promotions should be slowed down in the government sector.
- Social allowances and other similar allowances should be capped.
- New national government employees should be given fixed-term contracts where extensions would be subject to job performance.

Civil Service Reform
Civil service reform is an area where much can be accomplished. The constant barrage in the media about the inflated size of the government and its glaring inefficiency should provide support to this effort. Some of the proposed policy changes include the following:

- Redistribute government employment to reach an optimal allocation of manpower vs. needs. While some administrative sections may be overstaffed, there are others that are under-staffed. The latter may be sup-ported by shifting the excess labor to the areas that need bolstering; e.g., small business administration, patent offices, postal services, traffic mon-itoring, recreational facilities, consumer protection, environmental con-trols, etc.

- Redistribute government employment to reach an effective balance among the different regions within each country. Remote areas are nor-mally understaffed while urban areas are over-staffed. This is true even in small countries.
- Limit recruitment of new nationals to replace retirements, but only if politically required. Otherwise, it will be best if retirements are not refilled to effect a gradual decline in the size of the government sector.
- Abolish all vacant positions. Each new addition should be based on its own merits.
- Remove 'ghost' workers from the government ranks. This is a serious problem in many GCC states.
- Simplify salary structure.
- Advertise new job openings and enhance transparency of the recruitment process through the administration of entrance examinations.
- Relax job-termination conditions for nationals.
- Encourage the development of private training centers, employment agencies, and employment advertising agencies.
- Promulgate a procedure through which the highest two rungs on the civil service ladder immediately below the ministerial level would submit their resignation whenever there is a change at the Cabinet-of-Ministers-level.
- Streamline training programs by emphasizing "Training by Objectives" techniques.

Retirement and Overtime

Alternative options for possible early retirement cash-ins should be evaluated. The cost of that approach could be modest in the presence of the prevailing extensive social non-wage payments. This policy option ought to be evaluated periodically, however, to make sure that it is not negatively impacting the con-tribution of experienced, senior, national manpower in the government sector, nor is it leading indirectly to increasing the number of expatriate workers hired in the government as replacements for early retirees. Limitation on overtime and on secondary employment by government workers would also generate new employment prospects for young people.

In considering these initiatives, however, the authorities must be cognizant of the costs in foregone income and growth from such substitutions. Unless replacements have commensurate skills or can quickly develop such skills on the job, these programs are likely to result in slower economic growth.

Restrict Bans on Immigration

Almost all of the GCC countries have placed bans on the importation of certain skills from overseas. The bans are in response to the government's evaluation of the areas in which there seems to exist an excess supply of qualified national workers. Over the years, the list of the bans has been expanding. Experience shows that the imposition of bans has not been effective in stemming the tide of expatriate workers into the GCC, as shown earlier. Interwoven with this phenomenon is the illegal, but lucrative trade in work permits as a result of the restrictions imposed on them by the state. With the introduction of bans, the rents on these bogus sponsorships increase, as does the number of foreign workers.

Therefore, it is recommended that the *labor policy should not rely on bans, particularly firm-specific quotas.* Instead, solutions must be market-driven in order to become effective. Raising the cost of imported labor through our suggested mix of fees and subsidies, as an example, will deter fake sponsorships, for they will be responsible for paying the fees annually. In case the entire fee is passed on to the foreign worker in terms of annual dues, this may tip the balance for some foreigners in favor of working at home instead of moving to the GCC.

Improve the Job-Finding Process

At present, there are no specialized agencies that offer job search services. Existing employment agencies are primarily involved in the importation of low skills such as maids, cooks, drivers, etc. The vast majority of new jobs in both the private sector and the public sector are filled through personal contacts[13] or employment agencies overseas. Clearly, this system is sub-optimal, non-transparent, inefficient, and may turn out to be more expensive than working with employment agencies if the wrong candidate is hired. To improve this process, the following may be established or encouraged:

- Private job-hunters, referrals, and placement services;
- Government job centers;
- Career offices;
- Newspaper advertising;
- Registration of all vacancies with state employment services, as is the case in most European countries (except the UK);
- Job counseling—because the process of finding a vacancy is usually tedious and stressful.

The effects of introducing these services on employment could be substantial. Potential outcomes include: directing nationals to rewarding job opportunities in the private sector, shortening the process of finding jobs, matching vacancies with available skills in an efficient manner where suitable candidates are selected from the widest range of possibilities, enhancing productivity, reducing the duration of unemployment, and humanizing the job-seeking process in general.

Labor Market Information

An active labor market capable of adjusting to economic changes—both new opportunities and adversities—must contain mechanisms for the rapid transmission of information about job vacancies and persons available for employment. Labor economists generally divide job- and employee-search activities into two types, formal and informal. Both of these types of activities appear to be poorly developed in the GCC states. Both should be developed further in order to improve the functioning of the labor market.

The apparent underdevelopment of public employment services is traceable in part to the labor market duality that has grown over time. While most nationals expect to find employment in the government sector and private employers seek the services of foreigners, there is little need for a comprehensive employment service. In most developed nations, the public employment service is an important method of formal search. But, in order for it to function effectively, the private sector must be involved in a meaningful way. Through an active public employment service, prospective employers and employees may obtain important information and services such as the following:

- Up-to-date lists of job openings and job-seekers;
- Job counseling;
- Aptitude and performance tests;
- Referrals and placement services.

In a well functioning labor market, these activities supplement the information provided by other formal methods of job or employee search, such as private employment agencies, newspaper advertisements and placement services at educational institutions.

The second method of job search is of even greater importance. Research around the world has indicated that *most jobs and most employees are found via informal methods.* Those include referrals by current employees and information about job prospects from friends and relatives. In contrast with formal search techniques, informal channels of information provide much more comprehensive and trusted information about the nature of job opportunities and/or prospective applicants. Studies in labor market areas as different as Chicago, Illinois and New Delhi, India, testify to the effectiveness of these informal methods.[14] It follows that informal methods will provide useful information to GCC nationals about job prospects outside the government sector only when nationals are employed there. That, of course, is not generally true in the GCC states. The arrangements proposed above for preferential employment and on-the-job training of nationals are intended to remedy this deficiency.

Reciprocity
GCC governments have long relied on moral persuasion to convince private employers to employ more nationals. This approach has failed, as evidenced by the rising ratio of expatriate workers in the total work force since the early 1970s. On the other hand, industrial and commercial incentives are offered to all firms without regard to their response to government appeals. Even in the face of the recent rise in unemployment among nationals, available evidence reveals only a minimal change in their response. While this behavior is normal, to be sure, the experience of other countries in this regard points to the need to *link incentives to the achievement of certain measurable national targets.* Firms in this case are not coerced to behave in a certain manner, for they would be free to choose. The choice, however, is based on the principle of reciprocity, where a firm may benefit from existing incentives or be allowed to win a government contract only if it meets some pre-specified national/total employment ratio. Asian countries have made extensive use of this principle. The targets, however, must be reasonable, manageable, and demonstrable.

Stage III: Long Term: The Market-Oriented Job Creation Phase
Existing unemployment problems in the GCC are the product of a prolonged process of government interventions in the labor market, an over-sized public sector, institutional rigidities, labor immobility, dual labor markets, and reduced labor productivity, among other factors. These are long-term symptoms reflecting structural imbalances that cannot be solved by short-term measures alone. Short-term measures seek to create jobs for national workers through *replacement* of foreign workers using fiscal instruments such as subsidies and fees. On the other hand, long-term policies should seek to do the same but without resorting to the use of fiscal policies. They focus more on creating *new* job opportunities through economic expansion, diversification and the like than on replacement *per se.* Because the main components of this phase of the strategy have been addressed at length by national, regional, and international

organizations through conferences and research studies over the last two decades, they are treated briefly below.

- Deregulation and trade liberalization;
- Consumption subsidies reforms;
- Economic diversification;
- Privatization of government-owned public utilities and commercial SOEs;
- Attracting foreign direct investment;
- Promoting the growth of small and medium-sized establishments;
- Education reforms;
- Promoting special projects designed to generate meaningful job opportunities for national GCC workers.

The most important objective of long-term reform policies is to *reduce the extent of price distortion* in the factor and product markets. Thus, government efforts to liberalize the trade sector, labor market, banking sector, industrial-licensing mechanism, rules governing *kafalas* (sponsorship), and exclusive business agencies, etc., are quite critical to the process of freeing the region's resources. These resources should be allowed to freely search for the highest rates of return, which should in turn increase productivity, cut down on waste, and further the process of economic development. This is a *qualitative* growth that can be accomplished with very little additional physical investment. Opening up the economy, eliminating long-established institutional rigidities, allowing competition in the marketplace, and gradually reducing consumption subsidies will all have a salutary impact on the labor market, without adding new fiscal burdens on government budgets.

The structure of consumption subsidies must be revisited.[15] There is little doubt that special privileges and substantial social benefits reduce work incentives and alter the allocation of labor vs. leisure. For this reason, they must be reshuffled so that non-productivity-enhancing subsidies (such as electricity, water, sewage, communications, and transportation) are eliminated gradually, while shifting the freed resources towards improving the *quality* of productivity-enhancing subsidies (such as education, health, and housing).[16]

There are other macroeconomic policies that will further improve the outlook for the labor market. Aside from its many benefits already articulated in the economic literature about the GCC, *economic diversification* is necessary to enhance the chances of the national workers to obtain job opportunities outside the government sector. Diversification opens new and interesting fields with high value-added jobs that will in effect provide attractive and promising employment avenues for university graduates in particular. This trend will be supported by the proposed subsidy-removal fee, which will make it uneconomical to operate low-wage-intensive activities in the GCC, as their wage rates will be elevated by the regressive fee.

Economic *growth* is another factor certain to lead to higher employment. The issue in the GCC, however, is not creating employment *per se*. We recommend that GCC governments promote *private business projects* that are intensive in the use of the types of skills most available among national manpower. This interventionist stance is consistent with the envisioned role of the public sector as one limited to directing, planning, and providing the appropriate signals for the free forces of the market to move in targeted directions. In this context, it is useful to stress the importance of attracting *direct foreign investment* to the region. Excluding oil and its derivatives, special provisions and market liberalization steps should be pursued to bring in new technologies and foreign expertise in other sectors of the economy. As part of the proposed National Renewal Program, the GCC economies would benefit greatly from integration with the world economy, partly through FDI. This, however, requires that current foreign-investment laws, rules, and regulations in the GCC be redrawn to make them more friendly toward foreign investors.

In addition, we recommend that *small and medium-sized establishments* (SMEs) be promoted as a means of creating job opportunities for nationals as managers, owners, and professionals. Past policies of the public sector have crowded out the private sector and caused an excessive reliance on public employment. Based on the results of recent research in developed countries (US, Japan, and Europe) as well as newly industrialized countries (NICs), SMEs have created more jobs than large-scale establishments. Not only that, there are more "small" innovations and technological progress generated from SMEs than from large firms. To the extent that this is a relatively new concern in the GCC, it is perhaps an area that needs attention, institutions, development, and promotion.

Perhaps more importantly, qualitative educational reforms are the *sine qua non* for solving long-run unemployment problems on a self-sustainable basis. Based on the characterization of the corps of national unemployment given in Section 1, the following is a brief list of new ideas that should be examined in each GCC country:

- The general requirements of formal education (K-1 to K-12) should emphasize basic sciences, computer literacy, and foreign languages.
- Parallel secondary education in different business fields (accounting, marketing, bookkeeping, etc.) should be tailored for practical market-related needs.

- Post-secondary education in specialized vocational areas with emphasis on hands-on, workshop-type training should be expanded.
- Parallel intermediate and secondary education should be provided for gifted and advanced students.
- Vocational education generates a cadre of technical skills that are highly required in the following stages of development in the region. Therefore, vocational education should not be considered as the "back door" toward formal university education.
- Focus should be placed on vertical (qualitative) rather than horizontal (quantitative) expansion in view of the considerable progress made in the latter over the last two decades.

In sum, labor market reforms should focus on the following targets:

(a) Emphasize productivity growth.
(b) Revive good work ethics and a commitment to high-quality work.
(c) Be market-driven, whenever possible.
(d) Be transparent and applicable to the public and the private sector with an eye to reducing duality.
(e) Keep a watchful eye on the costs and risks associated with each program.
(f) Improve the image of the public sector as a strategist, whose role is limited to directing, influencing and overseeing labor market reforms using proper fiscal policies.

Finally, the institution of comprehensive labor market reforms requires cooperation among the various agencies responsible for its implementation. Perhaps the worst that can happen is to have a well-conceived plan only to falter due to turf disputes and overlapping responsibilities among labor-related governmental institutions. In order to streamline the implementation of policy recommendations, it may be prudent to establish a High Council on Labor and Human Resource Development composed of all those involved in this area (Ministries of Finance, Planning, Labor and Social Affairs, Industry, Education, and Vocational Education). As a group, they should be able to direct and coordinate comprehensive labor market reforms.

Section 3: Regional Implications

The political economy of the suggested reforms invokes a number of caveats that must be borne in mind. First, it may be argued that the reforms represent a zero-sum situation where GCC's gains are offset by losses sustained by displaced workers and, hence, their respective countries. However, in view of the geopolitical realities of the Middle East as well as existing political alliances, they may strain the GCC's regional relationships, depending on the degree to which the reforms will worsen current unemployment rates and financial exigencies of labor-exporting countries.

On the other hand, one may counter-argue that the substitution policy has already been in operation for some time. Past calls for the nationalization of jobs, bans on the importation of certain skills, and firm-specific quotas are all indications of this trend. This is also evidenced by the fact that the inflow of expatriate labor force slowed down significantly during the last decade and their absolute number in some GCC countries had actually declined. What these reforms imply is a continuation of past practices, albeit in a more structured, less bureaucratic and certainly more market-oriented manner.

Factually, available data indicate that the number of expatriate workers is about 7.8 million in 1999, of whom 3.5 million are Arabs (or about 45%), and 4.3 million are Asians. The former group is dominated by workers from Egypt and, to a lesser extent, Palestine, and Sudan. The latter group is made up primarily of workers from India and Pakistan and, to a much lesser extent, Iran. Based on an estimated average wage rate of expatriate workers in Kuwait, Bahrain, and Oman of US$564 (KD 182), it is estimated that replacing about 500,000 foreign workers would result in an annual income loss of about US$282 million. Assuming that remittances average about 70% of earned income,[17] the total loss of foreign exchange to labor-exporting countries may reach about US$200 million annually. Not only that, the unemployment level in the same countries would rise by as much as the number of the displaced workers.

Further analysis of skill distribution among Arabs and non-Arabs gives rise to the following conclusion: the impact is likely to be disproportionate where nationals would tend to be more substitutable for Arabs than for Asians. This is true for a number of reasons:

- A large number of Asians are employed in either menial jobs that are not in demand by nationals—e.g., household services, sales, and factory positions; or they are employed in jobs that are difficult to fill by nationals due to the lack of similar experience—e.g., machine operators, maintenance and repair of electric and electronic machinery, etc.
- A large percentage of Arab workers hold jobs that can be performed readily by nationals—e.g., teachers at all levels, clerks, cashiers, engineers, lawyers, translators, sales managers, executives, accountants, physicians, researchers, economists, etc.

- To the extent that Arab workers typically earn higher wages than non-Arab expatriates, the financial burdens of the reforms are likely to be disproportionately onerous to Arabs.

On balance, unless major strides are made to invigorate the rate of economic development and to diversify the economic base of the GCC economies, neighboring labor-exporting countries are well advised to anticipate less remittances, less foreign exchange, and more workers returning from the GCC region in the future. This is an eventuality that is inevitable.

Notes

1   The GCC countries consist of Bahrain, Kuwait, Oman, Qatar, Saudi Arabia and the United Arab Emirates. Among them, they established a free trade area in May 1981, which was ratified in 1983.
2   This type of unemployment is termed by some as 'voluntary'.
3   In the US, frictional unemployment is generally accepted in the range of 4–6 percent of the labor force.
4   The profile of the new job-seekers is based largely on Bahrain's unemployment data; See Central Statistics Organization, *Statistical Abstract 1994*, Bahrain.
5   Based on a detailed breakdown of the structural unemployment in Bahrain in 1991; see CSO, 1993, *The Population, Housing, Buildings and Establishment Census – 1991*; Summary results, Part two. It is interesting to note that Bahrain, in a sense, has led the GCC in terms of having experienced the highest education levels among its national manpower, nationalized a much higher percent of the economy's jobs, encountered the unemployment problem and then addressed it earlier than most.
6   This ushered in a new, low value-added pattern of development, which embodied low levels of productivity.
7   SOEs throughout the GCC, notably in the oil sector, have demostrated their discerning skills in preparing nationals for supervisory/managerial positions with higher earnings and recognition.
8   In Kuwait, the General Assembly is currently deliberating a government-proposed law that aims at reducing the wage gap by raising the cost of expatriate workers and subsidizing the cost of nationals.
9   Since there are no data available on the extent to which these services are used by nationals vis-a-vis expatriates, a conservative approach is employed whereby it is assumed that i) a foreign worker typically consumes ? the amount of electricity and water; ii) a Kuwaiti worker utilizes health care facilities twice as much and iii) an expatriate worker uses the transportation system twice as much. While these assumptions may need some fine-tuning, the results are not likely to differ materially. Results are computed from data in CSO, 1994, *Annual Statistical Abstract*,

Kuwait and Public Authority for Civil Information, 1994, *Population and Labor Force*, Kuwait.

10 Based on an analysis of the manufacturing sector's cost of production components, as reported in CSO, *1993 Industrial Survey*, Kuwait, excluding the petroleum refining sub-sector, the impact of raising the cost of expatriates as per the schedule given above would be mimimal due to the relatively small ratio of wages to output. When the fee is fully implemented, sectoral wages will rise by 9.17% and output (sales) by 1.11%.

11 It is noteworthy that the GCC has long subsidized private businesses through soft loans, reduced electricity and water charges, nominal rents, protective tariffs, price preferences in government procurements, cash subsidies, and exemptions from import duties, among others. *This package in effect subsidizes every input in the production process except national labor.* To the extent that subsidies signal the producer to use those inputs that are most subsidized more extensively, and vice versa, the prevailing subsidy program should be modified or reshuffled to support the suggested National Renewal Plan.

12 The Human Resource Development Support (HRDS) program in Bahrain, administered by the Ministry of Finance and National Economy, may be used as a catalyst for this policy. See Maurice Girgis, 1992, A *Proposed Program of Industrial Incentives for the State of Bahrain*, Ministry of Finance and National Economy, Bahrain.

13 While this phenomenon is not unique to the GCC countries, it seems to be much more prevalent there than in other countries. Several surveys conclude that about one-third of new recruits find their jobs through friends and personal contacts; see Whiting, Edwin, 1987, *A Guide to Unemployment Reduction Measures*, Macmillan Press.

14 See Chapter 6 for further information on the economics of labor market search in Robert M. Fearn, 1981, *Labor Economics: The Emerging Synthesis*, Winthrop Publishers, Cambridge, MA.

15 LTC Techno-Economics, 1997, *Public Policy Reforms of Consumption Subsidies in the GCC*, prepared for the World Bank.

16 If consumption subsidies are reduced or removed, the foreign labor fee should be adjusted accordingly.

17 According to conventional wisdom, Arab workers tend to remit a much smaller percentage of their earned income vis-à-vis Asian workers. The ratio of remittance to earned income also varies across skills, falling as one moves up the skill ladder.

5

Social Protection in the Middle East and North Africa: A Review

Zafiris Tzannatos*

From the Macroeconomy to Individuals

Social protection has to be placed within its macroeconomic and social contexts. The unique socioeconomic characteristics of each region determine the nature of vulnerability and scope of social policies. In the MENA region, oil markets have had a large effect on country incomes and have determined movements in labor markets, public policies, as well as socioeconomic trends. Households have adjusted accordingly their coping mechanisms such as migration (internal and emigration) or informal networks at the family and community level.

* This chapter is based on the broader overview of social protection programs and policies in the Middle East and North Africa that is currently under preparation at the World Bank. It reflects a personal synthesis of the author, and the findings, interpretations, and conclusions expressed in the chapter should not be attributed in any manner to the World Bank, its affiliated organizations, the members of its Board of Executive Directors, or the countries they represent. The author would like to acknowledge the valuable inputs of Bahjat Achikbache, Richard Adams, Petros Aklilu, Arbi Ben-Anchour, Jacques Baudouy, Judith Bradsma, Concepcion Esperanza Del Castillo, Daniel Dilitzky, Sophal Ear, Peter Fallon, Yasser El-Gammal, Guillermo Hakim, Sonia Hammam, Robert Holzmann, Steen Jorgensen, Iqbal Kaur, Rekha Menon, Robert Palacios, Qaiser Khan, Bassam Ramadan, Setareh Razmara, David Robalino, Elizabeth Ruppert, Jamal Saghir, Lorenzo Savorelli, George Schieber, Kutlu Somel, David Steel, George Tharakan, Patrizia Tumbarello, Julia Van Domelen, and Dimitri Vittas, whose contributions are greatly appreciated, without implicating them in any errors or omissions.

The Rise and Fall of Oil Markets

The MENA region outperformed all other regions (except East Asia) in terms of income growth between 1960 and 1985. This growth was largely based on the increase in oil prices in 1973. The region's reliance on oil revenues reduced the pressure to open up its markets to the world economy. Inward-looking industrialization implied that capital inflows were not actively sought, and foreign investors were reluctant to expand their operations in the region. By the end of the oil boom, the countries were largely closed off from the international market because of high tariffs and considerable non-tariff barriers. They also lacked institutions and know-how for penetrating the global economy—for example, financial services and export promotion strategies.

The situation reversed with the collapse of oil prices in the mid-1980s. The falling oil prices depressed disposable income and led to sharp decreases in the level of investment. Non-oil countries in the region also felt spillover effects from collapsing oil prices through lower migrant worker remittances and reduced foreign investment. Since 1985, virtually all countries in the region have experienced lower GDP growth, compared to that of the previous decade. In general, the low growth of the late 1980s continued into the 1990s, although some reversals starting taking place towards the end of the decade. (Table 5.1).

The region had a sizeable and rigid public sector, a marginalized (rather than leading) private sector, and economies relatively isolated from global trade. Following the decline in the price of oil, investment and growth rates collapsed, as did regional capital and labor markets. Over the last 30 years, growth of economy-wide productivity or Total Factor Productivity (TFP) has declined, while population growth has remained high. Declining productivity, high population

Table 5.1. Real GDP Annual Growth Rates for Selected MENA
Countries (%)

	1976–85	1986–90	1991–95	1996–1998
Algeria	5.8	0.2	0.2	3.0
Egypt	8.5	4.2	3.3	5.6
Jordan	10.5	-1.1	7.5	2.2
Lebanon	na	na	6.5	3.5
Morocco	4.8	4.4	1.2	4.2
Tunisia	5.3	3.0	3.9	5.2
Yemen	na	3.3	8.2	4.6

Source: *World Bank Database*

growth, and falling oil prices contributed to an average regional decline in real per capita incomes of 2% per year since 1986, the largest decline in any developing region during this period. In some oil-exporting countries the decline was more than 4% per year.

The economic decline has created some daunting challenges, including:

- How can productivity increase, unemployment decline, and labor incomes increase?
- What mix of formal and informal social protection mechanisms can protect the welfare of the poor and decrease the vulnerability of both the poor *and* the fragile middle class?
- What policies can restore a *sustainable* growth path in the region? How can the results of growth be equitably distributed among the population?

These questions are addressed in the following sections.

Labor Market Performance

The contractionary effect of the decline in oil prices affected labor markets in at least three ways. First, *investment* fell as a proportion of GDP across the region, leading to lower and outdated capital stocks. Second, *public budgets* came under pressure, and earlier policies of using the public sector as an employer of last resort were halted or reversed, leading, in some countries, to a decline in public sector employment (i.e., Algeria and Egypt). Third, countries with significant *out-migration* (such as Egypt and Jordan) faced falling demand for their citizens abroad and substantial repatriations, particularly after the Iran-Iraq and Gulf wars.

Labor supply growth continued to be high by international standards in most MENA countries. This largely reflects high population growth rates between 2.5 and 3.0%, and additional inflows to the labor force from increasing female participation rates. In addition, labor-supply increases in urban areas are particularly great in some countries (such as Morocco and Egypt) where natural urban labor supply growth is strongly augmented by ongoing rural-urban migration.

The labor market characteristics in MENA countries have been shaped by the macroeconomic and trade policies implemented during the oil boom that are now out of tune with economic reality. Expansion of the public sector due to the need for additional teachers, state-owned enterprises (SOEs), and public administration played a substitute role for "social protection" through over-recruitment. The private sector got little boost from international markets due to high tariffs and anti-export bias. These rigid institutional structures have led to a rather inflexible response to labor market pressures.

In the formal sector, employment growth—though high in some countries in the mid-1980s to the early 1990s—did not match labor supply growth. For example, in Algeria private sector employment grew at nearly twice the rate of public sector employment from 1985 to 1989—7.2% per year and 3.8% per year, respectively—but the overall economic growth rate of 4.7% was insufficient to absorb more than 50% of the new labor force entrants. In Morocco in 1986–95, urban formal employment increased by one and a half million jobs, but the urban labor force increased by nearly two million. In contrast, Egypt's public sector employment continued to grow at an annual rate of 3.7% in 1986–95, but the private sector grew by only 1.9%. Overall, however, employment growth in Egypt was only 2.6% annually, slightly below the annual growth rate of the total labor force (2.7%).

There is little evidence that real wages fell dramatically while the labor market imbalance grew. Public sector wages in Algeria declined by about 1.7% per year on average between 1988 and 1995, while real private sector wages declined by only 4% between 1991–94. In Morocco, real wages stagnated between 1985 and 1995, although real increases from improved labor force composition occurred after 1990. Similarly, in Tunisia, real wages remained unchanged between 1983 and 1993 despite growing unemployment. Wage changes in Egypt, however, present a major exception to the general pattern, as real wages fell considerably in every sector between 1982 and 1985, almost halving on average.

Informal employment, in contrast, has generally grown in the region. In Morocco, about half of all employment created in 1985–93 was in the private informal sector. Little is known about the behavior of informal wages over time, although it is likely that these have fallen, as the formal sector became increasingly less able to absorb new labor market entrants.

Recent labor market trends seem to have raised the incidence of poverty in most countries. First, the increased informalization of labor markets represents a relative shift from high-paying to low-paying jobs, and has reduced labor incomes for many households. Second, declining informal sector wages—such as those in Egypt—directly reduce household incomes further. Third, rising unemployment among older workers and among the less educated pushes non-poor households below the poverty line, and makes some poor households even poorer.

Urban unemployment is high and probably still rising in many MENA countries. In 1995, unemployment rates in urban areas ranged from 11% in Egypt to 21% in Algeria (Table 5.2). Generally, unemployment is worse among females and among persons between the ages of 15 and 24. The incidence of unemployment in countries with major labor market imbalances, such as Egypt and Morocco, seems to be worsening more quickly among older workers, thus shifting the

Table 5.2. Labor Force Indicators for Selected MENA Countries (circa 1995)

	Employment in Agriculture (%)	Employment in the Public Sector (%)	Urban Unemployment Rate (%)	Unemployment (%)
Algeria	28	59	21	28
Egypt	35	35	11	11
Jordan	17	47	18	13
Morocco	45	8	18	16
Tunisia	23	35	11	15
WBG	na	20	na	na
Yemen	13	18	na	30

Source: *World Bank Country Reports*

center of the problem away from one of unemployed dependents towards one of unemployed household heads. Rising unemployment among the less educated, as seen in Algeria and Morocco, is also of great concern, particularly from a poverty perspective. Poverty, risk diversification, and overall economic development have had a strong impact on migration.

Migration

Rural-Urban Migration

Demographic pressures and limited land availability have led to significant migration into cities (including peri-urban areas), where rural migrants often settle for inferior employment opportunities and have limited access to social services. Since income fluctuations in the urban or external labor market are not linked with those of agriculture and livestock, a household can reduce its exposure to income variability by "investing" in migration. This is aggravated by underemployment in the agricultural sector. The share of the labor force in agriculture in the region declined from 50% in 1970 to 35% in 1996, while the share of urban population increased accordingly. However, rural-urban migration frequently has resulted in migration from rural poverty to urban poverty.

Intraregional Migration

The greater financial returns from working abroad, as well as the common language which MENA countries share, led to increased regional migration. Expected wages in the oil-rich Arab Gulf and industrialized countries of Europe are often four to five times higher than those earned in the urban areas of most non-oil countries. At its peak in 1985, the number of migrant workers in the oil-exporting countries of the region exceeded five million. Around 3.5 million came from the Middle Eastern countries of Yemen, Egypt, and Jordan, of which two million came from rural areas. However, by 1990, with the decline in oil prices, the expulsion of Yemeni and Jordanian workers from Saudi Arabia and Kuwait caused the Arab share in non-national employment in the oil-exporting countries to fall to less than 35%. Moreover, migration patterns and remittance flows in the MENA countries were affected by cyclical changes in economic activity and political changes in their host European countries; the economies of Europe are undergoing a socioeconomic transformation.

International Migration
Migration from the Maghreb countries to Europe has gone through several phases. During the 1960s and until the oil crisis in 1973, only males migrated. However, when EU countries reduced the import of manpower in the 1970s, three types of migration emerged. The first, *family reunion migration* (which already existed), has become more significant since 1974. As a result, the ratio of young men and women migrating to Europe has risen. The second, *seasonal migration* (workers employed under short-term contracts), represented only a small fraction of migrants. The third, *illegal migration*, has risen since the adoption of the Schengen Agreement[1] in 1990. In 1993, the number of legal immigrants from the Maghreb to Europe was more than two million. However, the decrease in employment in traditional industrial sectors (automotive, steel, textile, chemical), which have traditionally employed significant numbers of unskilled foreign labor, has had repercussions on the demand for workers from the Maghreb. This has reduced inter-Arab labor movements and made skilled and more educated Asian immigrants more attractive to these countries. These changes not only resulted in the return of expatriates, but also reduced the flow of hard currency remittances (see next section).

Migration and Remittances (macro)
At the macroeconomic level, remittances have accounted for a large percentage of foreign exchange resources, and have also helped relieve balance of payments deficits. Official remittances received by the major labor-exporting countries increased from a very low level in 1970 (US$0.4 billion) to over US$6 billion in 1990. In Morocco, remittances have at times accounted for over 5 to 8% of the GDP, and in Tunisia, over 4%. Until 1985, a considerable share of government expenditures in labor-exporting countries was financed by remittances from the oil boom. A main beneficiary of remittance flows was the public sec-

Table 5.3. Workers' Remittances in Selected MENA Countries,
1970–1995 (in US$ million)[1]

Countries	1970	1980	1985	1990	1995
Algeria	211	241	313	321	n.a.
Egypt	29	2,696	3,212	3,744	3,417
Jordan	16	n.a.	1,022	500	n.a.
Morocco	63	989	967	1,995	1,890
Syria	7	774	293	375	385
Tunisia	89	207	351	539	590
Yemen	60	n.a.	1,391	1,366	n.a.
Total	415	5,004	7,469	8,892	6,351
TOTAL*	188	4,666	4,823	6,653	6,282

Notes: 1) Official international remittances include both monetary
   transfers to banks and exchange imports.
   * Sum of remittances for countries for which data is available for all five years,
   1970–1995.
   n.a. = Not available
Source:World Bank, *World Development Report* (various years)

tor, which redistributed these new resources to absorb the large number of new job-seekers. This led to labor market distortions, which became exposed when the oil boom ended. These countries then found it difficult to reverse the trends of earlier years and to reform their economies.

At the microeconomic level, remittances often can be critical to the economic survival of poor households. The fact that uneducated and unskilled people can and do migrate means that remittances can have an important positive impact upon poverty. Thus, most of the international manpower flows between MENA countries have consisted of unskilled labor.[2] The poorest income quintile group in rural Egypt was able to produce more than its proportionate share of international migrants (Table 5.4). Since international remittances can account for between 10 and 30% of total household income, remittances can represent an important means for lifting poor households out of poverty. For instance, when remittances are included in total household income, the number of poor households in rural Egypt declines by 10%.

Linkages Between Remittances and Investment. Often the bulk of remittances was spent on personal consumption, not productive investment. However, in more recent years, studies in Egypt, Pakistan, and Turkey have shown that migrant households do use the income derived from remittances to invest. These investments generally tend to be in jewelry (a form of savings), real estate (especially land), and housing, which, however, may fuel inflation

Table 5.4. Distribution of International Migrants Among Income
Quintile Groups in Rural Egypt, 1986–87

Income quintile group[1]	% of international migrants[2]
Lowest	22.9
Second	18.5
Third	22.9
Fourth	18.4
Highest	17.4

Notes: 1) Based on per capita income, excluding remittances.
2) There were a total of 363 international migrants in the
sample of 1000 rural households.
Source: Adams (1991).

instead of stimulating development.[3] In Morocco, housing and real estate are also among the preferred channels of investment for migrants. Remittance-receiving households invest in land because the expected rates of return to land purchases are high; similarly, they invest in housing to improve the housing stock of their immediate and extended families. In order to encourage productive investments, governments should ensure favorable rates of return on small enterprise development and agricultural crops. Moreover, when a country maintains a favorable exchange rate, migrants will remit more of their earnings through official banking channels. When an exchange rate is overvalued, though, migrants tend to send more of their earnings home through private, unofficial channels.[4]

The impact of the expected increases in migration on economic development over the next few decades will depend on:

(a) how governments harness these flows with growing formal global production networks; and

(b) liberalization in regimes regulating trade and foreign direct investment.[5]

Household Coping Strategies

The structure of social organization throughout the MENA region is characterized by kinship-based networks. These are reliable and stable relationships, and households activate these networks both to offset the effects of crises and to conserve or maximize the acquisition of resources. These networks are of vital importance (a) in spreading the risks, and as insurance against them in the case of localized catastrophes; and (b) in strengthening over the long term the economic and social capital within a group that can be accessed in times of shock or stress.

Relatives can be sources of refuge during or after environmental or political catastrophes. Studies conducted in the West Bank and Gaza illustrate that kinship is a strong element of informal support, where the better-off households give to those in need. The closer the kinship and community ties, the higher the incidence of sources of informal support. Informal support is lowest in the camps where dispersal and dispossession have weakened kinship relations. For example, in the case of the West Bank and Gaza, informal support, although limited in scope, provides a cushioning effect on the economic shocks on poorer families and is a tangible source of relief.[6]

Coping with Short-Term Crises and Risks
Short-term crises are often related to unexpected death, or illness requiring the intervention of doctors and hospital care. In both rural and urban areas, households living precariously at the subsistence level rarely have savings to meet such crises. Their only savings may be in the form of livestock, jewelry, or household items such as rugs. If additional resources are needed, the household has limited options such as loans, or services from the closest kinsmen against payment in the future. This assistance is mutual and the tacit rules are that the amount of a loan or the service given will be repaid or reciprocated when the crisis is over, or at the most opportune moment for both parties. See an example from Yemen (Box 2).

Box 1

Informal Social Support Systems in the West Bank and Gaza

A study on informal support systems in WBG found that nearly half the households reported giving assistance, but most of this was in the form of gifts for religious and social occasions. Only 10% of households provided any regular informal support (no assistance was provided by institutions—government or local—and there were no set rules that were binding in a legal or institutional sense) to other individuals or their families within their kinship group, while less than 4% gave regular assistance to individuals or families outside their kinship group. Strategies adopted by poor households tend to be formed mostly within the framework of kinship, local community, and the workplace. Those who are structurally denied access to the labor market or have no access to it for a prolonged length of time are more likely to seek assistance from formal support institutions, such as the Ministry of Social Affairs, UNRWA in the case of refugees, and various charitable organizations (such as *zakat* committees).

Source: Hillal (1998), "The Limits of Informal Social Support Systems in the West Bank and Gaza Strip," Presented at the Mediterranean Development Forum, September 3–6, 1998 based on a study conducted by the Palestine Economic Policy Research Institute (MAS) on a representative sample of 1458 households June–September 1996 in the West Bank and Gaza.

Coping with Medium-Term Crises and Risks
The most typical medium-term risks are seasonal demands, which can become crises if there are insufficient household means to provide resources for religious festivities or special social occasions. The availability of information about resources or opportunities is key for adapting to seasonal crises and risks. Networks of migration opportunities, for instance, are one form of response to seasonal or mid-term risks. In addition to the informal mechanisms used to cope with seasonal stress, the range of responses goes beyond the immediate kinship and community networks, and there is an appeal to formal mechanisms that may or may not be accessible to individual households. These include access to seasonal or short-term loans for agricultural inputs and technological advice. In general, however, one common characteristic is that this kind of stress requires a social network greater than the immediate circle of kinsmen.

Box 2

Coping Strategies of Poor Communities in Yemen

To assess the coping mechanisms of poor communities, in 1998 a social protection field study was conducted. This study targeted very poor communities that were identified in advance by their very low levels of household income—less than 5000 riyals per month ("food poverty line" estimated by the statistical office of Yemen is around 2500 riyals per month, per capita or for a family of three adults and five children, is around 20,000 riyals per month per household). To leave no doubt that the field study had reached the "very poorest," we asked the study participants to prioritize how they would spend an additional 5000 riyals per month. Over 85% of the participants indicated that they would spend the entire amount on food. A further 4% would spend some on clothing, and 4% on repaying loans. Less than 1% would spend on medicine or medical treatment.

How do these families survive? More than half the participants indicated that they were in debt through borrowing, predominantly from relatives/neighbors (47%) and local retailers/traders (42%). The debt levels ranged from around 20,000 riyals (60%) through 40,000 riyals (15%) up to 100,000 riyals (9%). In such poor communities, the capacity to repay is extremely low. Around 65% have not paid back their debts, 15% have partially repaid their debts, and only 20% have repaid in full. The field study revealed that the unpaid or partially paid debt (particularly in the case of retailers/traders) was generally part of a running line of credit, with the debtors paying off what they could when they were able. Family/neighbor debts were usually much smaller and tended to be repaid quickly (or "borrowed back"). It appeared that these informal lines of credit were the major coping strategy of the poor. Public programs of assistance (cash or in-kind) were not mentioned as regular—or even irregular—sources of urgently needed income. Indeed, very few programs of public provision had reached into these communities, and none were aware of opportunities available under the Social Development Fund.

Coping with Long-Term Risks
These risks arise from the policies dealing with land tenure, access to land for women, water availability, changes in land use, restrictions on imports and exports, controls or pricing of agricultural products, marketing mechanisms, and rural development strategies. In addition, there may be country legislation dictating or precluding the formation of local organizations, potential mechanisms for improving agricultural productivity and contributing to the decline of rural poverty (Box 3). The adaptive strategies of poor households for coping with macro-level policies are difficult to evaluate because the impact of these strategies can be assessed only over the long term.

The Ability to Cope with Policies at the Local Level Depends on Several Factors
First there are the cohesiveness and rationality of the forms and relations of production, strong local ability to provide coping mechanisms over the long term, and the roles of cooperatives and farmer organizations. Second, there are forms of access to the productive base, restrictions on the size of land owned, and access to water. Third is the degree of confidence and awareness in the state's policies; the state is often perceived as distant, and the main contributor to rural poverty.

Reducing Vulnerability

The reduction of vulnerability depends not only on social protection policies conventionally defined (see section 3), but on the coordination of all social policies and public expenditures. A range of the latter are reviewed below, including population, education and training, health, water, land, and infrastructure policies.

Table 5.5. Trends in Fertility, Mortality, and Life Expectancy, 1970–1996

Indicator	1970	1980	1990	1996
Total fertility rate	6.8	6.1	4.9	4.0
Life expectancy at birth, female (years)	53.6	59.8	66.6	68.1
Life expectancy at birth, male (years)	51.9	57.3	63.5	65.8
Infant mortality rate (per 1000 live births)	134.5	96.2	61.1	50.0
Under-5 mortality rate (per 1000 live births)	192.8	141.4	92.9	62.7
Total population (millions)	131.9	175.4	236.9	276.3

Note: The summary measures for MENA region for the above indicators are weighted by population or subgroup of population, except for infant mortality and population. IM is weighted by the number of births, and population is calculated by simple addition of populations of all MENA countries. Source: *World Development Indicators,* 1998.

Box 3

Coping with Liberalization: Egypt's Small Farmers

One key intervention in Egypt's efforts to liberalize its economy was the agricultural reform strategy. Linking agricultural reform to broader social and economic results has resulted in the removal of a range of social security benefits to which the poor formerly had access.

Shifting Household Consumption Patterns

Initial evaluations of the effects of these reforms on poor farm households show that there has been an overall attempt to prioritize the security of assets that guarantee future survival. The most direct impact of this strategy resulted in a decline in food consumption and a change in dietary patterns. This led to the consumption of food with lower nutritional value, as families opted for the purchase of cheaper commodities.

Women's Intensification of Participation in the Labor Process

While men can opt for migrating outside the rural areas in search of employment, or even consider international migration, women are required to increase their participation and also to diversify activities in order to compensate for male absenteeism. With diminished revenues, women had to spend more time in search of cheaper foodstuffs. They also had to spend more time waiting for health services as the budgets and personnel in the rural health services were reduced. Women had to increase their participation in agricultural activities, but among the better-off households in the rural areas, where women's involvement in such work would result in a loss of household prestige and status, women increasingly turned to the production and sale of handicrafts. As change became institutionalized, the women's income-generating activities became a pivotal part of rural households' survival strategies.

Social Repercussions

With increasing prices and diminished opportunities for employment in rural ventures, the reforms resulted in diminished social life among the villagers. The costs of festive occasions have become prohibitive for many households. There has been a diminution of cultural manifestations and associations, and concomitantly, an increase in crime, including rising petty thievery—particularly for tools, hand pumps, and crops.

State and Peasants' Interests

The above are illustrations of the different perspectives and interests of the state and the people who are on the receiving end of the policy reforms. There is an alarming gap between the interests of the two sides. What is called for to redress some of these impacts is a recognition of the different productive capabilities, or coping strategies, for examining the areas where there are common grounds and where there are differences that undermine rather than provide conditions for the improvement of agricultural productivity. The Egyptian agricultural crisis is *not* one of prices and inputs; it is a crisis of social and political dimensions, rooted in the history of the *fellahin*.

Source: Ray Bush. 1995. "Coping with Adjustment and Economic Crisis in Egypt's Countryside." *Review of African Political Economy* 66.

Population

The population of the MENA region has been growing faster than output. Most countries in the region, however, are in the midst of a demographic transition: their populations are expected to double again in the next 30 years, though fertility rates have begun to drop substantially. Even if fertility declines dramatically to reach the replacement level, with 40% of women of child-bearing age, the number of births will continue to increase.

In terms of labor supply, the working-age population in the region is expected to increase at a rate one-third higher than that of population growth by 2020. The estimated total number of youths entering the work force annually is currently around 7.4 million. While the current proportion of the population engaged in the labor force is not the highest in the world (in fact, it is among the lowest in the world), the increase in the proportion of the population flowing into the labor force between 1990 and 1997 (2.3%) was higher than for any other region of the world.

At the micro level, population growth burdens the poor disproportionately in the short run in terms of spending on food, education, health, and clothing. The poor typically have more children than do the non-poor and can be affected disproportionately, as they face tougher choices between current consumption and investment for future generations. In Algeria 50% of the members of poor households are under age fifteen, compared to about 40% for non-poor households. In addition, rapid population growth with high fertility rates as seen in Yemen, Iraq, and the West Bank and Gaza can result in high infant and maternal mortality rates and shorter life expectancies.

At the macro level, population growth puts pressure on the provision of basic services (e.g., health, education, water, sanitation, and public infrastructure) and the creation of adequate employment opportunities. In Yemen, the number of students enrolled in basic education is expected to more than double by 2020 (from 2.1 million in 1995 to 5.7 million in 2020). Providing reproductive health services for all women by the year 2020 would require more than doubling annual expenditures on health. Both figures, for education and health, dwarf the expected rates of economic growth in Yemen.

Some governments have adopted policies for managing population growth with significant success:[7]

- *Tunisia's* Family Planning Association was established in 1968, and, in addition to conventional measures, it promoted the importance of birth-spacing for the health of both mother and child. Laws were enacted that raised the age of marriage to 17 for women and 20 for men.

Family benefits were limited to the first three children of a household. Basic education is provided free of charge, and girls have equal access and practically identical enrollment rates as boys. The total fertility rate in Tunisia was 2.8 children per woman in 1996, compared with 6.4 children per woman in 1970.

- The population growth rate of *Iran* was 3.2% in 1986. A Population Committee was established by the Ministry of Health and Medical Education to study the implications for food, health, education, employment. and other services. Subsequently, the government's first and second Five-Year Development Plan included a policy to reduce population growth through an increase in contraceptive coverage, girls' education levels, and participation of women in the society as well as the family. The contraception prevalence rate (for women aged fifteen to 49, using some form of contraception) stands now at 55%, and girls' enrollment in basic education is universal. The program succeeded and the annual population growth rate has been halved (1.4%); TFR has decreased from 6.4 children per woman to 3.8 children per woman in 1996.

- *Egypt* has had a formal population policy since 1966, with the establishment of the national family planning program. The first national population policy was introduced in 1973. Between 1980 and 1996, the TFR dropped from 5.1 children per woman to 3.3 children per woman, and the contraceptive prevalence rate rose from 21% to 50%. The population program still remains a national priority for the government.

Education and Training

Most MENA countries have achieved universal primary enrollment and significant secondary enrollment rate increases. Nonetheless, the number of out-of-school children is expected to grow by over 40%, with disproportionate shares among the rural poor and girls. Nearly five million children aged 6–10 and another four million children 11–15 were out of school in 1995. By 2015, these numbers are expected to grow by over 40%—to 7.5 million and 5.6 million, respectively. In Egypt, the enrollment rate for children in the top quintile remains above 80%, whereas enrollments in the poorest fifth of the households are close to 50%. In Morocco, net primary enrollments in rural areas are 58%, compared with 85% in urban areas. Tunisian secondary enrollments in rural governorates are as low as 19%, while in Tunis they are 78%.

The quality of teaching and learning has suffered, as the number of teachers expanded quickly to meet growing enrollments. Education in the region does not effectively impart the higher-order cognitive skills, such as flexibility and problem-solving. While most countries provide basic inputs, maintenance is usually poor and severe deterioration of physical infrastructure is common throughout the region.

Although most MENA countries allocate a large share of their government budgets to education, both investment and recurrent resources are often not used efficiently. There are policies that impede optimal employment, hiring, promotion, remuneration, and termination of contracts, which in turn limit the education system's prospects for efficient operation, as 90% of recurrent funds are normally spent on human resources.

Table 5.6. Total Education Expenditure as Percentage of GDP

	1990	*1991*	*1992*	*1993*	*1994*	*1995*
Algeria	6.9	—	—	7.0	7.0	7.0
Egypt		4.2	3.9	4.5	5.1	4.7
Iran	4.1	—	—	5.3	4.5	4.5
Jordan	—	—	—	4.1	3.7	6.0
Morocco	5.3	5.0	5.3	5.9	5.4	5.5
Tunisia	6.0	—	—	6.1	6.2	6.5
West Bank & Gaza						
Yemen	—	7.6	5.9	6.2	6.4	5.1

Source: *UNESCO Statistical Yearbook* 1997

Private sector participation is often hindered by the lack of facilitating legal, regulatory, and accreditation frameworks, particularly for post-compulsory education. While governments have the responsibility of guaranteeing access to high-quality basic education for all, and of maintaining standards in post-basic levels, public budgets are limited and financing all education levels cannot take place without a serious deterioration in quality. In addition, high repetition levels and drop-outs add to the inefficiencies of the system that hit children from poor families particularly hard.

Vocational training programs tend to cater to those who have dropped out of the education system for academic reasons. Furthermore, those who complete these programs are often ill prepared to meet the demands of the modern labor market, and remain unemployed for long periods. For example, in Egypt, of the 52,000 students who graduated in 1996, less than 10% are absorbed by the labor markets each year. The rest engage mostly in low-paying jobs in informal markets or seek dependence on government programs.

The system is still expanding without an analysis of market requirements, with no coherent national strategy and low private involvement. In Tunisia, there are 411 private training centers with 26,000 students, offering more than 50 different specializations with no relevance to the job market. Algeria has the largest training system with 290,000 training posts, 260,000 of which are provided by public training centers and 15,000 by public enterprises. In Egypt, there are 120 publicly run training centers serving 36,000 students with weak links to the private sector and no management or financial structures in place. In the West Bank and Gaza, there are 29 centers outside of MOE and MOHE, with around 3000 trainees and 24 specializations, again with little coordination with job markets. In Yemen, there are fifteen public training centers with 5000 students, focusing primarily on industry and commerce. In most countries, the system is fragmented, with too many systems overlapping with the same purpose but distorted and varied approaches, lacking any coordination.

Training focuses on pre-employment services, not lifelong training. Programs focus mainly on pre-service training, and the cost-benefit tradeoff to enterprises provides no incentive for them to provide in-service training, though in some countries (such as Tunisia) in-service training benefits from tax rebates.

Overall, the end result is a supply-driven vocational training system. Programs are mainly publicly funded and administered, and do not correspond to labor market realities. The system does not meet the evolving needs of the economy, as there is little interaction with the private sector. In Tunisia, for instance, the private sector provides training for the tertiary sector, and the public sector is in charge of industrial training. In Egypt, the private sector has limited capacity either to identify the skills it needs or to fund skill-development programs.

Education and Training: The Way Forward

- Developing a comprehensive strategy that links the education system with the training system, the public with the private sector in view of emerging labor market requirements. This entails the adoption of policy frameworks for long-term programs of development and reform. These frameworks should be objective-driven and insulated against major policy shifts caused by minor changes in government;
- Improving performance at all levels of education and training by focusing on standards rather than delivery processes, and adding coherence to curriculum and assessment;
- Increasing private sector participation through regulatory and accreditation frameworks;
- Improving internal efficiency by controlling and managing unit costs;

- Building a community of learners willing to continuously review the best experiences, methodologies and technologies, and analyze educational and training problems;
- Disseminating information that is critical for building consensus around education and training reforms, and for continued support of national comprehensive policy frameworks.

Health

Living standards and health status in the region have improved significantly in the past 30 years, but disparities between rural and urban, as well as wealthy and poor, are widening. In 1995, except in Yemen and Morocco, over 90% of the population had access to health services. Although mortality and morbidity rates have declined, countries in the region are at substantially different stages of epidemiological and demographic transformation. Yemen, for example, has high mortality rates (101 per 1000 live births compared to a regional average of 37 in 1995) and an epidemiological profile comparable to the least developed countries of the world. Yemen and parts of rural Egypt and Morocco continue to suffer from high mortality rates from infectious diseases, especially among children and mothers. The low health status of the population is a consequence of poverty (e.g., low income, poor sanitation, lack of safe drinking water, poor nutrition, and low educational attainment level), as well as lack of access to health services.

On average the MENA region spends 6.1% of GDP on health care, with a significant share of private outlays. The public share ranges from just below 25% in Yemen to over 70% in Algeria, and possibly over 80% in UAE. This wide variance reflects differences in government provision of health financing, as well as in the size of the public sector relative to national income.

Private insurance accounts generally for only a small fraction of private spending. The reliance on out-of-pocket spending signifies that most individuals and households directly bear a substantial proportion of health care costs, but have little or no financial protection (i.e., insurance) in the event of a catastrophic illness or injury. Low-income households in particular allocate a higher share of their expenditures to health care services. In Algeria, for instance, household health expenditure for the poorest 10% of the urban population is three times as large as for the richest 10% of the same population; for the rural population, it is twice as large. In Tunisia, for the poorest 5% of the urban population, health expenditures account for about 1.2% of total expenditures, while the expenditure share increases to about 2.1% for the corresponding rural population. In the future, as the proportion of elderly will rise above 10% of the population in most countries, health care costs will be more acutely felt among the aging population.

Table 5.7. Health Expenditures

	Real Per Capita (US$)		Per Capita (PPP$)		Health Expenditure			Public
	1994 GDP	Total Health Expenditure	GDP	Total Health Expenditure	% of GDP Total	Public	Private	% of Total
Low- and middle income	1654	83	3027	139	5.0	2.4	2.6	42.3
EAP	753	27	3023	106	3.6	1.7	1.9	50.7
ECA	2464	138	4331	315	5.4	4.4	1.1	72.8
LAC	3435	248	6153	425	6.7	2.9	3.9	49.0
MENA	**9336**	**433**	**4888**	**211**	**4.6**	**2.4**	**2.2**	**49.6**
SA	407	21	1348	64	5.0	1.2	3.9	38.5
SSA	1814	55	1729	87	2.9	1.6	1.6	55.4
Low-income	623	22	1893	78	4.2	1.5	2.7	36.8
Excluding China & India	939	18	1518	47	3.1	1.1	2.0	36.7
Middle-income	3761	209	5198	264	5.1	4.3	2.4	52.3
High-income	24022	2404	21788	2227	9.6	6.9	3.7	62.0

Note: Regional averages do not add up due to incomplete coverage of data for private health expenditures. Averages in columns may not correspond due to differences in coverage of data.
Source: World Bank (2000)

Health: The Way Forward

- Changing the role of the state. With the expansion of private providers, instead of expanding publicly managed delivery systems, governments may reduce their role as direct service providers but expand their capacities as purchasers of private health services, as well as regulators of the health sector;
- Improving the performance of the public delivery system through better intersectoral coordination on policies that affect health;
- Dealing with the consequences of epidemiological and demographic transitions by strengthening maternal health services, health education programs, and support from women's organizations or other community-based efforts;
- Improving equity and expanding health coverage to the poor and marginal groups through greater government partnerships with non-governmental organizations and local communities;

- Improving private sector efficiency and regulating private insurance;
- Restructuring health systems involving the design of a coherent, systematic reform plan.

Water

The level of water reserves is the lowest in MENA compared with other world regions, and water resources are being depleted fast. The MENA region is the driest in the world, and its water reserves are shrinking. Though Iraq and Lebanon appear to have adequate renewable water supplies relative to their populations, Yemen's water availability per capita today is a little more than 170 cubic meters, Jordan's is 200 cubic meters, and the West Bank and Gaza, 103. In 1993, annual water consumption within Yemen, Libya, Saudi Arabia, and the Gulf States, and more recently Jordan, exceeded renewable supplies. Jordan and Yemen withdraw 25 to 30% more from their aquifers than is being replenished annually.

Figure 5.1. Renewable Water Resources in Cubic Meters per Capita by Region

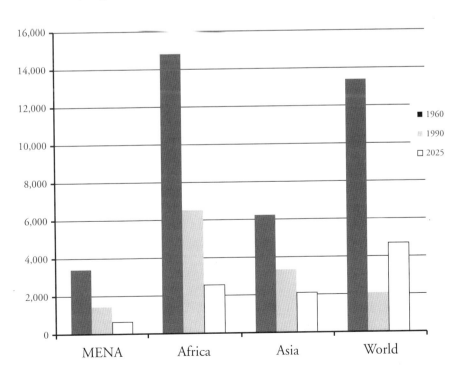

Urbanization increases per capita water consumption and the competition for water between human consumption, irrigation, and industrial use. The urban areas in the region are growing at a rate of more than 4 % per year. By 2025, the share of the population living in urban areas will increase from 60 to 75%. The absorbed share of renewable water supplies in urban areas would rise from the current 6% to more than 20% in 2025. In addition, the growth in population would limit water consumption to only 1250 m^3 on average per person, compared with 7500 m^3 in Africa and 23,000 m^3 in Latin America.

Agriculture is the largest water-user in the region, yet only one quarter of the cultivated land is under irrigation. 87% of the water withdrawn went to irrigation, and only 13% to industrial and municipal uses, compared with 69% and 31%, respectively, worldwide. Irrigation is extremely inefficient in most countries; in flood irrigation only 30% of the water reaches the crops. The long-run marginal cost of irrigated water in Jordan, for example, is an estimated US$0.32 per cubic meter, higher than the estimated value added from most agricultural production. In Yemen, agriculture supports nearly 81% of the population and produces only 18% of GDP. Because of the decline in water sources, farmers can no longer make a living from farming alone.[8] For example, a typical farmer near the capital of Sana'a has deepened his well by 50 meters over the last twelve years—increasing his costs—while the amount of water he can extract has dropped by nearly two-thirds.

Inefficient water management aggravates the water problem.[9] The resultant inadequate supply of safe water in urban areas is forcing even the poor to purchase water from private vendors at very high prices (Box 4).

The scarcity of water also imposes serious public health risks. About 45 million people in the region—nearly 16% of the population—lack access to safe water, and nearly 80 million lack access to safe sanitation. Children below the age of fourteen are particularly vulnerable, and they account for nearly 43% of the MENA region's population. Waterborne diseases, especially diarrheal diseases, are second only to respiratory diseases in causing mortality and morbidity among this group of children. In the region, five of the six leading causes of disease are waterborne.[10] According to a recent study by UNDP, increasing the availability of uncontaminated water supplies can reduce the incidence of waterborne diseases in rural and urban areas by one-third.

Water: The Way Forward

- Pricing water appropriately is necessary, albeit unpopular. Willingness-to-pay studies with user participation can help design tariffs that cover costs while protecting the poor;

- Countries in the MENA region need to seek alternatives to fresh water, such as wastewater treatment and reuse, and desalination;
- Defining national water strategies and improving institutional frameworks. This should include:
  - (a) enhancing cost recovery;
  - (b) strengthening local capacity in water resource management and planning (through formation of water organizations);
  - (c) promoting awareness of water issues and programs;
  - (d) reducing water use in agriculture while maintaining or adding

---

Box 4

The Economic Costs of Inadequate Water Supplies to Meet Domestic Use and the Community's Response

Economic Costs

Yemen's total annually renewed water resources are an estimated 2.1 billion cubic meters. With a population of around 14 million, available resources amount to a little more than 170 cubic meters per capita each year. In Yemen, the urban poor often have to buy water from private vendors at a price nearly ten to 25 times the price of water from the National Water and Sanitation Authority.

Jordan's per capita availability of water resources amounts to around 200 cubic meters per year and is expected to be reduced to nearly 91 cubic meters per year by 2025. Increasing population, inefficiency of water distribution, and inadequate infrastructure has lead to a shortage of water resources available for household use. This has an adverse impact, especially on the urban and rural poor. In Jordan, water consumption in urban areas is rationed and is generally available only two times a week in summer, less in some communities. To meet household demand, even the urban poor are compelled to purchase water from tankers supplied by the Water Authority of Jordan at a price of 1.5 to 1.7 JD/m^3 or from private tankers at a wider range of prices.

Community Response

In an *Egyptian* village in the Nile Delta, village women helped facilitate water, sanitation and environmental health improvements by working with an action research team. The village had a population of 5,000 and had not sewage, solid waste or sullage disposal system. It had access to three water sources: piped water through public standpipes, shallow wells with hand pumps, and canal water. The women identified two problems: a malfunctioning standpipe (forcing women to walk far everyday to fetch water) and a highly polluted canal. Gastrointestinal and eye diseases were widespread among the children of the village. The women organized the village to repair the standpipe and formed two women's committees: one to maintain the repaired standpipe and another to monitor the cleanliness of the canal.

Source: World Bank. (various sources). Assad, M., S. el Katasha and S. Watts, "Involving women in water and sanitation initiative: an action/ research project in an Egyptian village." *Water International* 19.

agricultural value-added and shifting water resources to high-value usage and controlling ground water use;

(e) introducing regulations to improve water quality;

(f) financing innovative approaches to managing water resources;

(g) developing low-cost technologies; and

(h) identifying and increasing use of alternative or non-conventional sources of water—treated wastewater, river cleanup, desalination and water imports, encouraging population management policies to reduce demand for water.

Infrastructure, Land, Transportation

In addition to population, education, health, and water services, pressures on the land and existing systems of land tenure, as well as transport and other infrastructure services, bring their own complications and often act as impediments to adequate social protection.

Land

Land tenure is generally a sensitive issue, and the following characterize the land tenure situation in the region:

(a) landholders tend to be small and, for many, farm size is economically inadequate;

(b) uneven distribution of land has led to widespread poverty among the landless and small-holders;

(c) there is a fragmentation of holdings and prevalence of joint ownership due to inheritance laws;

(d) insecurity of tenure and lack of land titles cause unsustainable exploitation, as well constraints in access to official credit (due to the collateral issue);

(e) common lands—those without any titles—are exploited through customary rights;

(f) small-holder agriculture coexists with a structure of tenancy and share-cropping; and, finally,

(g) land markets are virtually nonexistent and are encumbered by costly and time-consuming bureaucratic processes. In Morocco, 69% of the rural farmers have less than five hectares per farm and own only 23% of the land, while less than 1% of farmers have 50 hectares or more and own 15% of the land. In rural Tunisia, 43% of farm families own less than five hectares and control only 6% of the arable land. In Jordan, land tenure is characterized by a large number of small holdings. Three-quarters of farmers either have no land or have land holdings of less than five hectares.

Transportation

Improved transportation facilities can have many beneficial effects, e.g., from increasing attendance in primary schools to opening up access to markets and facilitating worker mobility. Road transportation often lacks adequate attention for maintenance and affects mainly the rural population, most of whom are poor. Major challenges include:

(a) a better understanding of the needs of the rural poor by conducting surveys;

(b) the creation/improvement of rural access infrastructure (tracks and trails), which can be used by non-motorized transport aids;

(c) the promotion of affordable transport aids (e.g., bicycles); and

(d) improved community involvement in the identification and improvement of rural access projects.

Infrastructure

There are many schemes for providing basic physical infrastructure, such as electricity and sewerage. Governments tend to keep the prices of these services low to make them affordable, but cannot often afford maintenance or expansion, which leaves large segments of the population—generally the poorest ones—unserved. In many cities, especially in the poorer areas, the municipal solid waste disposal and sewerage are inadequate: In Jordan and Morocco, one-third of the urban population lack adequate sewerage services. This inadequacy can lead to disease, traffic congestion, environmental degradation, crime, and—through the creation of peri-urban poverty—unemployment. Major challenges include:

(a) improving the targeting of these services to the poor, particularly in rural and remote areas, through greater involvement of the communities and civil society;

(b) introducing a cost recovery system for the better-off, particularly in urban areas;

(c) allocating sufficient budgetary funds to programs which benefit the remote areas; and

(d) involving the private sector.

Increasing Protection

The broad social policies discussed previously (Section 2) can play a significant role in protecting human capital, and households can continue supporting themselves even in the midst of crises (Section 1). Nonetheless, social protection programs can further foster human development and provide social safety

Table 5.8. Social Sector Expenditure in 1995 (% of GDP)

Country	Food Subsidies	Social Assistance[2]	Public Works	Public Pension	Health	Education	TOTAL	TOTAL (excl. Health and Education
Algeria[1]	0.9	0.7	0.6	1.9	1.2	7.0	12.3	4.1
Egypt	1.3	0.5	0.3	2.5	1.6	4.7	10.9	4.6
Iran	2.9	1.2	—	1.5	2.0	4.5	12.1	5.6
Jordan	1.4	1.0	—	4.2	3.5	6.0	16.1	6.6
Morocco	1.7	0.1	0.3	1.8	1.1	5.5	10.5	3.9
Tunisia	1.7	1.0	0.4	2.6	2.2	6.5	14.4	5.7
Yemen	4.9	0.2	0.2	0.04	1.2	4.9	11.4	5.3

Notes: 1) Pre-reform

2) Social assistance includes cash and kind transfers, but exclude public works

Source: *World Bank Reports* (various)

nets. This section assesses existing programs (those in Table 5.8 plus training, social funds, and others) and explores their impact on reducing vulnerability. It also makes key recommendations to improve the programs and develop a sustainable social protection system. Key issues include the management of public provision, the quality of services, and the synergy between governments and civil society rather than the level of public spending per se (Table 5.9).

Microfinance

Microfinance is potentially useful, and the main bottleneck is not the lack of funds for on-lending, but rather the lack of local capacity to efficiently deliver microfinance services. There are over 7.5 million poor households in MENA (over 60 million poor people), of which less than 2% have access to financial services.[11] The estimates of the outreach gap—people needing financial services and willing to pay for them, who nevertheless lack access—lies between two and four million households. The funding gap—funds needed for on-lending—lies between US$750 million and US$1.4 billion, less than 1% of total lending of the formal financial sector in the region. There are over 60 microfinance programs, the majority being NGOs. Together these programs serve over 112,000 active borrowers, 75,000 of which live in Egypt. 14% of active borrowers live in rural areas and 36% are female. Of the 60 programs, only two are fully sustainable,[12] and eight are well underway towards sustainability.[13] Another seven are designed and implemented according to best practice guidelines, but it is too soon to evaluate their sustainability. The seventeen best practice programs together serve the majority (70%) of current active borrowers. However, most of the remaining 43 programs are funded by the government and charge subsidized interest rates, lack sustainability, and demonstrate low performance.

Programs that are part of a larger socioeconomic program are difficult to implement. In general, it is very difficult to implement a best practice microfinance program as a component of a larger, more socially oriented program, such as a Social Fund (see below) or relief program. Although the initial umbrella of a larger organization ensures financial and institutional support, "culture" clashes can occur as the microfinance program adheres to sound business and banking practices while the larger program does not.

Programs that target both men and women tend to marginalize women. Experience in MENA shows that women tend to become marginalized in programs that target both men and women. However, programs that target women exclusively do not only reach the poorest but have also achieved sustainability.

The role of banks in the delivery of microfinance can be improved. Banks may be the most effective in filling and funding the outreach and funding gap because they have a wide branch network, systems in place, and, usually, a business orientation. Subsidized lending programs through banks—often imposed under political pressure—have proven largely unworkable in, for instance, Morocco, Tunisia, and Egypt. Borrowers are often selected based on their poverty or unemployment status and not their entrepreneurial capability, and banks did not receive technical support to develop the loan screening and monitoring systems required for successful micro and small business lending. As a result, repayment rates remain low and banks incur high loan losses.

Microfinancing: The Way Forward[14]
In the medium term, microfinance can deepen and widen the financial system in a country, and the development of the microfinance industry should be part of a country's financial sector development strategy. *At the program level,* some micro-programs in MENA countries are already being spun-off from their larger, socially oriented mother organizations, and a similar strategy should be developed at the macro-country level. Microfinance should be a joint responsibility between financial and social development policy-makers and a joint responsibility between the financial sector and donors. More specifically:

- Microfinance programs, when they are part of broader social programs, should be established as an independent legal entity. This will help avoid future legal, operational and administrative problems.

- Well informed policy dialogue can avoid backlashes on the issue of interest charged; loans should not be free or subsidized.
- Microfinance services can be successfully provided based on Islamic banking principles.
- Banks should be part of the delivery mechanism. Banks or financing companies with a retail focus, operating in a competitive environment, are the most likely to be effective, as is shown by emerging developments in Morocco and Lebanon.

Public Work Programs

Public Work Programs (PWPs) provide income-earning opportunities through the creation of temporary jobs for the unemployed and underemployed. These programs also provide poor communities with basic infrastructure and can become a permanent feature in the sense that they are dormant when not needed, but are triggered once there is an increase in poverty (such as in the case of crop failure).[15] Morocco and Tunisia both have a long tradition of public work policies (Box 5). In other cases, public works have been introduced as needed, such as in Algeria and Egypt in the 1990s, following structural adjustment measures. In MENA countries, public work programs can be an effective mechanism to alleviate poverty and to provide short-term employment for unskilled or semi-skilled labor, while improving the infrastructure in poorer communities.

Box 5

Public Work Programs in Morocco and Tunisia

In *Tunisia*, public work programs (*chantier public*) are an important source of employment for the poor. In urban areas, activities include road maintenance, sewer cleaning and installation, removal of wastewater, and cleaning of public roads. In rural areas it covers road work, soil conservation and forestry activities. These programs, which provide short-term jobs for unskilled workers in an attempt to reduce underemployment and unemployment, are a key vehicle for transferring income to the poor. Participants are primarily in agriculture (66%) and construction (28%). Overall, during 1987–91, the programs employed on average 75,000 workers per year, of which one-third were in urban areas and two-thirds were in rural areas.

In *Morocco*, the Promotion Nationale (PN) has managed for about 30 years projects located mostly in disadvantaged rural areas, such as reforestation, well-water caption, dam and road construction, paved roads, etc. Overall, less than 20% of the budget allocated to PN is genuinely spent for labor-intensive programs in poor areas, and less than 10% of employment created is labor-intensive. Moreover, a large share of resources is spent on staff salaries, assisting local governments in the payment of wages of administrators instead of reaching the low-income groups in poor communities.

However, PWPs are often supply-driven: They can neglect the needs of the poor and do not add to much to productivity or economic value of assets. Although generally useful as short term mechanisms for transferring income to the poor, the share of wages in total cost is about 60% in Tunisia, 50% in Morocco, and between 40 and 60% in Algeria. In Egypt, where program activities are mainly capital-intensive (i.e., water supply and sewerage), the wage share is 30% of total cost. Experience throughout the world shows that the most cost-effective and well targeted PWPs provide highly labor-intensive work for wages at or below the market rate for unskilled labor,[16] entail a high wage share in total cost, and create productive assets that are maintained either by the program itself or by some other mechanism.[17] In general, programs in the region are not very successful when measured in terms of productivity and the economic value of assets created, with a lack of attention to the quality of assets created, and to maintaining those assets. The effect of these programs on net employment creation and poverty are unknown, due to the absence of reliable monitoring and evaluation indicators. More recently, however, there has been a tendency for the governments to decentralize and increase participation of the private sector in managing the programs as well as an emphasis on community demands.

Can PWPs Benefit the Poor or the Poorest of the Poor?

- Improving self-targeting. PWPs should mainly concentrate on poor areas and use self-targeting mechanisms to attract only the poor through appropriate levels of payment (no higher than the market wage for unskilled labor), type of work (labor intensive activities), and regional distribution of work sites of the program;
- Better monitoring and evaluation. Often little is known about the number of jobs created, the cost and the impact of these programs on poverty, and program characteristics (in terms of costs, duration of benefits, and managerial requirements) are determined in an ad hoc manner;
- Encouraging greater participation among women. PWPs in MENA countries have created employment predominantly for men, but international experience shows that there is potential to employ women in public work programs through piecework or task-based payment, providing work close to beneficiaries' homes and offering flexible work schedules;
- Increasing the economic returns of public works by taking into account the general development of basic infrastructure in poor regions. It is desirable to estimate economic rates of return to different projects in different regions prior to project selection, integrate the program with

broader national development plans, and introduce a component to maintain the assets created;

• Increasing the participation of the private sector. Involving the private sector and small contractors can increase the efficiency of programs vis-à-vis the public sector in undertaking and supervising works.

Social Funds

Social funds have been used to mitigate shocks and their effects on the most vulnerable groups, and also as compensatory mechanisms to increase access to, and the quality of, basic services used by the poor. Traditional public expenditures on the social sectors have been recently supplemented with social investment funds (SIF),[18] an increasingly common feature of the region's social protection portfolio. Social funds cover a range of programs, including public works, community development projects as well as microfinance, which had been previously undertaken as stand-alone programs.

To date, social funds have been instrumental in transferring resources to target groups. Poor communities and beneficiaries received a far greater degree of government support than would have been the case in the absence of social funds. However, the operations are small compared to the magnitude of poverty conditions in MENA. In terms of total level of resource transfers, as a percentage of GDP, Egypt's SIF is the most important, but still its annual expenditures amounted to only 0.2% of GDP in 1993–96. Egypt also has the largest per capita transfers, as well as the largest total transfers per poor person, estimated between US$83 and US$125. However, if every poor person received an equal value of social fund transfers, the annual amount transferred by the MENA social funds would represent less than 4% of their average income.

Table 5.9. MENA Social Fund Spending in Relation to Target
       Population

	WBG–CDP	WBG–NGO	Yemen	Egypt[1]	Algeria
Total US$ per capita	$11.11	$6.30	$5.23	$25.03	$2.91
Total US$ per poor person	$46.30	$26.23	$27.52	$83.45–$125.17	$17.96
Average annual US$ per poor person	$15.43	$4.37	$5.50	$11.92– $17.88	$4.49
Average annual US$ as % of poverty line	2.4%	0.7%	3.4%	N/A	1.2%

Note: 1) Includes SFD Phase I and Phase II. Poverty headcount
       index information varies from 20–30%.

The social funds within the region use a variety of intermediaries. For instance, in community infrastructure, Egypt works mainly with governorates; Yemen with NGOs and community groups; and the West Bank and Gaza work with a combination of the two. Within the project cycle, funds differ widely in the extent to which projects are demand-driven, and participation is built into operating procedures. In general, there are very few mechanisms that build in beneficiary participation in the identification and supervision of the social fund investments,[19] except in cases where local project committees are eligible as sponsors. Moreover, coordination and collaboration with beneficiary communities and intermediary organizations are central to the impact and effectiveness of social fund investments. Gaps in coordination have reflected poorly on the sustainability of certain social fund investments.

Social funds have been able to absorb foreign assistance in a number of ways. With their emphasis on locally driven investments, funds have offered an innovative approach for building a modern civil society and promoting self-help mechanisms. In the region, social funds have successfully contributed to miti-

---

Box 6

Social Fund Operations in MENA

The main social funds in the MENA region are: the Egyptian Social Fund for Development, the Yemen Social Fund for Development, the West Bank and Gaza Community Development and NGO Projects, and the Algerian Social Development Agency.[20]

The weight of social funds in the overall safety net vary from one country to another: it is of moderate importance in Egypt; negligible in Algeria. Social funds have been successful in terms of generated outputs. The Egypt SFD, for its size and number of years operating, has generated the largest level of outputs. As of June 30, 1998, the small business support program assisted over 63,000 small businesses with loans, averaging US$5000, and over 40,000 micro-entrepreneurs receiving smaller loans (average US$500) through the Community Development Program. About 30 percent of small business loans went to women. Over 1 million adults had benefited from literacy training. Communities were given greater access to and quality of infrastructure and services. Even in countries with newer and smaller social funds, delivery of significant benefits is notable.

In Yemen, most targets of what have been surpassed. By the end of 1998, 269 communities have received support compared to an expected 25, and SFD has supported 2168 micro-entrepreneurs compared to an expected 2000.

In the West Bank and Gaza, the CDP is a follow-up to the first phase project, and will continue to improve infrastructure services. Nevertheless, the strategy will be redefined to target marginal and poor communities with emphasis on poor areas identification, focusing on labor-intensive micro-projects, which will preserve capital assets as well as promote local job opportunities.

Source: World Bank: *Project Appraisal Reports*

gating risk—or the reduction of the variability of income if a shock were to occur—through support for household and community portfolio diversification and asset accumulation through the provision of social and economic infrastructure improvements and micro-enterprise development. Key factors in the efficiency of the funds are autonomy (legal and operational) and the presence of highly motivated and efficient managers.

Social funds have created employment though their exact size is debatable, as little is known about the permanence of jobs created. In the West Bank and Gaza, Yemen, and Algeria, the amount of employment generated is far below 1% of the total labor force. The Egypt SDF accounted for an estimated 25% of the non-agricultural jobs generated in the nation between 1993 and 1996. This would have absorbed about 10% of the estimated 2.2 million unemployed if they were net jobs. Temporary employment would have provided jobs to an additional 2% of the unemployed.

Efficiency in generating these jobs is difficult to estimate. Public works under social funds have opted largely for medium labor-intensity projects, as they have been as concerned about the type of infrastructure created as the employment benefits they generate. For example, improving access to services has often meant new construction, usually far more capital-intensive than routine repair and maintenance. In addition, wage rates are administratively set at levels comparable to those prevailing in the labor market. Therefore, unit costs appear to be higher than other national programs that may prescribe lower wages, particularly in such cases as Algeria, where social benefits and minimum wage regulations are followed. In addition, there has been little systematic evidence on the impact of social funds on the living conditions of beneficiaries—such as income, skills development, or health indicators.

Sustainability depends heavily upon donor money. To date, there has been little provision for maintaining social funds from domestic finance, should international donor money be exhausted. Leveraging community and local resources could help sustain social funds. In the West Bank and Gaza this has reached up to an average of 25% in the CDP program, higher than initial appraisal estimates. In Egypt and Yemen, the average is about 10% in the public work program. At the initial stages, social funds are concerned more by the emergency situation and are preoccupied with outputs, rather than the need to ensure their sustainability.

Social Funds: The Way Forward

- Improving sustainability. Sustainability will depend on the evolution of national policies in terms of fiscal decentralization, implementation of sectoral cost recovery policies, and greater community inputs.

- Measuring and enhancing impacts. Social funds need to improve the accuracy and reliability of enumerating beneficiaries and better identify benefits, through the application of solid evaluation methodologies.
- Seeking an optimal portfolio mix. In all cases, social funds will need to experiment with the composition of the services they offer (e.g., community development, public works, microfinance) in order to identify which groups are or are not reached and what programs have the greatest impact on the most vulnerable groups.
- Promoting learning across organizations. The experience of social funds in managing demand-driven portfolios, working with NGOs, community groups, and small-scale contractors, encouraging community participation and cost-sharing, and using beneficiary assessments and other participatory evaluation methodologies all have interesting implications for local governments and line ministries.

Social Safety Net Programs

Consumer Food Subsidies (CFS)
The design and objectives of CFS vary across countries, ranging from universal subsidies to self-targeted systems, and from rationed schemes to alternative targeted safety nets. In Morocco, subsidy programs were introduced to stabilize prices of strategic goods, with no explicit focus on the poor. This was achieved through subsidy, taxation, and a reallocation of resources among commodities to adjust for international price fluctuations (Box 8). In Tunisia, the system aimed to stabilize prices of basic food staples, protect the purchasing power of the poor, redistribute income to the poor, and improve the nutritional status of the poor—as well as that of the population at large—with multiple interventions along the marketing chain from importers to refiners to distributors. In Egypt, a ration scheme was introduced initially to ensure the supply of essential goods to the population at large. However, over the course of the 1980s, policy objectives were reoriented towards poverty alleviation, and measures were adopted to reduce the number of goods subsidized and improve the targeting through emphasis on inferior goods. In Yemen, the subsidy schemes were introduced through the application of a preferential exchange rate for imports, and in Iran they were conducted through maintenance of multiple official overvalued exchange rates and controlled prices. Algeria and Jordan used to have food-subsidy schemes but abandoned them in the late 1990s.

Subsidies have a larger relative impact on the poor, but the non-poor absorb most of the public funds distributed in this way. Food commands a larger share of total spending by lower-income than well-off households. Subsidized foods contribute an important share of caloric intake and protein consumption to the poor since they provide about 40% of total caloric intake. In 1990, subsidized foods' share of Tunisia's per capita expenditure was five times higher in the lowest quintile than in the highest. A 1987 Jordanian household survey showed that subsidies represented about 14% of expenditures for the lowest quintile, compared to 8% for the top quintile. However, higher-income groups benefit more in *absolute* terms than do the poor, because they consume greater quantities of subsidized goods.[21] In Morocco, for example, people in the top quintile consume twice the amount of subsidized food that those in the lowest quintile consume. In Yemen, the wealthiest 10% of the population spend ten times more than do the poor on subsidized wheat and flour; they benefit ten times as much.

Table 5.10. Absolute Incidence of Food Subsidies

Country	Targeting	1	2	3	4	5
Tunisia (1993)	Self-Selection	21	20	21	20	18
Morocco	Universal Subsidies Self-Selection	15	19	20	21	25
	Extraction Rate Flour	23	24	22	18	13
Algeria (1991)	Universal Subsidies	13	17	19	22	29
Egypt	Self-Selection	21	21	22	19	17

Sources: World Bank (1999) and other World Bank Reports.

In the MENA region, government spending on Consumer Food Subsidies (CFS) is comparable to public spending on education and health, ranging between 1% and 5% of GDP. However, food-subsidy schemes do have a significant opportunity cost. Although much progress has been made in controlling the cost of food subsidies, the program in MENA countries is expensive and subject to international prices and exchange rates.

Food Subsidies: The Way Forward

- Link food-subsidy reform to a broad poverty-alleviation strategy. From a poverty-alleviation perspective, reform of food subsidies can vary among MENA countries based on the overall system of social protection and other social policies.
- Successful reforms that introduce compensatory measures for the poor

while phasing out subsidy systems. Cash transfers compensating for subsidy elimination may have a similar or greater impact on poverty.
- Provide a convincing rationale for reforms through publicity. The public is more likely to accept a policy change if its rationale is provided through advance publicity, indicating the savings that are being sought while the poor are protected (Algeria, Egypt, Tunisia).
- Reform consumer subsidies while reducing producer protection. When a system is structured to protect domestic producers by inducing domestic prices that are higher than world market prices, and compensate consumers for the welfare loss created by this protection, subsidy reforms can be pursued simultaneously with a reduction of producer protection.

Cash Assistance: Direct Transfer Programs in Cash and in-Kind

In addition to food subsidies, many governments provide cash and in-kind transfer programs in their direct effort to reduce poverty. These programs include: (a) in-kind transfers such as food aid through schools (Tunisia), food aid to elderly and handicapped (Morocco), nutritional programs for mothers and children (Tunisia and Morocco), training centers for illiterate and/or drop-out girls, and shelters for school-age children and orphans (Morocco); (b) financial aid to the hard-core poor who cannot support themselves, such as the elderly and handicapped (Algeria, Egypt, and Tunisia); and (c) means-tested cash transfers to poor families who need income support (Jordan, Tunisia, Yemen). These programs are usually publicly administered, but in some cases they take the form of partnerships with local charities (i.e., Entraide Nationale in Morocco).

The amount spent on transfer programs is smaller than that spent on food subsidies, ranging between only 0.2% and about 1% of GDP. Transfer programs are small compared to food subsidies. Though they are targeted to the "categorically" poor—that is, those who cannot work for physical or other reasons—they are often paid to the non-poor, as there are no developed mechanisms for assessing whether an individual is working or what his/her income level is. In Jordan, a recent clean-up operation eliminated one-third of the beneficiaries of transfers who were receiving benefits without being eligible. Finally, transfer programs are not coordinated with other social programs, leading to overlaps between programs. Their administration is hampered by weak management, and they are characterized by high administrative costs for each beneficiary they assist.

Transfers: The Way Forward

- In spite of their limited coverage, transfer programs have the potential to provide more effective assistance to the poor.
- Transfers should reach the poor by delivering fewer but of adequate value and better-focused programs in a more cost-effective way.
- Partnerships and complementarities with other agencies and the civil society at large should be explored and utilized in implementation.
- The institutional capacity to monitor and evaluate the impact of transfers needs to be sound.

Pensions

The MENA region faces the challenge of population aging like the rest of the world. Nevertheless, the demographic structure suggests that there are still five to ten

---

Box 7

Direct Transfer Program in Morocco and Tunisia

Morocco

Entraide Nationale (EN) is a public establishment under the tutelage of Morocco's Ministry of Social Development and Social Solidarity. Its mission, since its creation in 1957, is to support the poor. It manages a number of different programs to address the needs of the poor, often working in partnership with local charities. It also has the authority to raise its own funds. But of an estimated five million poor, EN reaches only 60,000 (1.3%). Lack of coordination with other agencies (such as the ministries of health education, vocational training agencies) often implies that EN deals with issues that nobody else in the Government wishes to handle. This results in duplication (e.g., "*garderies*" and vocational training programs) and stretches too thinly EN's activities, which tend to be scattered and often unfocused. The share of the wage bill has increased from 69% in 1993 to 81% in 1996, while the budget allocated to the programs has dropped to 14% in 1996 from 27% in 1993. Currently, the budget allocated to EN's activities is small (about 0.1% of GDP in 1996) and most is spent on staff salaries for its 6300 employees (1900 are permanent staff and 4400 are temporary, paid around the minimum wage). On average, there is one staff for nine assisted poor. Overstaffing and low pay is associated with poorly qualified individuals: about 24% of EN staff are illiterate. The EN's recurrent expenditures are high compared to its number of beneficiaries, and some centers are generously overstaffed. These problems are found in other government agencies as public sector employment is used as an indirect way of social protection. Administration is highly centralized, allowing little room for decision-making at the local level. The *délégué* (regional coordinator at the provincial level for EN programs) has no power to make decisions about personnel or their activities. There is no system for monitoring the cost of each program, the performance of the centers and their impact on the poor.

years before the aging process will begin to take off. Therefore, the region should take this opportunity to reform the system before demographic pressures force benefit cuts and/or contribution increases that are politically difficult and economically harmful. Although the rising proportion of old people in the population will be important in the long term, the number of people taking early retirement and dependency ratios will rise in the short run.

As the number of elderly rises compared to the working-age population, it increases the need for better family, societal, or public-based support mechanisms to prevent the group from falling into poverty. In MENA, by 2025 it is expected that the number of elderly will rise by an annual growth rate of 4%, compared with the rest of the population, which is expected to grow by 1.4%.

Countries in the region have mandatory pension schemes. However, they are inefficient and mismanaged, such that services are often not distributed as they should be. These schemes are based on partially funded systems and operate as pay-as-you-go (PAYG) systems with defined benefit plans. However, in most countries,

---

Tunisia

In Tunisia, the Ministry of Social Affairs provides direct transfer programs to the hard-core poor unable to support themselves. Direct transfers provide cash assistance to poor families who need income support (about 101,000 *familles nécessiteuses* in 1992). Although the number of households benefiting from direct cash transfers has been increasing, coverage is still inadequate, including in the poorest regions—the northwest and center-west. In its first year, 1986, the program covered about 65,000 families, about 81% of the eligible population. In 1994, coverage had reached 107,000 families, about 72% of the eligible population. If the program had attained full coverage, providing transfers to all those meeting its eligibility criteria, coverage would have reached almost 700,000 people, nearly 100,000 more than the 1990 household survey estimated to be below the poverty line. Partial comparison of the number of households benefiting from cash transfers and the number of households below the poverty line (as defined at the national level by the 1990 Household Consumption Survey) confirms that coverage under the cash transfer program is not fully satisfactory and that there is margins for improvement. In addition, administration of transfer programs is complex, and eligibility lists are rarely updated. Even when the lists are updated, coverage is not always extended to those newly identified as eligible. And because of lack of information on the characteristics and determinants of poverty, the eligibility criteria are very general, and entitlement to benefits is not always fully defined. As a result, some of the truly needy do not benefit from the program, while others receive multiple benefits from various social assistance and insurance programs. The lack of distinction between the group-based and need-based approaches also leads to overlap between programs. Direct transfers have been provided to defined groups, without distinguishing between benefits awarded to individuals and those to families. Moreover, the screening process bypasses the transitional poor and the newly poor (poor unemployed and those between jobs). Because of lack of information, the impact of these programs on poverty is not known. Finally, financial constraints also have kept cash transfers to needy families consistently below subsistence.

Figure 5.2. Formal Pension Cost and Population over 60 in MENA

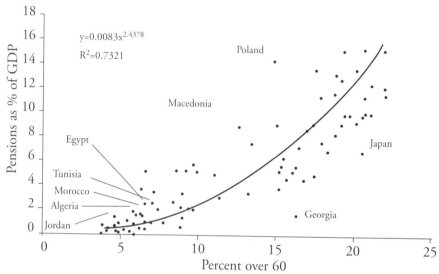

they are poorly designed PAYG schemes, and reserves are inappropriately managed. In addition, evasion of contributions is widespread, individuals can be treated unequally, and the systems are rigid and offer little choice.

The parameters of pension schemes are poorly designed. In MENA countries, for most workers the benefit formula *appears* generous, promising 70 to 80% of the worker's wage at the end of his career. However, because none of the schemes has a formal indexation mechanism, benefits are actually dependent on inflation and discretionary adjustments. Absence of formal indexation and rules increases the level of uncertainty related to the value of the ultimate benefit, and workers perceive contributions as a tax.

Payroll taxes for pensions are set at fairly high levels, compared to international benchmarks. This is done in order to generate surpluses and smooth the long-run contribution rate under the scaled premium concept. Payroll taxes for pensions as a share of total labor costs[22] range from around 8 to 9% in the main schemes of Algeria, Libya, Morocco, and Tunisia, to more than 23% in Iran and Egypt. If other social insurance contributions are taken into account, the range is between 13 and 36% of total labor costs. Important differences emerge, however, when considering details such as whether or not there is a ceiling on taxable earnings.[23]

Based on eligibility criteria, it is relatively easy to obtain a pension in the MENA region. The normal retirement age is particularly low for women in the main schemes of Algeria and Jordan. The extremely high ratio of pensioners to older persons in Egypt (241% with small agricultural pensions or 133% without agricultural pensions) suggests that early retirement (along with broad survivorship rights) is also available and often used (compared to 111% in Jordan, 73% in Tunisia, 49% in Iran and 36% in Morocco).

Although coverage rates are low, they are comparable to what is found in countries with similar income per capita levels. In MENA countries, coverage rates range from 20% of the labor force in Morocco to about half in Egypt, or between 18 and 34% of the working-age population.[24] While some of the uncovered population may not be required to contribute by law, most of the uncovered population evades the payroll and other taxes of the formal sector.

Pension finances are deteriorating due to out-of-line pension system dependency ratios (the ratio of pensioners to contributors) with the old-age dependency ratio (the ratio of old to working-age persons). Available data suggest that there are more than ten persons between ages 20 and 59 for every person over age 60. At the same time, the system dependency ratios in the region range from 18 to as high as 36%, or between three and five workers per pensioner. The other reason is the inefficient public management of reserves. Many of the MENA countries' pension systems have substantial reserves that tend to dominate local capital markets. In most instances, the return from the investment is lower than private investments with comparable risk, and in some systems the rate of return is even negative. In Tunisia, Egypt, and Yemen, returns have been significantly negative for long periods of time.[25] This is due largely to the use of pension reserves for subsidizing other government priorities, a phenomenon found in many countries around the world (e.g., in Algeria they finance social assistance programs; in Tunisia they financed social housing until 1992, and they are still financing a small unemployment assistance program).

Most pension systems in the region create labor market distortions. Due to poorly designed benefit formulae and large implicit taxation on labor force participation after a certain age, the system provides incentives for workers to enter into the large informal sectors, which are less productive, and encourages experienced workers to retire early. In addition to the incentive to move to the informal sector, most MENA countries' pension systems generate poor microeconomic incentives that discourage labor supply of those workers who cannot avoid being in the formal sector. Finally, since the system gives full benefits at a relatively early retirement age, incentives to retire early are increased.

Large informal sectors are also a serious public finance problem. Given the design of the system, a large fraction of the work force is not paying taxes and is not contributing to the pension systems. For instance, a very large part of the agricultural sector is informal (ranging from 18% of total male employment in

Algeria to 50% in Yemen), and in many countries, the largest part of the formal labor market is in the public sector. Informality among non-agricultural workers is around 57% in Morocco, 47% in Tunisia, and 40% in Egypt.

Pensions: The Way Forward
Preparing for pension reform involves two phases. The first phase includes the following steps:
   (a) systematic collection of information on existing schemes;
   (b) assessment of the current issues;
   (c) proposition of possible reform measures and their quantified impacts, based on international experiences; and
   (d) consultation with domestic interest groups.

The second phase involves:
   (a) informing the public;
   (b) generating political consensus;
   (c) spelling out key details of the reform;
   (d) drafting legislation; and
   (e) reform implementation.

Reform options within the current framework
Within the current framework, reforms could include the rationalization and revamping of the benefit formula, the integration of schemes or the harmonization of benefits across schemes, and a reconsideration of the scope for social action of the pension system. Since some of these reform measures are likely to affect vested interests, a clearly specified and publicized plan is necessary:

- Changes in the benefit formula, which can reduce the pension liability significantly by the time the aging process begins to accelerate. This can be achieved by gradually raising effective retirement ages (through various means) and gradually reducing target benefit levels;
- Indexation of benefits, which will eliminate the inflation risk that presently threatens the purchasing power of pensioners Indexation of past earnings in the calculation of initial pensions can be automatic, especially as the number of years counted in the average is extended;
- Changes in portfolio allocation of reserves and increased investment in diversified capital markets will improve returns and achieve fiscal sustainability;
- Increasing links between contributions and benefits by applying actuarially fair reductions or increases for early or later retirement, allowing for

easy portability between existing schemes or merging them, and avoiding policies which use the pension system as a substitute for unemployment or severance schemes in the context of economic restructuring or privatization.

Reform: Moving to multipillar schemes
This constitutes a substantial departure from the existing schemes, especially for those countries that already have an advanced system (such as Jordan, Tunisia, Morocco and Egypt). In this case the following issues/advantages can arise:[26]

- Transition from PAYG to funding in the future would involve making explicit a much larger liability than would be the case in the MENA countries today. This window of opportunity, however, closes further as each new cohort of workers acquires pension rights under an increasingly unfunded system.
- Moving to a multipillar system can help generate good returns reflecting more productive use of capital in the economy by shifting a significant portion of the pension contribution to privately managed and funded schemes.
- A privately funded component can create labor market efficiency gains. A well designed, funded scheme with competitive and regulated private asset managers can provide younger workers with better returns and a portfolio which diversifies their risk between the different pillars. This should improve compliance at the margin and would resolve portability problems in countries with multiple schemes.
- Introducing a market-based savings element can reduce the political backlash, although it certainly will not eliminate it completely. There is the fundamental issue of political economy.

Nevertheless, the multipillar reform involves more than simply making marginal changes to the existing system. In particular, the planning and implementation of the transition from one system to another would require an intense technical and political effort. Most countries that have made the transition have given current workers an option between the two types of schemes. New labor market entrants with no rights accrued under the old scheme, on the other hand, are channeled into the new system from the outset. There is by now considerable experience of other countries in these matters and other important areas (e.g., supervision of private pensions) that is available for consultation by countries contemplating pension reform.[27]

Conclusions

General Directions for MENA

The MENA economies have two distinct characteristics for designing policies to reduce vulnerability and lead their economies toward sustainable growth: large public sector and significant informal sector safety nets. The state has an important function that cannot be underplayed—its ability to enhance growth and redistribute its benefits. The state can increase the synergy between the public and the private spheres. Formal social protection mechanisms, for example, will reduce social risks if they build upon, enhance, and do not crowd out informal mechanisms. A more active civil society means a different—not necessarily smaller—role for the state. For example, social protection in the form of secured employment in the public sector can have adverse macroeconomic implications and can increase insecurity in the informal sectors. The state can reduce its role as producer (in parastatals) and provider of services, and increase its role as a regulator (enforcing competition rules and maintaining a level playing field among public and private providers, such as in the area of social services). Through adherence to competitive exchange rates and reducing trade protection, long-term efficiency will increase. Supplementary measures could be introduced for those who would be adversely affected in the short run. For example, governments can introduce measures that balance the increase in population with the more efficient use of the water sector and the depletion of water. These are system-wide concerns and are unlikely to be met by the independent actions of the private sector. Help for the poor can be more coordinated and effective. Public works and other employment-support schemes and income-generating programs can become better administered and more focused on the objectives of poverty reduction through the creation of sustainable employment. New mechanisms, such as social funds, can be designed more efficiently to target the poor. The interface between formal and informal mechanisms can be complemented with selective cash transfers and other direct-assistance programs to the categorically poor. This would require systems that enable the verification of employment or the income status of beneficiaries, in addition to better databases for timely analysis and effective policy design. Reducing vulnerability is not just for rural inhabitants, informal sector workers, or the poor. Particularly with increasing urban unemployment and poverty in the region, additional measures can be introduced for those in urban areas and employed in the formal sector. The increasing reliance on market forces suggests that employment would be subjected to higher variation—such as a cyclical type—or some short-term shock—such as adjustment. This can be mitigated through labor market insurance mechanisms such as unemployment insurance. Some economies in the MENA region have these schemes already, but they are characterized by high payroll taxes and significant tax evasion. Other separation benefits (such as severance pay) are often independent of unemployment insurance schemes, and none of them are well coordinated with social assistance benefits. The MENA economies, therefore, have many options to reduce vulnerability, stabilize welfare, and foster conditions that would lead to sustainable income growth. Coordinated public policies can lead to better social risk management, help fight poverty, improve consumption-smoothing over time, achieve greater equality, and support economic development through broad-based growth. In particular, bearing in mind (a) the need for greater efficiency of public spending, (b) the necessity to crowd in private expenditures, and (c) the usefulness of greater cooperation in the public/private and formal/informal spheres, the MENA economies can:

- Reduce the vulnerability of the poor by enabling them to help themselves through fostering land rights and implementing land reforms, encouraging efficient water use, and improving infrastructure policies; removing obstacles to employment creation in agriculture and in the formal sector, and improving access to microcredit; creating/expanding social funds or new types of programs to reach the poorest; encouraging greater synergy between formal and informal mechanisms, and government, private sector, and civil society activities.
- Improve equality in opportunity, through better quality of and access to education; higher performance of public health services; and equality in public and private life (e.g., family law and gender differences).
- Smooth consumption by enhancing formal and informal insurance mechanisms, through labor market insurance (unemployment insurance, disability benefits, and unemployment assistance); agricultural and rural development programs; pension and social insurance/assistance systems; and migration and expansion of the use of community arrangements/ participation.
- Contribute to macroeconomic performance and improved governance, through raising productivity growth by means of skills formation and privatization of public enterprises; reducing the size of the public sector while protecting public expenditures in key social services; encouraging export growth through trade liberalization and greater participation to the global economy; allowing wages and employment conditions to be more determined by the market; an increasing transparency and efficiency in administration.

Three Key Areas for Social Protection in MENA
The general directions for MENA outline the range of areas and interventions that could be included more or less permanently in the regional agenda. A strategy calls, however, for a decision on prioritizing and sequencing. What are the areas that the region should start to address in the three-to-five-year horizon? While many issues can be handled on a day-to-day basis, some require more time to be planned and executed, some have greater weight in the economy, and some have better known solutions than others. On these criteria the paper proposes: First, address formal social insurance. Though many other areas of interventions refer to issues which are cyclical or short-term in nature (i.e., they may wither away—albeit at a cost—in the absence of specific policies), social insurance is deeply embedded in the socioeconomic structures of the region. Labor insurance and pensions are already under strain, and five arguments point to the urgency of addressing them immediately:

- The certainty that social insurance systems in all economies will require reforms sooner rather than later, as, despite favorable demographics at present, pension funds have reserves well below what they should have, some are already in deficit, and there is steady deterioration in the old-age dependency ratio;
- Their size and (under-) performance have a significant adverse effect on growth, arising from poor outcomes in labor, product, insurance, and capital markets;
- Because the programs are publicly managed and yield low returns, funding them presents a sizeable obstacle to a more efficient and effective use of public social spending;
- The systems are bound to mature and expand further (due to urbanization, growth, and so on), making reforms more costly over time due to increasing deficits;
- The international experience suggests that reforms in this area take a long time, have heavy statistical and analytical requirements, and require substantial stakeholder consensus-building.

In short, a good first step for revamping a social protection system can start with an *assessment of the formal social insurance systems and the functioning of both formal and informal labor markets.* These have direct linkages, not only to pensions, but also to safety nets and labor markets. In turn, policy decisions taken in one of these three social protection areas can have important implications in the other areas. Finally, a proper assessment of the labor and social insurance system, which typically fails to reach families who do not work in the formal labor market, would indicate the required resource allocation decisions across these three program areas, as well as between the formal and informal sectors. This is particularly important, as, despite the size of social insurance systems, the share of the formal sector labor force, or the covered sectors in most economies in the region, is quite low. Given limited public resources, this integrated approach permits programmatic tradeoffs to be considered when deciding budgets for pensions, safety nets, and labor market interventions.

Second, *improve training systems.* Though training cannot be blamed for much of the high (and still rising, in some cases) unemployment rates in the regional economies, current training schemes tend to absorb considerable funds (often raised from payroll contributions), deprive the education/human development sector of valuable resources, and have generally poor results. Regional systems tend to be publicly dominated, supply-driven, expensive, and are often designed to act as a program of last resort for dropouts from the formal education system. But market-relevant training can help increase the employability of the young or those who lost their jobs because of economic restructuring. The way skills are created, financed, and managed can, therefore, have important implications for productivity, employability/unemployment, and poverty. National reviews of the training systems and analyses of labor market data can pave the way for meaningful reforms with far reaching effects on economic efficiency and poverty. Reforms in the training sectors would have sizeable and deep effects on product and regional markets and productivity, on the one hand, and household earnings, unemployment, and poverty on the other.

Third, *design safety nets as developmental and community-based, not just assistance and centrally administered, schemes.* While the MENA region has the lowest incidence of poverty, the risk of becoming poor—either temporarily or permanently—will continue as a result of the unfinished economic agenda. Also problematic are additional effects from globalization, such as transition and possible economic downturn in the short-run, aging populations, and natural disasters (and perhaps sporadic conflict situations). While to date, informal arrangements have acted as a significant safety net, they have been supplemented by substantial, albeit declining, formal support. This support may be compromised further, and can also put informal arrangements under additional stress, unless there is an upturn in economic performance. In this respect, there is plenty of room to improve the design of social protection instruments. For example, evaluations suggest that social funds reach many poor but generally fail to reach the poorest and, often, women. Microfinance granted at low or even negative interest rates is more of a transfer than a contribution to sustainable development. Public works that pay high wages or have low labor shares in their total costs are unlikely to meet poverty objectives efficiently. Food subsidies can create significant economic distortions and, if universal, are appropriated by the non-poor. Finally, child protection (including child labor and disability) schemes, though embryonic in most regional economies, are an area of potentially promising developmental activities, with strong participation of civil society.

———

Notes

1   Schengen agreement allowed for one visa for travelling anywhere in Europe.
2   It likewise seems true that most of the migrants from the MENA region to Europe are also unskilled.
3   For Egypt, see Adams (1991); for Pakistan, see Adams (1998); and for Turkey, see Russell (1986).
4   The propensity of international migrants to remit will also be affected by the differential existing between official exchange rates and black market exchange rates in the origin country. In other words, the larger this differential, the more migrants will tend to remit through unofficial, black market channels. For more details see Swamy (1981).
5   Castles 1998.
6   See Hilal, 1998.
7   *World Bank (1994a); Egypt: Demographic and Health Survey (1995); Ministry of Health, Iran (1998).*
8   World Bank, 1997a
9   The difference between the volume of water delivered into a supply system and the volume of water accounted for by legitimate consumption, whether metered or not.
10 The six leading causes of disease are acute respiratory infections (ARI), diarrheal diseases, intestinal helminthes, malaria, trachoma and tropical cluster (includes schistosomiasis, trypanosomiasis and filariasis).
11 Microfinance practitioners prefer to use the household as unit of analysis because household activity and microenterprise activity are highly intertwined. It is also a common rule that no more than one member of a household should be eligible for a micro loan.
12 The Alexandria Business Association program and the National Bank for Development program, both in Egypt.
13 These include the spun-off Save the Children programs in Lebanon, The West Bank Gaza and Jordan (resp. Al Majmoua, JDWS and Faten), the UNWRA program in The West Bank Gaza, Zakoura and Al Amana in Morocco and two programs in Egypt (Cairo, Sharkia) designed along the lines of the Alexandria Business Association.
14 See *Study on microfinance in the MENA region* and outputs of a four-day workshop (MDFII) with over 100 microfinance practitioners from the region (Marrakech, September 1998).
15 See Ravallion (1998).
16 A PWP's labor cost share must be over 60–70 percent to be considered high. For example in Chile, which operates one of the best PWPs in the world, labor cost was set at a minimum of 80

percent of total cost, virtually mandating selection of labor-intensive activities. Wages were also maintained at about 70 percent of the minimum wage, thus facilitating self-targeting of the poor.

17 See "Safety Net Programs and Poverty Reduction—Lessons from cross country experience," Subbarao, Bonnerjee; Braithwaite; Carvalho; Ezemenari; Graham; Thompson; The World Bank, 1997.

18 This review uses the broad definition of social funds as "agencies that finance small projects in several sectors targeted to benefit a country's poor and vulnerable groups based on a participatory manner of demand generated by local groups and organizations and screened against a set of eligibility criteria."

19 These general conclusions do not apply to the programs to support small and micro enterprise, where the nature of working with individual clients is by definition highly demand-driven and participatory.

20 In addition, there are several projects that are either in the pipeline or very similar to social funds, such as the proposed Moroccan social fund and the on-going Jordan Community Infrastructure Project (for its targeted nature rather than its operational mechanism).

21 See "Consumer Food Subsidies in MENA region," World Bank, Yellow cover, June 1999.

22 These figures refer to total payroll tax rates as a share of gross wage plus employer payroll contributions.

23 The answer is "yes" in Egypt and Morocco, no in Algeria, Jordan and Tunisia.

24 In Yemen coverage is even lower than in Morocco. A recent report showed that fewer than one third of eligible private sector employees participated in the pension scheme and that the informal sector is likely to be very large.

25 While data on returns are not available for the rest of the countries, reserves have been channeled to socially desirable purposes in Iran and Algeria with predictable consequences.

26 See: Averting the Old Age Crisis", World Bank, 1996

27 See Palacios and Whitehouse (1998) and Demarco and Rofman (1999).

Bibliography

Adams, Richard, Jr. 1991. *The Effects of International Remittances on Poverty, Inequality and Development in Rural Egypt.* Research Report 86. Washington, DC: International Food Policy Research Institute.

Adams, Richard, Jr. 1995. *Sources of Income Inequality and Poverty in Rural Pakistan.* Research Report 102. Washington, DC: International Food Policy Research Institute.

Adams, Richard, Jr. October 1998. "Remittances, Investment and Rural Asset Accumulation in Pakistan." *Economic Development and Cultural Change* 47: 155–73.

Aiyer, S. R. 1997. *Pension Reform in Latin America: Quick Fixes or Sustainable Reform?* Working Paper No. 1865. Washington, DC: The World Bank.

Ahmad, Z. 1994. "Islamic Banking: State of the Art." *Islamic Economic Studies* 1 (2).

Amerah, M. S. 1990. "Major Employment Issues in Arab Countries." Prepared for the senior Policy Seminar on Employment Policy in Arab Countries. Amman: The Royal Scientific Society.

Arrau, P., and K. Schmidt-Hebbel. 1994. "Pension System and Reforms: Country Experiences and Research Issues." *Revista Analisis Economico* 9 (1).

Asher, M.G. January 1998. "Investment Policies and Performance of Provident Funds in Southeast Asia." Paper presented at Workshop on Pension System Reform, Governance, and Fund Management.

Azam, J. P. "The Agricultural Minimum Wage and Wheat Production in Morocco, 1971–1989." Mimeo.

Banque Centrale de Tunise. 1994. "Tunisian Financial System." *Journal of Economic Cooperation* 15 (3–4).

Birks, J.S., A. Holt and C.A. Sinclair. 1990. *Employment and Unemployment in Jordan: A Review*. Geneva: International Labour Office.

Bisat, A., M. A. El-Erian, and Th. Helbling. 1997. *Growth, Investment, and Saving in the Arab Economies*. IMF Working Paper 97/85.

Bonnerjee, A., and M. Morett. 1997. *Kingdom of Morocco: A Simulation Analysis of the Long-Term Pension System of CNSS*. The World Bank Social Protection Team, Human Development Network.

Bos, E., M.T. Vu, E. Massiah, and R. Bulatao. 1994. *World Population Projections, 1994–1995*. Washington, DC: The International Bank for Reconstruction and Development/The World Bank.

Börsch-Supan, Axel. 1992. "Population Aging, Social Security Design, and Early Retirement." *Journal of Institutional and Theoretical Economics*. 148: 583–657.

Börsch-Supan, Axel. 1998. Germany: A Social Security System on the Verge of Collapse." In Horst Siebert, ed., *Redesigning Social Security*. Tübingen: Mohr.

Börsch-Supan, Axel. 1998. "Incentive Effects of Social Security in Germany and Across Europe." *Journal of Public Economics*.

Börsch-Supan, Axel. 1998. "Capital Productivity and the Nature of Competition." Brookings Papers on Economic Activity, Microeconomics.

Börsch-Supan, Axel, and Peter Schmidt.1996. "Early Retirement in East and West Germany." In Regina Riphahn, Dennis Snower, and Klaus Zimmermann, eds., *Employment Policy in the Transition to Free Enterprise: German Integration and its Lessons for Europe*. London.

Börsch-Supan, Axel, and Reinhold Schnabel. 1998. "Social Security and Declining Labor Force Participation in Germany." *American Economic Review*.

Botka, A.U. 1994. "Some Features on Current Pension System Reform in Latin America." *Revista Analisis Economico* 9 (1).

Caisse Nationale de Sécurité Sociale. 1996. *Rapport d'activite 1995*. Royaume du Maroc.

Cashin, P. and C. J. McDermott. 1995. *Informational Efficiency in Developing Equity Markets*. IMF Working Paper 95/58.

Charmes, J. 1991. *Employment and Income in the Informal Sector of Maghreb and Mashreq Countries*. Cairo Papers in Social Sciences. Cairo: The American University in Cairo Press.

Corsetti, G. 1994. "An Endogenous Growth Model of Social Security and the Size of the Informal Sector." *Revista Analisis Economico* 9 (1).

Corsetti, G. and K. Schmidt-Hebbel. 1995. "Pension Reform and Growth."

Cox, D., and E. Jimenez. 1992. "Social Security and Private Transfers in Developing Countries: The Case of Peru." *World Bank Economic Review* 6 (1): 155–70.

Davis, E. Ph. 1996. "The Role of Institutional Investors in the Evolution of Financial Structure and Behavior." In *Proceedings of a Conference on the Development of Financial Systems*. Reserve Bank of Australia.

Davis, E. Ph. 1997. *Public Pensions, Pension Reform and Fiscal Policy*. Staff Paper No. 5. Frankfurt a.M.: European Monetary Institute.

Diamond, P. 1994. "Privatization of Social Security: Lessons from Chile" *Revista Analisis Economico* 9 (1).

Diamond, P. "The Economics of Social Security Reform." Paper presented at NASI Conference, March, 1998.

Disney, R. 1996. *Can We Afford to Grow Older?* Cambridge: Cambridge University Press.

Diwan, I., and L. Squire. 1992. *Economic and Social Development in the Middle East and North Africa*. The World Bank Discussion Paper Series No. 3.

El-Erian, M.A., and M. S. Kumar. 1995. *Emerging Equity Markets in Middle Eastern Countries*. IMF Staff Paper 42 (2).

Feiler, Gil. March 1991. "Migration and Recession: Arab Labor Mobility in the Middle East." *Population and Development Review* 17: 134–55.

Feldstein, M. 1977. "Social Security and Private Savings: International Evidence in an Extended Life-Cycle Model." In M. Feldstein and R. Inman, eds., *The Economics of Public Services*. International Economic Association.

Feldstein, M. 1995. *Social Security and Saving: New Time Series Evidence*. NBER Working Paper No. 5054.

Gilani, Ijaz, M. Khan, and Munawar Iqbal. 1981. *Labor Migration from Pakistan to the Middle East and its Impact on the Domestic Economy*. Research Report 126. Islamabad: Pakistan Institute of Development Economics.

Gelos, G. 1995. *Investment Efficiency, Human Capital & Migration: A Productivity Analysis of the Jordanian Economy.* The World Bank Discussion Paper Series No. 14.

Gruber, J., and D. Wise, eds. 1998. *Social Security and Retirement around the World.* Chicago: University of Chicago Press.

Hall, R.E., and C.I. Jones. November 1996. *The Productivity of Nations.* NBER Working Paper No. 5812.

Handoussa, H. 1991. "Crisis and Challenge: Prospects for the 1990s." In Heba Handoussa and Gillian Potter, eds., *Employment and Structural Adjustment: Egypt in the 1990s.* ILO, The American University in Cairo Press.

Heller, P.S., J. Amieva-Huerta, B. Clements, and P. Tinios. 1996. *Jordan: Pension Reform Issues.* International Monetary Fund.

Holzmann, R. 1994. "Funded and Private Pensions for Eastern European Countries in Transition?" *Revista Analisis Economico* 9 (1).

Holzmann, R. 1995. "Pension Reform, Financial Market Development and Endogenous Growth: Preliminary Evidence from Chile?" Mimeo. IMF. (Updated and shortened version was published as IMF Staff Paper, 1997).

Holzmann, R. 1999. "Financing the Transition from PAYG to Fully-funded Pension Schemes."

Hsin, P. L., O.S. Mitchell. 1994. "The Political Economy of Public Pensions: Pension Funding, Governance, and Fiscal Stress." *Revista Analisis Economico* 9(1).

Iglesias, A., and Palacios, R. 1998. *Public Management of Pension Reserves.* Social Protection Working Paper Series. Washington, DC: The World Bank.

International Bank for Reconstruction and Development. 1997. *Contractual Savings Development Loan to the Kingdom of Morocco.* Report No. P-7176-MOR, Washington, DC: The World Bank.

International Development Association. *Country Assistance Strategy of the World Bank Group for the Republic of Yemen.* Report No. 15286-Yem, 1996.Washington DC: The World Bank.

International Finance Corporation. 1997. *Emerging Stock Markets Factbook.*

Jbili, A., K. Enders, and V. Treichel. *Financial Sector Reforms in Algeria, Morocco, and Tunisia: A Preliminary Assessment.* IMF Working Paper 97/81.

Keely, Charles, and Bao Tran. Fall 1989. "Remittances from Labor Migration: Evaluations, Performance and Implications." *International Migration Review* 23: 500–25.

Khan, M.F. 1994. "Comparative Economics of Some Islamic Financing Techniques." *Islamic Economic Studies* 1 (2).

Kim, J. I., and L.J. Lau. 1994. "The Sources of Economic Growth of the East Asian Newly Industrialized Countries." *Journal of the Japanese and International Economies* 8: 235–71.

Klevser, H. 1994. "Financial Structure of Egypt." *Journal of Economic Cooperation* 15 (3–4).

Knowles, James, and Richard Anker. April 1981. "An Analysis of Income Transfers In a Developing Country: The Case of Kenya." *Journal of Development Economics* 8: 205–26.

Levine, R., and S. Zervos. May 1996. "Stock Market Development and Economic Growth." *The World Bank Economic Review* 10 (2).

McKinsey Global Institute. June 1996. *Capital Productivity.* Washington, DC.

Ministère des Finances et des Investissements Exterieurs, Royaume du Maroc. May 1997. *Développement de l'Epargne Institutionelle en vue de la Dynamisation des Marches de Capitaux.* Bossard Consultants.

Ministry of Planning. 1997. *Report to the Ministry of Planning on Provident Funds in the Hashemite Kingdom of Jordan.* Provident Funds Working Group.

Musalem, A. 1999. *Contractual Savings and tie Capital Markets.*

OECD (1988). "Reforming Public Pensions." Paris.

Ogaki, M., J.D. Ostry, and C.M. Reinhart. 1996. *Saving Behavior in Low- and Middle-Income Developing Countries.* IMF Staff Paper 43 (1).

Palacios, R., and R. Rocha. 1998. *The Hungarian Pension System in Transition.* Social Protection Discussion Paper Series No. 9805. Washington, DC: The World Bank.

Palacios, R., and E. Whitehouse. 1998. *The role of choice in a shift from PAYG to Fully funded pension schemes.* Social Protection Discussion Paper Series No. 9815. Washington, DC: The World Bank.

Pissarides, Ch.A. 1993. *Labor Markets in the Middle East and North Africa.* Discussion Paper Series No. 5. Washington, DC: The World Bank.

Queisser, M. 1996. *Pensions in Germany.* Working Paper No. 1664. Washington, DC: The World Bank.

Queisser, M. 1998. *Financial Liberalisation in Asia: Analysis and Prospects.*

Ribe, F. 1994. "Funded Social Security Systems: A Review of Issues in Four East Asian Countries." *Revista Analisis Economico* 9 (1).

Rodriguez, Edgard. January 1998. "International Migration and Income Distribution in the Philippines." *Economic Development and Cultural Change* 46: 329–50.

Russell, Sharon. June 1986. "Remittances from International Migration: A Review in Perspective." *World Development* 14: 677–96.

Said, M. 1995. "Public Sector Employment and Labor Markets in Arab Countries: Recent Developments and Policy Implications." Workshop on Labor Markets and Human Resources Development. Cairo: Economic Research Forum.

Sachs, J., and A. Werner. 1996. "Achieving Rapid Growth in the Transitional Economies of Central Europe." Mimeo. Harvard Institute of Economic Development.

Schmidt-Hebbel, K. 1998. "Chile's Takeoff: Facts, Challenges, Lessons." *Economic Development.* Institute of the World Bank, Washington, DC. Mimeo.

Schmidt-Hebbel, K. August 1998. "Does Pension Reform Really Spur Productivity, Saving, and Growth?" Mimeo.

Schwarz, A. 1998. "The Moroccan Pension System." The World Bank. Mimeo.

Social Security Administration. 1997. *Social Security Programs Throughout the World—1997.* Research Report No. 65, SSA Publications No.13-11805.

Social Security Corporation. 1997. *Annual Report 1996.* Amman.

Social Security Research Group. 1997. *Social Security in Iran.* Tehran.

Stark, Oded. 1991. *The Migration of Labor.* Cambridge: Blackwell Press.

Stark, Oded, J. Edward Taylor, and Shlomo Yitzhaki. September 1986. "Remittances and "Inequality." *Economic Journal* 96: 722–40.

Swamy, Gurushri. 1981. *International Migrant Workers' Remittances: Issues and Prospects.* World Bank Staff Working Paper No. 481. Washington, DC: World Bank.

Vittas, D. 1993. *Options for Pension Reform in Tunisia.* Policy Research Working Paper 1154.

Vittas, D. 1997. *The Case for Partial Privatization of Pensions in Jordan.* Washington, DC: The World Bank.

Vittas, D. 1997. *The Argentine Pension Reform and its Relevance for Eastern Europe.* Working Paper No. 1819. Washington, DC: The World Bank.

Vittas, D. 1998. *The Role of Non-Bank Financial Intermediaries (with Particular Reference to Egypt).* Working Paper No. 1892. Washington, DC: The World Bank.

Whitehouse, E. 1997. "Pension Reform in Britain." Mimeo.

Whiteford, P. 1995. "The Use of Replacement Rates in International Comparisons of Benefit Systems." *International Social Security Review* 48 (2).

The World Bank. 1993. *Republic of Tunisia: The Social Protection System,* Report No.11376-TUN.Washington DC: The World Bank.

The World Bank. 1994a. *Averting the Old Age Crisis: Policies to Protect the Old and Promote Growth.* Oxford University Press.

The World Bank. 1994b. *The Democratic and Popular Republic of Algeria, Country Economic Memorandum: The Transition to a Market Economy.* Report No. 12048 DZ. Washington D.C: The World Bank.

The World Bank. 1994c. *Hashemite Kingdom of Jordan: Poverty Assessment,* Report No. 12675-JO. Washington, DC: The World Bank.

The World Bank. 1995. *Kingdom of Morocco, Country Economic Memorandum: Towards Higher Growth and Employment,* Report No. 14155-MOR. Washington, D.C: The World Bank.

The World Bank. 1996. *Report on Social Security Corporation of Jordan.* Washington DC: The World Bank.

The World Bank. 1997a. *Democratic and Popular Republic of Algeria: Growth, Employment and Poverty Reduction.* Washington DC: The World Bank.

The World Bank. 1997b. *Arab Republic of Egypt, Country Economic Memorandum: Issues in Sustaining Economic Growth.* Summary Report No. 16207-EGT. Washington DC: The World Bank.

The World Bank. (Undated). "Macroeconomic Development and Employment in Egypt." Washington DC: The World Bank. Mimeo.

The World Bank. (Various years). *World Development Report.* Washington, DC: The World Bank.

The World Bank. *Consumer Food Subsidies Program in MENA,* Report No. 19561-MNA, 1999. Washington DC: The World Bank.

The World Bank. Draft MENA Health Strategy Paper, 2000, MNSHD. Washington DC: The World Bank.

6

Poverty and the Labor Market in the Arab World: The Role of Inequality and Growth

Ali A. G. Ali
Ibrahim A. Elbadawi

Section 1: Introduction

Despite being a very diverse region in terms of overall economic indicators, the achievements of the Middle East and North Africa (MENA)[1] in the area of human development have been considerable. In particular, the region is characterized by low poverty and relatively equal income distribution by international standards. A recent World Bank (1995, 2–3) report on the region observes that "during 1960–85 the MENA region outperformed all other regions except East Asia in income growth and the equality of income distribution." The report then points out that these achievements have made it possible for the region to realize enormous social benefits: "infant mortality more than halved, and life expectancy rose by more than ten years. Primary school enrollment shot up from 61% in 1965 to 98% in 1991. And adult literacy improved from 34% in 1970 to 53% in 1990, with particular progress made in the oil-exporting countries." The report also credits the region's governments with reducing poverty effectively, "by 1990 only 5.6% of the population in MENA lived on less than $1 a day—the global benchmark for absolute poverty—compared with 14.7% in East Asia and 28.8% in Latin America. And whatever the wealth, poverty was lower in MENA countries than elsewhere." Finally, the report, in our view, correctly attributes these achievements to both accelerated growth (in the 1970s and early 1980s) and distribution, with the latter being in terms of "generous transfers to large parts of the population."

This chapter, which agrees with the above analysis, uses a simple, nontechnical framework (drawn from a dynamic model of poverty, growth, and income inequality taken from Ali and Elbadawi (1999a), hereafter AE) to explain the observed experiences of six Arab countries (Algeria, Egypt, Jordan, Mauritania, Morocco, and Tunisia). Among all countries of the MENA region, only the above six countries have high-quality data on income distribution.[2] In view of this data limitation, further analysis will be confined largely to the six Arab countries, which will be throughout this chapter liberally referred to as the "Arab world" or the "Arab region." The analysis of this chapter will extend on that of AE by examining, as well, the impact of the labor market in the poverty and income inequality outcomes. The framework will also be used to motivate future strategies for further poverty reductions in the six countries, based on their economic performance during 1986–96 as well as the prevailing labor market conditions during the period.

Section 2 provides a brief discussion of some aspects of the diversity of the Arab region. The objective of this discussion is to underscore the need for developing a variety of strategies for dealing with poverty in the region, given its underlying economic diversity. Also, this section is aimed at motivating subsequent analysis of the potential roles of growth and distribution in poverty reduction, given the initial conditions of the labor markets in the region and the current economic slump, which has impacted the region since the second half of the 1980s. Section 3 describes a nontechnical framework for the analysis of poverty, growth, and income inequality, while section 4 discusses some estimated results of these three pivotal variables, based on AE. Section 5 briefly describes the labor market conditions in the region and draws linkages between income inequality and poverty. Given the poverty, growth, and income inequality performances, as well as the labor market conditions during the 1990s, section 6 identifies policy strategies for poverty reduction in the six Arab countries. Section 7 offers conclusions.

Section 2: Economic Diversity in the MENA Region

To highlight the economic diversity of the region, we follow ERF (1998) and group the countries of the region into four broad categories: mixed oil producers (MOP: Algeria, Iran and Iraq); Gulf Cooperation Council (GCC: Bahrain, Kuwait, Oman, Qatar, Saudi Arabia and UAE); diversified economies (DE: Egypt, Jordan, Morocco, Syria, Tunisia, and Turkey); and, primary producers (PP: Mauritania, Sudan and Yemen).[3] The 1996 distribution of population and

GDP over these categories was such that DE accounted for 49% of the population and 39% of GDP; MOP's share of the population was equal to its GDP share at 31%; PP's population share was 12% while its share of GDP was only 2% in contrast with that of GCC with a population share of only 7% and a GDP share of 29%. Excluding Iran and Turkey—the two non-Arab countries in ERF's definition of MENA—it is an easy matter to show that the Arab countries display a similar distribution to that of larger MENA. Thus, Arab DE had a population weight of 48% and a GDP share of 28%; MOP had a population share of 21% and a GDP share of 24%; PP had a population share of 20% but a GDP share of only 3%; and, GCC with a population share of 11% and a GDP share of 46%.

The above diversity is captured also by differences in per capita GDP. Not surprisingly, GCC ranks at the top of this scale with a per capita GDP of US$9045 in 1996, followed by MOP (US$2478). DE ranks third with a per capita GDP of US$1280 while PP's per capita GDP amounted to only US$276. The production structures of the four groups differ as well. Thus, in 1996 the agricultural sector accounted for 24% and 23% of GDP in PP and MOP, respectively, and for 16.2% in DE, while it accounted for only 2.4% of GDP in GCC. The manufacturing sector accounted for 14.4% of GDP in DE, 11% in MOP and GCC, and 9% in PP. Thus, none of the country groups of the region could be considered as industrialized (defining this stage in terms of a manufacturing sector contribution of 20% of GDP). Extractive industry, however, contributed fairly large shares in GCC (35% of GDP) and MOP (27% of GDP).

Having noted the above, we also need to note that the most recent growth performance of the countries of the region was judged to have been below potential (ERF 1998). Thus, over the period 1991–1995 the best performing group was PP with an average growth rate of GDP of 3.8% per annum, followed by DE (3.4% GDP growth rate). GCC recorded a growth rate of 2.9% while MOP's growth rate was a mere 0.8%. Given population growth rates for the respective groups, only PP and DE recorded marginal improvements in GDP per capita over the period (at a rate of 0.7% per annum). Therefore, aside from the performance of the economically marginal PP group, current per capita growth in the region is either negative or zero. With such conditions of economic stagnation but low inequality, it has been argued that even modest growth will have a dramatic effect on poverty (as measured by US$1 per person per day). According to some estimates (e.g., World Bank 1995, 8), "moving from zero growth to 1% annual growth in the MENA region would reduce the number of poor in the region by 8 million over the next decade." On the other hand, the report also estimates that, "without the higher growth that the reform can bring the number of poor (those living on less than $1 a day) would rise by 15 million by 2010." We hasten to point out, however, that a strategy for poverty reduction which is exclusively centered on growth—such as the one described above—can be successful only in the context of the limited development objective of dealing with *abject* poverty. This concept of poverty, which assumes a fixed poverty line relative to mean income, has been coming under intense criticism from labor movements, NGOs, and other stakeholders in developing countries. Also, recent contributions to the development literature support the view that the poverty line should be responsive to growth in mean income (for a review, see Ali and Elbadawi 1999b).

Section 3: Growth, Distribution and Poverty: A Framework

To guide subsequent policy discussions, we draw from AE to describe below a simple framework for the analysis of the linkages between growth, poverty and distribution. The essence of this framework is that poverty and growth are allowed to depend on the inequality in the distribution of income for both the short and longer runs.[4] In a much longer horizon, inequality in the distribution of income is assumed to be determined by the growth performance of the economy, as envisaged in a long-run development transformation process. The poverty, growth, and inequality components of the framework can be solved jointly to determine an equilibrium rate of growth consistent with a long-term fixed level of poverty (i.e., a stationary level of poverty). In addition, the solution generates a level of inequality consistent with both stationary poverty and a constant long-term rate of growth. Moreover, depending on initial conditions, the framework allows interesting patterns of interactions, which could inform broad strategies for dealing with poverty in the future.

The Growth Component

Long-run target growth is assumed to be determined by the degree of income inequality and a host of other growth fundamentals—reflecting policy variables, external factors and initial conditions. Following recent advances in the literature (see, for example, Alesina and Rodrik, 1994) we assume that growth in the long run is negatively associated with initial degree of inequality (initial level of Gini). The theoretical literature established this negative link by showing that less equal societies (as measured by high Gini coefficients) are susceptible to grow at lower rates due to the economic distortions created by the redistributive polices (e.g., high tax rates). The logic behind this is that the essentially low-income majority of the population in these societies is likely to force such policies. Such economic distortions will be expected to reduce the rate of returns to investment and hence discourage investment and growth. At the empirical level there exists evidence to support such a prediction. Further justification for the negative relationship is also reported in terms of the more encompassing concept of "distributional conflicts." Under this approach, "distributional conflicts" are envisaged to reduce the productivity with which a society's resources are utilized (hence reduced growth) through: delaying needed adjustment in fiscal policies and key relative prices (such as the real exchange rate or real wages), generating uncertainty in economic environment, and diverting activities from the productive sphere to the redistributive one (Rodrik 1998, 2).

The Poverty Component
Following the literature, the poverty component of the framework is derived from the standard general specification of poverty measures as being dependent on the standard of living in society (e.g., per capita expenditure); inequality in the distribution of expenditures among the population (as measured, for example, by the Gini coefficient); and a threshold below which people are identified as poor (i.e., a poverty line). For a wide range of poverty measures, it is expected that poverty would decline as per capita expenditure increases, for a given inequality. On the other hand, for a given per capita expenditure, poverty is expected to increase as the degree of inequality in the distribution increases. Thus, changes in poverty over time can be looked at in terms of those due to economic growth (through the increase in the per capita standard of living) and those due to distribution (through changes in the measure of inequality). The extent to which poverty responds to growth and distribution is usually measured by the elasticity of the poverty measure with respect to the relevant variables.

The Inequality Component
One of the most celebrated propositions relating to the long-run transformation of developing economies is the so-called Kuznets Hypothesis (1955). Simply put, the hypothesis asserts that as development proceeds (increase in per capita income), income inequality will tend to increase at first, reach a maximum, and then decrease. The hypothesis is based on historical observations pertaining to the sectoral shifts of population from a low-inequality, low-productivity sector to a high-productivity, high-inequality sector. Despite the fact that the hypothesis has been subjected to extensive empirical testing, controversy abounds as to whether or not it exists (for a review of the empirical and theoretical Kuznets literature, see Ali and Elbadawi 1999b). In recent years renewed interest in the Kuznets Hypothesis has been expressed from a policy perspective, especially the perspective of the effect of economic policy reforms on the poor.[5] A careful review of recent theoretical advances should serve to illustrate the position that

the Kuznets Hypothesis is meant to describe a long transformation process during which not only production structures change, but also institutions change. In short periods of time different economies may find themselves on either side of the Kuznets curve, assuming that it exists. The side on which economies find themselves will have important implications for the reduction of poverty.

Therefore, subscribing to this view of the Kuznets relation, we assume that income inequality (Gini) is endogenous to mean income and a time trend, where the structure of the dependence of the Gini on income produces an inverted U-shape. This would suggest that starting at low levels of development (low mean income) the Gini would initially rise as income increases before the relationship between Gini and income eventually becomes negative at high enough levels of development (high mean income).

The Long-Term Equilibrium Solution
The long-run equilibrium solution decomposes the rate of change in poverty into two components. The net "growth effect" is given by the direct growth effect on poverty minus the indirect income inequality effect, operating through the growth channel. Under most conditions, the net effect of growth on poverty change is negative (i.e., with income inequality unchanged, higher growth normally reduces poverty). The second component is the "pure income inequality effect," which is positive.[6] The implication of this solution is that under conditions of high and rising income inequality, positive income growth may actually be associated with rising poverty, or at best, an inconsequential reduction in poverty.

The equilibrium level of inequality is given as a fraction of the difference between the share of the income growth rate explained by all determinants of growth (except initial income inequality) and the component of the rate of change in poverty explained by the "net inequality effect."[7] This expression suggests that a stationary level of poverty is not necessarily inconsistent with a high long-term equilibrium level of inequality, provided that the absolute rate of reduction in poverty due to growth fundamentals (not including initial income inequality) is higher than the rate of change (increase) in poverty due to the "net inequality effect." If, on the other hand, the difference between the two components of the rate of change in poverty is small, a much smaller equilibrium level of inequality would be required to prevent poverty from rising.

An analysis of the dynamic behavior of inequality, poverty, and growth around the long-run equilibrium suggests six plausible phases describing the initial conditions of the economy relative to the equilibrium. These phases motivate some broad strategies for dealing with poverty. An analysis of these phases and the associated strategies are discussed in section 5.

Section 4: Income Distribution, Poverty, and Growth

In this section we describe the key results as well as draw the policy implications of the empirical estimation of the growth, distribution, and poverty due to AE. These estimates are required for calculating the structural parameters of the framework.

The Growth Estimation Results
The results of the long-term growth model suggest that income inequality is negatively and significantly associated with growth, with a parameter value of -0.07. To underscore the significance of this result, assume that we have two countries (country A and country B), which have identical policies and other initial conditions except that country A has more equitable initial income distribution than country B (initial Gini in country A is half that of country B). This result would suggest that the rate of growth of country A will be higher than that of country B by about 5%. If in addition to having identical initial conditions (except for income inequality), the two countries also happen to have identical income levels in the initial period, the income of country A will be double that of country B in about fourteen years. Indeed, initial income inequality does have a profound effect on long-term growth.

In addition to initial inequality, AE's empirical analysis of the determinants of long-term growth also accounts for two pivotal macroeconomic growth variables (investment and government consumption). The two macroeconomic variables arguably could account for, or at least reflect, all the macroeconomic effects that matter for growth. The results suggest that high investment spurs growth, while excessive government consumption reduces it.

Income Distribution and Poverty
As is well known, high-quality data sets permitting the comparison of inequality across countries and regions have only recently became available. The currently agreed-upon criteria for high quality require that observations be based on household surveys that cover the whole population and use a comprehensive measure of income including consumption out of own production. For the MENA region only a limited sample is reported to have high-quality data sets. This is a limitation on this study as well. Thus, due to a lack of recent high-quality data, the MENA countries in this chapter exclude both Iran and Turkey, which have a combined weight of 34.4% and 38.6% of the region's population and GDP, respectively. Excluded also are countries belonging to the GCC category for the same reason (with a weight of 7.2% of the population and 28.6% of the GDP of the region) as well as Iraq, which has been in a rather abnormal

economic condition since the Gulf War. Of the remaining Arab countries, the sample used represents 68% of the population and 92.6% of GDP.

Given income distribution information, poverty results can be generated using appropriately specified poverty lines. To generate the poverty results, we use the high-quality expenditure distribution data of Deininger and Squire (1996) and the World Bank (1998). A summary of our results is reported in Table 6.1 for the four regions of the developing world with which we are dealing. To determine inequality we report the Gini coefficients, while for poverty we report the three standard measures: headcount ratio (H: to measure incidence or spread), the poverty-gap ratio (P1: to measure depth), and the squared poverty-gap ratio (P2: to measure severity).[8] We emphasize that these are meant to be illustrative results for the purposes of making our framework operational for policy analysis.

Table 6.1. Inequality and Poverty in a Sample of Countries by World Regions

Region	No. of Countries	Mean Expenditure* (US$)	Poverty Line* (US$)	Gini Coefficient (%)	Head-Count Ratio (%)	Poverty-Gap Ratio (%)	Squared Poverty-Gap Ratio (%)
Arab World	6	115.3 (45.1)	50.8 (13.7)	38.95 (3.61)	21.52 (8.80)	6.51 (5.83)	3.38 (4.91)
Africa	18	75.0 (70.4)	41.9 (24.2)	48.0 (10.07)	52.10 (13.78)	23.04 (8.06)	13.21 (5.87)
Asia	8	97.67 (45.62)	45.84 (13.37)	37.03 (7.18)	24.72 (12.22)	6.99 (4.25)	2.95 (2.03)
Latin America	16	172.7 (82.0)	73.6 (32.7)	50.38 (6.69)	34.83 (8.57)	14.40 (5.04)	7.94 (3.59)
Overall	48	109.1 (78.6)	52.0 (27.8)	45.83 (9.39)	37.96 (16.33)	15.42 (9.10)	8.51 (6.08)

* per person per month.
Source: Our own calculations.

Looking at expenditure distribution first, we note that Latin America boasts the highest degree of inequality in the distribution of income, as reflected by a Gini coefficient of about 50%. The next-highest inequality is reported for sub-Saharan Africa, with a Gini of 48%. The lowest inequality is reported for Asia, with a Gini coefficient of 37%, and the the Arab region registers a close second, having a Gini of about 39%. These results conform with the generally accepted ranking among world regions.

As is well known, these average results hide a lot of variation that exists between countries. Thus, for example, as far as inequality in the Arab region is concerned, the lowest inequality is reported for Egypt with a Gini coefficient of 30% in 1991 (i.e., a Gini of 37% for income distribution), followed by Morocco and Algeria, having Gini coefficients of about 39% each. The highest inequality is reported for Mauritania, with a Gini coefficient of 42.5%, followed by Jordan (40.7%) and Tunisia (40%).

Given our method of estimating the poverty line, the table shows that the Arab world boasts the lowest poverty for all measures except for severe poverty. Asia follows in second place as the region with lowest poverty in terms of incidence and depth, but ranks first in terms of severity. Africa is the highest poverty region for all poverty measures, followed by Latin America. Thus, according to the above results, about 22% of the Arab population were living below a poverty line of US$51 per person per month in the early 1990s. At the other extreme, 52% of Africa's population were living below a poverty line of US$42 per person per month in the early 1990s. Among Arab countries the highest incidence of poverty in the sample is recorded for Mauritania, where 39% of the population lived below a poverty line of US$33 per person per month. On the other hand, the lowest incidence of poverty is recorded for Egypt, with 14% of its population living below a poverty line of US$42 per person per month.

Similar results can be read for the depth and severity of poverty as recorded by the poverty-gap and the squared-poverty gap measures, respectively. From the table it is easy to calculate the average income of the poor where it can be shown that such an average comes to US$34 per person per month in the Arab region, compared to US$23 per person per month in Africa, and US$44 in Latin America. Among the Arab countries the lowest average income for the poor of US$18 per person per month is recorded for Mauritania.

An important issue for policy is the extent of the sensitivity of poverty to growth (changes in per capita consumption expenditure or income) and distribution (changes in the Gini coefficient). This is measured by computing the elasticity of poverty with respect to both growth and distribution (the percentage rate of change in poverty due to a 1% increase in growth (or inequality). Table 3.2 of AE provides estimates of these elasticities. The estimates suggest that the pattern of sensitivity of poverty is similar in the Arab region and Asia, where it is seen that poverty is responsive both to growth and distribution and where sensitivity to distribution is consistently higher than that to growth. The sensitivity of poverty to growth is marginally higher in Asia than in the Arab world, while the reverse is true for distribution. Thus, for example, a percentage point increase in per capita consumption expenditure would be expected to reduce poverty by 2.3 and 2.4 percentage points in the Arab region and Asia, respectively. A percentage point decline in the Gini coefficient, on the other hand, would be expected to reduce poverty by 6.2 and 5.7 percentage points in the Arab world and Asia, respectively. In contrast, the sensitivity of poverty to growth and distribution is lowest in Africa, followed by Latin America. However, the sensitivity of poverty to changes in the distribution of income in Latin America is almost double that of Africa.

To obtain the growth elasticity of poverty after allowing for changes in the distribution of income over time and for the functional dependence of the poverty line on mean income, one must specify the way in which distribution changes with income (the so-called Kuznets relation). The estimation of the Kuznets specification allows the calculation of the turning point of mean income, which is equal to about US$1111 of private per capita consumption in 1987 prices. Thus, countries with per capita consumption lower than this turning point would be expected to experience increasing inequality as their economies transform, other things being the same. Beyond the turning point, countries are experiencing declining inequality. This is the sense in which a Kuznets relationship is useful in the context of the dynamic interaction between growth, inequality, and poverty. Not surprisingly, most of the developing countries in the sample were found to be below the turning point, except for fourteen countries out of the 48 covered (see Appendix Table 1 of AE). The latter group includes only two Arab countries—Algeria and Jordan, with mean per capita consumption figures of US$1243 and $1352, respectively.

Section 5: The Role of the Labor Market

Rigorous analysis of the role of the labor market as it relates to poverty has been attempted only recently in the literature. This is especially true for the case of reforming countries, where reform programs incorporate direct and indirect policy measures that affect the working of the labor market. In this context it is recognized that the labor market is a crucial element in understanding poverty in view of the fact that most of the poor generate their income by hiring out their labor services. Indeed, assetless workers only have their labor as potential assets, which generates returns only if they are offered employment in the labor market. Therefore, the way the labor market operates conditions employment, quality of employment, and wage outcomes, all of which are affected by the package of policies and institutions in a given economy.

As already noted, the most widely used measure of poverty is the headcount ratio. An obvious linkage to the labor market would be to observe that the higher the unemployment rate the more widespread poverty would be. This is obvious for the simple reason that usually assetless workers would have no entitlement to income-earning opportunities except through wage employment in the labor market. And hence, by not earning any income they would be expected to be among those falling below the poverty line.

Despite the data problems surrounding information on unemployment rates in the region, available evidence suggests that indeed unemployment rates are relatively high. Thus, for example, according to Economic Research Forum (ERF) (1996, 90), "unemployment rates exceeded 20% in Algeria in the early 1990s and were close to 15% in Morocco, Tunisia, Jordan and Yemen …. In Egypt and Algeria, for which multiple year data are available, there appears to be an increasing trend in the unemployment rate for the early nineties." The most problematic feature of the labor market in the region from a poverty perspective is the observed consistent pattern in the unemployment profile along education and age lines. Thus, the "analysis of unemployment by age and education indicates that the primary cause of unemployment in the region is the inability of educated new entrants to the labor force to get the increasingly scarce public sector jobs, which were the main source of employment for that group in the past." (ERF 1996, 91). It is reported, for example, that in Syria and Egypt about 80% of the unemployed are first-time job-seekers. In Jordan, Morocco and Tunisia the first-time job-seekers account for 50% of the unemployed. The implications of this feature should be obvious for poverty, given that this type of unemployed worker would be the least equipped to hedge against falling below the poverty line.

Another linkage is the structure of the labor market, especially the urban labor market. A major characteristic of this market in the region is its dual nature of formal and informal employment. By its nature the informal sector is characterized by ease of entry and low productivity. The first feature explains why this sector has accounted for the bulk of job creation in the recent past. On the other hand, the low productivity implies relatively lower wages, compared to the formal sector. As such, therefore, the recently observed phenomenon of increasing urban poverty can be explained in terms of such structure and functioning of the labor market. As observed by ERF (1998), the informal sector played a major role in the process of job creation in the region over the last two decades. As a result of this, a sharp increase in the share of informal employment is recorded for most countries of the region. While it is acknowledged that there are severe statistical data limitations in this respect, it is estimated nevertheless that informal employment comprises between 30–35% of the urban labor force in Egypt, between 35–45% in Yemen, about 37% in Morocco and, about 33% in Jordan.

Moreover, the labor markets in the region are characterized by declining real wages. This also provides an obvious link to the depth of poverty, as measured by the poverty gap ratio. Thus even if there were no observed increase in the spread of poverty, the depth of poverty could increase as a result of declining or stagnant real wages. This is simply because the average real income of the poor would be increasing at a lower rate than the real cost of attaining the required entitlement to basic needs. There is evidence that most of the countries of the region experienced sharp declines in real wages in the recent past (see ERF 1996, 93–4). The decline is reported to have been led in most cases by public sector wages, thus for example, real government wages in Egypt in 1992 were equivalent to only 50% of their 1982 levels. Similarly, by 1993, public sector wages in Morocco accounted for only 77% of their value in 1975, while those in Jordan accounted for 85% of their 1985 levels. The above behavior in public sector real wages is also reported for the behavior of the real minimum wage for some countries of the region. For example, the real minimum wage in Algeria declined by 16% per annum over the period 1989–92.

Section 6: Labor Market Implications of the Poverty-Reduction Strategies

An analysis of the dynamic behavior of inequality, poverty, and growth around the long-run equilibrium configuration of the economy (i.e., the steady state) enabled the identification of six phases, two of which give rise to stable paths toward the long-run equilibrium state of the economy (i.e., the steady state). Based on average growth, poverty, and distribution performance in 1986–96 (see Appendix Table 1), the six Arab countries can be classified according to the phase they are likely to be associated with during the period (Table 6.2). We discuss below this classification and the implied strategy for poverty reduction in these countries and the implications of this for the labor market.[9]

First, the economic performances of Algeria and Jordan during 1986–96 were characterized by rising poverty, decelerating growth, and higher inequality than levels consistent with the long-run equilibrium of the economy (i.e., the steady state). According to our analysis, the performances of these two countries produced a "transitional low-level equilibrium trap," driven by an unstable path of rising poverty. For these two countries, both low growth and bad distribution are constraints on sustainable poverty reduction. However, redistributive measures are particularly important to move the two economies towards a phase in which the rise in poverty will come to a halt at the steady state along a stable path. Moreover, a combination of growth acceleration and efficient distributional measures could push the two countries further into the phase where poverty declines continuously along a transitional, unstable path of 'super-performance.' It must be noted that the implications for the labor market policies are obvious. As noted in section 4 above, the economies of these two countries

Table 6.2. Strategies for Poverty Reduction in the Arab World
(Based on Average Performance in 1986–96)

Countries	Phases	Phase Description (Performance 1986–96)	Predicted Performance/ Recommended Strategy
Tunisia	Phase I	1. Declining poverty 2. Decelerating growth 3. Inequality higher than levels consistent with steady state	1. Poverty would decline at a decreasing rate along a stable path toward the steady state. 2. Avoiding growth collapse and achieving more equitable distribution would prolong the cycle of declining poverty.
Egypt	Phase IV	1. Rising poverty 2. Accelerating growth 3. Inequality lower than steady state levels	1. Poverty would increase at a decreasing rate until it converged at zero in the steady state, where distribution would worsen over time. 2. Both distribution and growth are important, and equitable growth that avoids increased inequality could lead to declining poverty over time. This could push the economy into a divergent phase of continuously declining poverty (East Asia, until recently).
Mauritania, Morocco	Phase V	1. Rising poverty 2. Accelerating growth 3. Inequality higher than steady state levels	1. Divergent phase of continuously rising poverty: "transitional low equilibrium trap" 2. Growth is not an immediate constraint, but redistributive measures will be required to shift the economy to Phase IV, and possibly Phase III
Algeria, Jordan	Phase VI	1. Rising poverty 2. Decelerating growth 3. Inequality higher than steady state levels	1. Unstable path towards continuously rising poverty: "transitional low . equilibrium trap." 2. Both growth and distribution are con strains but redistributive measures will be required to shift the economy to Phase IV, and possibly Phase III

Source: Ali and Elbadawi (1999a)

were characterized by fairly high rates of unemployment that were increasing over time (from 17% in 1989 to 23.8% in 1992 for Algeria and from 14.9% in 1987 to 18.8% in 1991 for Jordan). In the case of Algeria, moderately high rates of inflation (slightly above 20% per annum) exerted further pressures on the poverty front. As such, therefore, the design of redistributive policies would have an important anchor in the labor market, with the objective of reducing the rate of unemployment in both countries. Moreover, in the case of Algeria, the strategy should aim also at stabilizing the economy.

Second, the economic performance of Mauritania and Morocco during the period 1986–1996 was characterized by rising poverty, and higher inequality than levels consistent with the long-run equilibrium of the economy (i.e., the steady state), but growth was accelerating. According to our analysis, these countries are likely to be located in the region characterized by "transitional low level equilibrium trap." Even though growth may be less of a constraint for these countries, they would, however, need redistributive measures similar to those recommended for Algeria. In the case of Morocco, we note that the historical performance of the economy produced negative labor market outcomes in the form of fairly high, and increasing, unemployment rates (from 14.7% in 1987 to 16% in 1992). Further, real wages in the economy have declined at an annual rate of 5.5% despite the stabilization of the economy where the inflation rate has declined from 4.9% as an average for the period 1985–1995 to 1.8% for 1996. Such evidence points to the importance of labor market policies to complement other redistributive measures.

Third, in terms of overall average performance during 1986–96, the Egyptian economy was one of equitable income distribution (relative to the steady state levels), but also rising poverty, as well as negative but accelerating economic growth.[10] According to our analysis, this phase would lead the economy along a stable path where poverty would rise at a decreasing rate until it converged at zero in the steady state. Distribution also is predicted to worsen over time. In this case both distribution and growth are important, where equitable growth that avoids increased inequality could lead to declining poverty over time. A combination of declining poverty, equitable income distribution, and positive growth acceleration would enable the Egyptian economy to embark on a path of continuously declining poverty. Once such conditions were established, only growth would matter for simultaneously reducing poverty as well as improving distribution over time. This would happen if this phase also produced a relatively sustained era of "transitional super-performance." However, for now the immediate strategy should be to accelerate growth and undertake direct measures for reversing the rise in poverty. Most of these measures must be anchored in the labor market. The labor market's performance in Egypt, however, has not been promising. Unemployment rates have been high and rising over time. Moreover, real wages in the manufacturing sector have declined at fairly high rates (an annual rate of decline of 9.5% for the period 1985–1992) despite the stabilization of the economy (the inflation rate declined from 14.8% for the period 1985–1995 to 9.1% in 1996). This not only threatens the past gains of a relatively equitable distribution of income, but it also points to the centrality of labor market policies in the context of sustaining growth in the future. Job-creating growth, especially urban job creation, will be an important challenge for policy-makers.

Fourth, the performance of the Tunisian economy over the period from 1986–1996 was characterized by decelerating growth, higher-than-long-run equilibrium inequality levels, but declining poverty. According to our analysis, poverty is predicted to decline at a decreasing rate along a stable path and, will therefore come to a halt at the steady state. Both distribution and growth are important. For example, a collapse of growth (negative rates of real growth) might push such countries into a transitional "low equilibrium trap," in which poverty rises over time. On the other hand, more equitable distribution and positive growth could move this country into a "transitional super-performance" phase, and hence produce a more sustained era of declining poverty. We note in this respect that the labor market outcomes in Tunisia have not been conducive to poverty reduction. The unemployment rate was relatively high and increasing over time: the rate increased from 14.1% in 1987 to 16.1% in 1993. On the macroeconomic front, Tunisia was able to establish and maintain a stable macroeconomic environment, where the annual inflation rate averaged 5.6% per annum for the period from 1985–1995, and declined to 4.8% in 1996. Despite this, however, there is evidence that the real manufacturing wage in Tunisia has declined over the period from 1980–1992 at an annual rate of 1.4%. Moreover, as noted in Section 4 above, government real wages have declined as well. Again, these observations point to the importance of labor market policies in the context of future strategies.

Section 7: Conclusions

This chapter analyzes the behavior of poverty, growth, and income distribution under the prevailing labor market conditions in the Arab world. The nontechnical framework of the chapter motivates broad strategies for poverty reduction in the case of six Arab countries (Algeria, Egypt, Jordan, Mauritania, Morocco, and Tunisia) for which high-quality data is available. A combination of average performance in the areas of growth, poverty, and income distribution, as well as prevailing labor market conditions during the 1986–96 period, provides the basis for classifying the countries into phases. Thus, the recommended strategies vary across the six countries, depending on the phase in which they were judged to be located during this period.

The main thesis of this chapter is that a strategy for poverty reduction which is exclusively centered on growth can only be successful in the context of the limited development objective of dealing with *abject* poverty. Taking a broader view of poverty, the analysis of this chapter shows that with initial conditions of low inequality and faltering growth, as well as worsening labor market conditions (high unemployment as well as declining real minimum wages) in the region, a strategy for poverty reduction must be much broader. The main elements of these strategies are described below.

First, for Egypt (in spite of its relatively equitable income distribution) the strategy should comprise direct policy measures for the immediate reversal of the rise in poverty, coupled with longer-term policies for generating equitable and sustained growth in the future. Once poverty starts to decline and equitable income distribution is sustained, growth acceleration, and especially avoidance of growth collapse, would position this country onto a stable, although possibly prolonged, path of declining poverty. However, sustaining high growth appears to be very much dependent on the future conditions of the labor market. The past performance of the economy, however, produced relatively high unemployment rates with a tendency to increase over time. Moreover, real wages in the manufacturing sector have declined at fairly high rates. This not only threatens the past gains of a relatively equitable distribution of income, but it also points to the future centrality of labor market policies in sustaining growth. In particular, job-creating growth—especially urban job creation—will be an important challenge for policy-makers.

Second, in the case of Tunisia our analysis suggests that poverty has declined at a decreasing rate along a stable path, and will therefore come to a halt at the steady state. In this case both distribution and growth are important for prolonging the phase of declining poverty, or even better, they could move this country into a "transitional super-performance" phase, and hence produce a more sustained era of declining poverty. Once again, this strategy very much depends on the labor market conditions in Tunisia. We note in this respect that the past performance of the labor market in this country—where despite high and rising unemployment real wages have been declining—suggest that this market will be the main battleground in the fight against poverty in the future.

Third, in the cases of Mauritania and Morocco, redistributive measures would be required before the two countries could escape the dire consequences of a possibly long, though transitional, "low equilibrium trap" of rising poverty. On the other hand, Algeria and Jordan would require both growth and redistributive measures to move their economies from paths of continuously rising poverty to a phase in which the rise in poverty would come to a halt at the steady state along a stable path. Moreover, a combination of sufficiently high growth acceleration and efficient distributive measures could push the economies of all four countries into the phase of continuously declining poverty along a transitional unstable path of 'super-performance.' An important point to make in this connection is that, at least for Algeria, Jordan, and Morocco, the relatively high income inequality levels are very much the outcome of labor market conditions that prevailed in these countries. As the analysis of the previous section makes clear, labor markets in these countries are characterized by high and rising unemployment as well as declining real wages. This suggests that policies aimed at sustaining growth in the longer run or achieving meaningful reductions in income inequality must be anchored in the labor market.

Finally, the central tenets of the recommended strategies are that—with the exception of Egypt, where only growth is likely to be the eventual constraint—both distribution and growth are constraints. Moreover, even in the case of Egypt, immediate and direct measures for poverty reduction would be required for reversing the current rise in poverty (see Box 1; for more detailed analysis on these measures, see for example, Fergany 1997, 98; and El-Mahdi 1999). A particularly interesting feature of the above analysis is that despite the differences that exist between the countries of the sample in terms of initial conditions and equilibrium configurations, the labor market implications of the analysis are almost identical. This is due to the almost identical labor market outcomes produced by past performance. As a result new forms of distributive policies would be required in the future, and such policies must be anchored in the labor market. As is clear from the analytical framework, the long-run equilibrium poverty level will be stationary where poverty is defined in terms of the headcount ratio. The depth of poverty, however, can increase despite the fixity of the headcount ratio on account of the differential behavior of the real wage rate and the real cost of basic needs. It is in this respect that labor market policies will be central to future policies. With changing structures of production, it is perhaps reasonable to argue that the skill mix of the labor force would need to be changed. The most relevant policy measure in this respect would be investment in education and training, including apprenticeship training in critical future industries. Moreover, while maintaining the stability of the macroeconomic framework will continue to be important for growth enhancement, the decline in real wages needs to be arrested. This may point to a possible future trade-off that would require judicious policy-making.

Box 1

The Labor Market and Strategies for Dealing with Poverty in Egypt

Egypt has entered a period in its demographic transition during which the working-age population is increasing relative to the rest of the population (it is projected that by the year 2010 the working age population will be twice the size of the dependent population). It has been argued that this type of demographic transition offers "a demographic window of opportunity," where the high shares of the working age population foster accelerated and sustained economic growth by increasing labor participation and saving (Yousif 1997). However, it must be emphasized that for Egypt to realize such an opportunity, growth must create enough jobs to absorb the huge growth in its working age population. First, without reducing the currently high level of unemployment (more than 10% since 1993) growth is not likely to be sustained in the future, even with the best economic programs. Recent evidence suggests that societies with major "latent" social conflicts (e.g., due to high inequality or high unemployment) are not likely to achieve stable growth. These societies, the argument goes, are likely to adopt growth-retarding policies in response to external shocks as the authorities try to accommodate conflictive interests of non-cooperative social groups (Rodrik 1998). Second, even if growth could be sustained with little labor absorption, it will likely be associated with rising poverty as was the case in the 1990s. Thus, future growth strategies in Egypt, indeed its overall future development strategies, will neither be sustainable nor would it be poverty-reducing if they were not anchored in the labor markets. Some elements of these strategies for Egypt (and other Arab countries) are discussed in the last two sections of this chapter. A successful labor market-based strategy for poverty reduction in Egypt must aim at achieving a radical restructuring of the labor market. Eventually, the formal private sector (currently employing just 3% of the labor force) should account for most of the employment growth in the future. This will require increased productivity and gradual formalization of the private informal sector, which currently account for 28% of total employment. The expansion of the private formal sector will permit growth in productivity and gradual reduction in employment in agriculture and the government sectors, which account for a combined share of 64% of total employment.

Job Creation:

In the medium-to-short runs, however, the proactive measures for job creation should be maintained, and if possible expanded and enhanced. These measures were put in place in the 1980s as part of the instruments for mitigating the social consequences of the Economic Reforms and Structural Adjustment Programs (ERSAP). This recommendation would be in recognition of the widely held view that lingering and high unemployment as well as the substantial reductions in the food subsidy programs, have been the main factors behind the worsening of poverty in Egypt in the 1990s. The effects on poverty of these two factors have clearly dominated the poverty-reducing impact of the positive per capita growth achieved during the period. In the context of Egypt's "intermediate" strategy for poverty reduction, the Social Fund for Development (SFD) has been an effective instrument. In assessing the role of SFD in job creation, Abda Al-Mahdi writes (1999, 36) "[o]ver a three year period of operation, the SFD succeeded in generating 630 thousand jobs of which 250 thousand were permanent ... While the absolute numbers are quite significant given the limited resources and the SFD's limited goal of alleviating unemployment associated with ERSAP, they are insufficient when compared to the number of unemployed. As stated previously, the number of unemployed in 1995 was estimated at 1.9 million or 11.3% of the labor force. This means that the SFD was only able to absorb 18% of the unemployed in permanent and temporary jobs.

Jobs created by the Fund are characterized by their low cost, pointing to effective use of donor funds. A World Bank report states that "the SFD met its employment creation objectives with annual expenditures equivalent to only .2% of GDP or about 6% of annual donor flows to Egypt. This job-creation cost compares favorably with other countries." The report estimates the cost of job creation at market exchange rate at US$1401. However, the question remains as to the sustainability and productivity of workers in these newly generated job opportunities.

Adapted from Al-Mahdi (1999).

Appendix

Table A6.1. Predicted Performance in the 1986–96 period:
Behavior of Poverty, Growth and Distribution in Six Arab Countries

Country	$\dot{g}$	G	g_F	$\bar{G}$	$\hat{P}$	$\dot{g}{>}0$	$\dot{g}{<}0$	$G{>}\bar{G}$	$G{<}\bar{G}$	$\hat{P}{>}0$	$\hat{P}{<}0$
Algeria	-0.0776	39.2813	1.1972	24.26	7.8057	X	X			X	
Egypt	0.2864	32.0057	3.9962	36.90	0.6804	X			X	X	
Jordan	-0.1722	40.6564	1.6606	24.26	7.9486	X	X			X	
Mauritania	0.0286	42.5346	3.9843	36.90	0.7200	X			X	X	
Morocco	0.5680	39.2002	4.7004	36.90	0.7176	X			X	X	
Tunisia	-0.1192	40.0013	6.6971	36.90	-0.4021	X			X		X

Source: Appendix Table D.1 and equation (10) of AE

$\hat{P}$=-αg+α_0, where α=(1-ϵ)η-θv is the elasticity of the growth effect on poverty net of the influence of inequality operating through the growth channel .
α_0 = component of change in poverty due to distribution.
g= average annual growth rate in 1986–96.
$\dot{g}$= average annual change for the rate of growth for 1986–96
G= level of Inequality in 1986–96
g_F=g+β_0G is the average annual growth explained by non-distributional fundamentals (1986-96)
$\bar{G}$=$\frac{1}{\alpha\beta_0}$(αg_F-α_0); where the parameters are obtained from Appendix Table D.1 of AE.

Notes

1 Our definition of the MENA region includes the two Arab countries of Sudan and Mauritania, which are not considered part of this region according to the World Bank, for example.
2 For more details, see Deininger and Squire (1996).
3 Libya and Lebanon are excluded due to a lack of data.
4 However, even though AE's model accounts for both the long- and short-run determinants of growth, only the long- run modeling of growth is required for the analysis of this policy-oriented framework.
5 See, among others, Lal and Myint (1996); Bruno, Ravallion and Squire (1998); but see also Horton, Kanbur and Mazumdar (1995).
6 Algebraically, the rate of change in poverty, which decomposes the change in the poverty index into a "growth effect" net of the distributional effect through the growth channel $(-\alpha=-(1-\varepsilon)\eta+\theta v)$ and a "trend distributional effect" $(\alpha_0=\theta v_0)$ is given by: $\hat{P}=-\alpha g+\alpha_0$, where P is an index of poverty; ε = elasticity of poverty line with respect to mean income; $-\eta$ = elasticity of poverty index with respect to mean income; θ is the elasticity of P relative to inequality (Gini index), v is the elasticity of the Gini relative to growth and v_0 is the component of the rate of change in the Gini that is does not depend on growth.
7 Algebraically, the level of inequality $(\bar{G})$ consistent with equilibrium (i.e. $\hat{P}=0$), is given by $\bar{G}=\dfrac{1}{\alpha\beta_0}(\alpha\bar{g}_F-\alpha_0)$, where α, α_0 as defined in footnote 6 above; β_0 is the negative of the coefficient of initial inequality in the growth equation; and $\bar{g}_F$ is the component of growth due to other fundamentals (not including initial inequality).
8 The reported results are averages over the results of individual countries generated by Povcal (a program used for grouped data: t-statistics are shown in brackets).
9 For a detailed exposition of strategies for dealing with poverty in the Arab world, see UNDP (1996); and for Egypt see Fergany (1997, 98).
10 Our model's prediction that poverty has risen in Egypt in the post-1985 period is corroborated by recent poverty studies on Egypt (for a review, see El-Mahdi 1999).

References

Alesina, A., and D. Rodrik. 1994. "Distributive politics and economic growth." *Quarterly Journal of Economics* 109 (2).

Ali, A.A.G., and I. Elbadawi. 1999a. "Poverty in the Arab World: The Role of Inequality and Growth." Prepared for the ERF Sixth Annual Conference, Cairo, October 23–31.

Ali, A.A.G., and I. Elbadawi. 1999b. "Inequality and the Dynamics of Poverty and Growth in Developing Countries." Unpublished mimeo. Nairobi: AERC.

Bruno, M., M. Ravallion, and L. Squire. 1998. "Equity and growth in developing countries: old and new perspectives on the policy issues." In V. Tanzi and K. Chu, eds., *Income Distribution and High Quality Growth*. Cambridge: MIT Press.

Deininger, K., and L. Squire. 1996. "A new data set measuring income inequality." *The World Bank Economic Review* 10 (3): 565–91.

El-Mahdi, A. 1999. "FEMISE Poverty Study: Egypt Preliminary Report." Unpublished mimeo. Cairo: Economic Research Forum.

Eoconomic Research Forum (ERF). 1998. *Economic Trends in the MENA Region*. Cairo.

ERF. 1996. *Economic Trends in the MENA Region*. Cairo.

Fergany, N. 1998. "The Growth of Poverty in Egypt." ALMISHKAT Research Notes: No. 12. Giza.

Fergany, N. 1997. "Poverty and Employment in Egypt and Sudan." Unpublished mimeo. Giza: ALMISHKAT.

Horton, S., R. Kanbur, and D. Mazumdar. 1995. "Openness and inequality." Paper presented to the IEA World Congress. Tunis.

Kuznets, S. 1955. "Economic growth and income inequality." *American Economic Review* 45 (1):1–28.

Lal, D., and H. Myint. 1996. *The Political Economy of Poverty, Equity, and Growth: A Comparative Study*. Oxford: Clarendon Press.

Rodrik, D. 1998. "Where Did All the Growth Go? External Shocks, Social Conflict, and Growth Collapses." Harvard University, John F. Kennedy School of Government. Mimeo.

UNDP. 1996. "Preventing and Eradicating Poverty: Report on the Experts' Meeting on Poverty Alleviation and Sustainable Livelihoods in the Arab States." February 28–29, 1996. Damascus,

World Bank. 1995. *Claiming the Future: Choosing Prosperity in the Middle East and North Africa*.

World Bank 1999. *African Development Indicators 1998/99*.

Yousif, T. 1997. "Demography, Capital Dependency and Globalization in MENA." Paper presented at ERF conference on "Globalization: Challenges and Opportunities for Development in the ERF region." Cairo.

7

Human Development and Poverty in the Arab States

Moez Doraid

From the Atlantic to the Gulf, people—women, men, and children—are the real wealth of the Arab countries. The purpose of development and growth in the Arab region should be to free people from deprivation and to expand their choices. Over the last four decades, remarkable progress has been achieved in reducing poverty and in advancing human development. However, much still needs to be done to address the backlog of deprivation and imbalance. The Arab region has the resources to eradicate poverty in less than a generation. Political commitment, not resources, is the binding constraint.

A strong, unequivocal commitment to clear human development and poverty-reduction objectives is critical. The political commitment should emanate from ethical, social, political, and moral imperatives as well as the region's religious and cultural traditions (Box 1).

As we begin the new millennium, critical lags persist, and in some cases widen, in the Arab region. First, there is the lag between the Arab region and other regions in terms of participatory governance. The wave of democracy that has changed the mode of governance in most of Latin America and East Asia in the 1980s and Eastern Europe and Central Asia in the late 1980s and early 1990s has not yet reached the Arab states.[1] Second, there is the lag between political reform and economic reform. In many Arab countries, political reform has not caught up with economic reform. Third, there is a gap between economic development and reform on the one hand, and social development on the other. This third lag is this chapter's main concern.

Human Achievements in the Arab Region

Over the past forty years, Arab countries have experienced unprecedented human development and poverty reduction.[2] Economic gains and purposeful action in the social sectors have contributed to substantial progress in health, education, nutrition, living standards, and other aspects of human development. Between 1970 and 1997:[3]

- Life expectancy increased by about fourteen years from 51 to 65.
- Infant mortality rates were more than halved.
- The mortality rates for children under five were reduced by nearly two-thirds. The Arab region was the first in the developing world where most countries reduced mortality rates of under-five children to the target of 70 per thousand by 1990, well ahead of the global goal.
- Adult literacy rates rose from 31% to 58.6%. Combined school gross

---

Box 1

Religion and Culture Against Poverty

The Islamic tradition has a long history of recognizing poverty and fighting it. In the *Qur'an*, a number of verses emphasize the virtue of *infaq*, the voluntary spending for the welfare of the poor. It is proclaimed that no man will attain piety nor enjoy heaven unless he spends freely from his wealth on the poor. The *Qur'an* specifically mentions the need to help the poor as a way of cementing social cohesion. A recurrent premise is that societies which fail to take care of their poor will disintegrate.

In Islamic society, there are numerous institutional devices for implementing *infaq*. One is the *waqf*. This implies setting aside certain assets, like land and buildings, to be used exclusively for specific purposes under a legal deed. Another institutional device is the *manihah*. This involves granting a productive asset to a needy person free of charge for a specific period. Also, the *Qur'an* emphasizes the importance of establishing a social security system for the poor. It accomplishes this feat through the use of *zakat*. This is a tax on the wealthy of a community, whose proceeds are used to help the poor attain their basic needs.

Social solidarity and compassion were an integral part of the message of the Prophet Muhammad, who reflected it in his saying: *I disavow any community in which a person becomes hungry.* Several Caliphs built on the tradition. Ali Ibn Abi Taleb, the Fourth Caliph, described poverty as "the greater death."

An Arab definition of poverty, written around the fourteenth century by Ibn Mandhur in *Lisan al-Arab*, defines poverty as the inability of the individual to satisfy his own basic needs and the needs of his dependents. Another source, *Fiqh al-Lugha*, written by Tha'aliby in the enrollments rose from 47% in 1980 to 58% in 1995.

• Daily caloric intake and access to safe water and sanitation are higher than in any other developing region.[4]

• Compared to other regions, the Arab states made the fastest progress in women's education by raising women's literacy rates threefold since 1970, and by more than doubling female primary and secondary enrollment rates, from 32% in 1970 to 74% in 1997.

Of course the above regional averages hide wide variations and uneven progress between—and within—Arab countries. In general, oil-rich countries made rapid advancements. Several countries from this group set world records in improving some social indicators (Tables 7.1 and 7.2). However, rapid progress was not limited to the oil-rich. Yemen and Tunisia were among the ten countries that experienced the fastest improvements in the world in raising life expectancy and reducing under-five mortality, respectively.

The multifaceted nature of human progress in the Arab region and its rapid pace are captured by the improvement of the Human Development Index (HDI), which measures progress in terms of life expectancy, educational attain-

---

eleventh century, identifies eight different levels of poverty: loss of savings; loss of assets or property due to drought or natural disaster, when an individual is forced to sell the decoration items on his sword, when the individual/household can only afford to eat bread of millet (which is cheaper than the usual wheat-flour bread), when the individual/household has no food available, when the individual/household has no belongings left that he/it can sell to purchase food, when the individual/household has become humiliated or degraded due to poverty, and, finally, when the individual/household is reduced to ultimate poverty.

Maimonides, the twelfth- and thirteenth-century Egyptian philosopher, codified the importance of charity and giving to the poor. Specifically, he suggested leaving part of an orchard or a field unharvested so the poor could help themselves. He also emphasized the need to collect charity funds and run food pantries in each local community. The most frequently quoted part of his writings involves the eightfold ranking of charity, from least to the most meritorious:

• Giving grudgingly;
• Giving cheerfully, but less than you should;
• Giving after being solicited;
• Giving without being solicited;
• Giving to a recipient unknown to you who knows you;
• Giving to a recipient you know who does not know you;
• Giving to an unknown recipient who does not know your identity; and. most interestingly;
• Helping a needy person become self-supporting through a gift, loan, or entering into partnership with or providing work for him or her.

Sources: Gordon 1996; Bremner 1994; Ahmad 1991.

ment, and income. Between 1960 and 1992 the Middle East and North Africa (MENA), compared to other regions, experienced the second-largest absolute increase in their regional HDI value after East Asia. During the same period, Tunisia and Syria were among the top ten performers in terms of absolute increase in HDI value (Table 7.3). Egypt, Jordan, and Morocco more than doubled their HDI values, and Yemen more than tripled its HDI.[5]

In assessing the human-development improvements in the Arab region, it is essential to remember that Arab countries started their progress from a very low base. This helps better understand the considerable extent of their achievement. Oman, for example, made very rapid advancements in order to catch up with the developing world human development averages (Box 2).

Arab countries overcame severe difficulties in expanding their social services following independence. For example, a glance at literacy rates for 1960 shows how far many countries have come since colonial days, when two-thirds to

---

Box 2

Oman: An Impressive Record of Accelerated Human Progress

Beginning in 1970, Oman undertook a comprehensive program of human development, achieving some of the most rapid advances ever recorded. Since that time life expectancy has increased by 24 years, from 47 years in 1970 to 71 years in 1997. Infant mortality has been reduced more than tenfold—from more than 215 per 1000 live births in 1970 to less than eighteen in 1997.

Improvements in education have been even more impressive. In 1970 there was no education system, and only three schools—all primary—provided an education for 900 pupils, all boys. By 1994 there were 454,000 students in 920 schools, and 49% were girls. Today 70% of primary school-age children are in school.

Most health problems associated with poverty and lack of education have been controlled or eradicated. Trachoma leading to blindness, once affecting more than half of schoolchildren, has virtually disappeared.

Rapid advances in other areas of human development have accompanied progress in health and education. Nearly three-quarters of houses now have running water and flushing toilets, and nine out of ten have electric light and electricity or gas for cooking. Pensions are provided for the disabled, the elderly, widowed or divorced women, and orphans. Oil revenues, of course, made possible such rapid progress and such a high standard of living. But without the commitment to human development, Oman might have been wealthy but unhealthy.

Oman has been a global pacesetter in human development. But there is still room to enhance human development by translating income growth into the lives of the people. The female literacy rate is two-thirds the male rate, and the fertility rate, at 6.9, is one of the highest in the world. Oman has established an ambitious strategy to take its people to the year 2020 and ensure a better quality of life for all of them.

Source: Updated from *HDR 1997*

three-quarters of the people of the region were illiterate. By way of comparison, when South Korea shifted its development strategy to export-led growth in the early 1960s, over 70% of the population could already read and write.

Table 7.1. Fastest Progress in Raising Life Expectancy in
Developing Countries, 1970–1995 (by age)

Country	Life Expectancy at Birth 1970	Life Expectancy at Birth 1995	Percentage Change 1970–95
Oman	**47**	**70**	**50**
Yemen	**41**	**57**	**39**
Saudi Arabia	**52**	**71**	**36**
Viet Nam	49	66	35
Indonesia	48	64	34
Nepal	42	56	33
Bolivia	46	61	32
Honduras	53	69	31
Bhutan	40	52	30
Lao People's Dem. Rep.	40	52	29

Source: UNDP, Human Development Report Office

Table 7.2. Fastest Progress in Reducing Under-Five Mortality Rate in
Developing Countries, 1970–1995 (per 1000 live births)

Country	Under-Five Mortality Rate 1970	Under-Five Mortality Rate 1995	Percentage Change 1970–95
Oman	**200**	**18**	**-91**
United Arab Emirates	**150**	**19**	**-87**
Korea, Rep. of	55	7	-87
Brunei Darussalam	78	11	-86
Chile	96	14	-85
Saudi Arabia	**185**	**32**	**-83**
Tunisia	**201**	**37**	**-82**
Singapore	27	5	-82
Iran, Islamic Rep. of	**208**	**40**	**-81**
Malaysia	63	13	-79

Source: Human Development Report Office, *HDR 1998*

Table 7.3. Top Performers in Human Development (1960–92)

Top Ten Performers (1960–92)	Absolute Increase in HDI Value
Malaysia	0.463
Botswana	0.463
Korea, Rep. of	0.462
Tunisia	**0.432**
Thailand	0.424
Syrian Arab Republic	**0.408**
Turkey	**0.406**
China	0.396
Portugal	0.378
Iran, Islamic Rep. of	**0.366**

Source: UNDP, Human Development Report Office

Backlog of Deprivation

Despite impressive progress and the great wealth of many parts of the region, a considerable backlog of human deprivation and poverty persists. In 1997:

• About 13% of the population were not expected to survive to age 40.
• 65 million adults were illiterate.
• A 40% increase was expected in the number of children out of school.
• 54 million lacked access to safe water.
• 29 million lacked access to health services.
• The unemployment rate was about 15%.
• Lack of access to safe water and safe sanitation translated into about ten million lost years of productive life each year.
• More than 50 million people breathe dangerously polluted air.

Between 1980 and 1995, the Arab states experienced economic decline, with GNP per capita decreasing by 1.2% per annum. The fall in oil prices and the Gulf wars contributed considerably to this stagnation. Only two Arab countries, Oman and Tunisia, had per capita incomes in the 1990s higher than ever before. In contrast, eight Arab countries had real per capita incomes in 1993 equal to what they had in the 1970s or before. In the 1990s, per capita income nose-dived falling by a staggering -4.5% per year between 1990 and 1994.

Regional estimates of the incidence of income poverty vary considerably. According to the World Bank, in 1994, 4% of the population of the MENA region or about eleven million people lived in poverty on less than US$1 a day. Forty million people lived on less than less than US$ 1.67 per day (1985 constant dollars adjusted for purchasing-power parity).[6] Most sources agree that the number and proportion of poor people has increased in the second half of the 1980s.[7]

Income poverty is much less pervasive than human poverty—or deprivation in basic human development. Human poverty is about 32.4%, as per the Human Poverty Index (HPI) which measures deprivation in terms of short lives, illiteracy, and lack of basic services.[8] The same applies for individual countries as evident in Figure 7.1 that shows that income poverty and human poverty do not coincide.

Several countries have national income poverty estimates (Annex Table 2). For the second half of the 1990s, national estimates of overall poverty ranged between 45% for Djibouti to 23% for Egypt. At 6%, Tunisia had the lowest incidence of extreme poverty among the Arab countries for which data is available.

Women and children suffer the most. The maternal mortality rate is 396 per 100,000 live births—double the rate in Latin America and the Caribbean, and four times the rate in East Asia. The tragic toll of female genital mutilation is a disgraceful indictment in many Arab countries. More than half of adult women

Figure 7.1. Human poverty and income poverty do not always move together

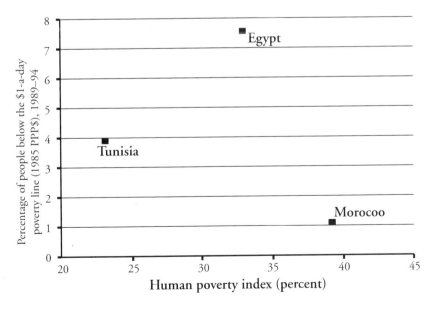

are illiterate, and women's literacy is only two-thirds that of men's. This is significantly lower than the average of 79% for all developing countries. In Egypt
female literacy is lower than in Malawi and Uganda, despite considerably higher
per capita incomes. In 1997, the majority of women were illiterate in six of the
fifteen Arab countries for which data on female literacy was available. In contrast
with Latin America, only in Haiti and Guatemala are most women illiterate.

About 15% of children from the relevant age group are out of primary school
(68% in Djibouti, 38–39% in Kuwait and Saudia Arabia, 28–29% in Oman,
and 20% in Qatar), and nearly 30% are out of secondary school.

Uneven progress has widened disparities within countries and between countries. Widening gaps between countries are evident when comparing the oil-rich
to the poorer countries that do not have the oil income and that have signifi-

Figure 7.2.

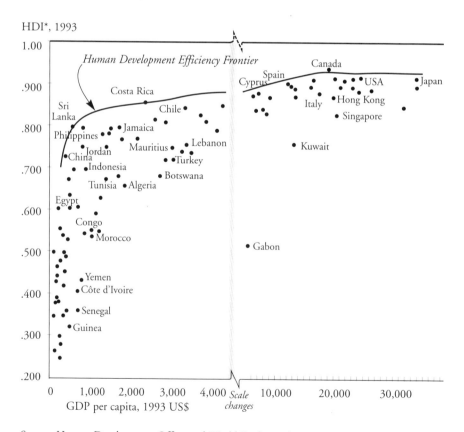

HDI*, 1993

Source: Human Development Office and World Bank 1994a

cantly larger populations. While the difference in GNP per capita was 2:1 in favor of the oil producers in 1960, it reached 9:1 in 1994. GNP per capita varied from US$260 in Yemen to more than $17,350 in the United Arab Emirates and Kuwait in 1995. The substantial contrasts in income levels in the region are matched by contrasts in human development. For example, life expectancy ranges from 50 years in Djibouti, to 76 years in Kuwait and adult literacy rates from 43% in Yemen to 87% in Jordan.

Pervasive imbalances contribute to the backlog of human deprivation in the Arab countries. The following is a discussion focusing only on imbalances related to the link between income growth and human development, public spending, and gender.

Imbalances

Development
Countries differ in how well they translate income into human development—their "human development efficiency." At each general level of income are countries that are on or close to the "human development efficiency frontier." They convert income into capabilities more effectively than others do. Countries that constitute the "human development frontier" of efficiency, include Canada, China, Costa Rica and Sri Lanka. These countries, together with others that lie very close to the frontier, such as Chile and Jamaica, have the highest efficiency (Figure 7.2). By comparison, Arab countries lie significantly below this frontier. They have not effectively translated wealth and income growth into human development.

The link between economic growth and human development has not been automatic in the region. Trends of economic growth and of human development progress have not been correlated and have varied from one Arab country to another. Figure 7.3 shows that among the four Arab countries for which data is available, Egypt had the highest rate of annual GDP per capita growth between 1975–97. However, it also had the second-lowest rate of human-development progress. The latter is measured by the reduction in the shortfall between levels of the HDI* (i.e., HDI without the income component) at the beginning of the period and their levels at the end of the period.

Levels of human development of Arab countries are typically lower than what we would expect given their per capita incomes. The imbalance is reflected in ranks according to HDI that are much lower than ranks according to per capita income (Annex Table 1). Among the Arab states, only two countries have HDI ranks better than their per capita income ranks–an indication that their human development levels are commensurate with their income levels.[9]

Figure 7.3. Long-term pattern of economic growth and human
development progress

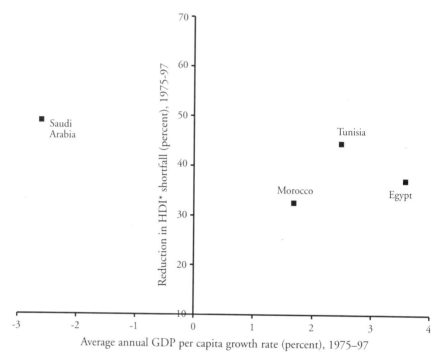

The average per capita income for the region is significantly higher than the developing world's average, while the average HDI value is lower. This shows that Arab states lag beyond countries with comparable per capita income levels. It also highlights the potential for using available income to enhance human development.

The potential is particularly evident in the oil-rich Arab countries. For these countries the negative difference between both the HDI and per capita income ranks remains among the greatest in the world, ranging from -6 for Libya to -47 in the case of Oman.

The lag between income levels and human development levels, and the potential for using available income to raise human development, is also evident in poorer Arab countries. The HDI ranks of Djibouti and Sudan are lower than their rankings according to per capita income. This also shows that the state of human development in these countries is still incongruous with their per capita income levels, despite the low levels of the latter. In spite of their scarce resources, these countries have the potential to improve their human development, even within existing constraints.

Middle-income Arab countries also could have translated growth to human development more effectively. In Egypt, for example, per capita GDP grew at 3.3% per year between 1960 and 1994, well above the world average. Yet improvements in health and education10 were significantly below the world's average. Thus Egypt was unable to fully translate its growth into broad-based education and health. Today nearly half of the adult population (47.3%) are illiterate. Illiteracy rates are higher than in Tanzania, Togo, and Zambia, though these countries have per capita incomes less than one-third of Egypt's. By the 1980s, the lack of broad-based human capital was acting as an important brake on Egypt's growth. Economic reforms accelerated growth rates in the 1990s. Experience shows that operationalizing the Egyptian Government's commitment to social development is needed to sustain growth.

Inefficiency in converting income to human development has been attributed to the maldistribution of either private or public resources, or both. In Latin American countries such as Brazil, maldistribution of private resources is largely blamed for human development levels that are incommensurate with per capita income levels. In contrast, maldistribution of private resources (both wealth and income) does not seem to be the prime suspect in Arab states. Distribution of private resources in the Arab region is more egalitarian than in most other regions of the developing world. The Gini coefficients (a measure of equality in which one denotes perfect inequality and zero denotes perfect equality) of several Arab states are among the best in the developing world. Thus, inefficiency in converting income to human development seems to be more attributable to the maldistribution of public rather than private resources. The next section sheds more light on this.

Public Spending
Shares of national budgets allocated to human development concerns varied considerably among countries and across time. On the positive side, by the mid-1970s Algeria was devoting close to 30% of its national budget to education. Political commitment by governments has often led to dramatic improvements in human development (Box 3). However, misallocation and maldistribution of public resources are to blame for much of the backlog of deprivation and lag of social development beyond income growth.

Education and health
Governments have made considerable efforts to improve health and education. In 1996, 5.2% of the GNP was spent on education in the MENA region—more than any other region in the developing world with the exception of Eastern Europe and Central Asia.[11] Countries undergoing structural adjust-

ment programs and reducing public spending, such as Egypt and Tunisia, have increased expenditure on education (in Egypt by nearly three-quarters in real terms in the 1990s). At 2.3% of GDP, public spending on health was significant though slightly lower than the world average.

Misallocation and maldistribution plague the education and health sectors. Public spending on education, for example, is over-concentrated on university education. Around a third of public spending on education goes to the tertiary level in Egypt, Jordan, Kuwait, and Turkey. Among developing countries, only Venezuela allocates a higher share of its education spending to the tertiary level. Per-pupil costs remain high. At US$1588 per student, spending on tertiary education in the Arab states is higher than in any other developing region.

The effect of all this is regressive and diverts substantial resources from broad-based expansion of education. For example, Egypt's National Human

---

Box 3

Oil for reading and a solution for life

The Iraqi literacy campaign illustrated what can be done when a resource-rich government is committed to education. The Ba'athists had both an ideological commitment to the goal of universal literacy and the resources that the oil boom of the 1970s provided. There had been literacy campaigns during the 1960s, but these had foundered due to lack of information on the characteristics of illiterates, inadequate and insufficient textbooks, paucity of funds, and low motivation of the adult learners.

From 1971 to 1978, the government conducted crash campaigns to train teachers. In November 1977 it undertook a census to determine the characteristics of the illiterate: 2.2 million illiterates, aged fifteen to 45, of whom 70% were women. The government then passed laws requiring attendance of adult-literacy classes, made extensive use of trade unions and other "popular organizations," daily use of TV, and so forth. Different textbooks were prepared for peasants, workers, housewives, and soldiers. To ensure female participation in classes, nurseries were provided.

The impact seems to have been considerable. 84% of the target population attended classes, and many women left home for the first time to attend. The cost was high: over US$700 million was spent, a cost of approximately US$350 per person reached by the campaign. But most development specialists would agree that the investment was well worth it. Political commitment often helped overcome constraints through cost-effective means. Oral Rehydration Therapy (ORT) is spreading in the region, with Syria, Tunisia, Morocco, and Egypt manufacturing their own packages of salt needed for the life-saving ORT solution. Use of this simple technique has cut Egyptian infant mortality from diarrhea by nearly half in only a few years.

Sources: *Iraq National Human Development Report 1995*, Sousa 1982, Richards and Waterbury, 1996.

Development Report, estimates that 54% of tertiary spending goes to the richest third of households, while only 10% goes to the poorest third.[12]

Subsidies to tertiary education have proven to be inequitable because students in these schools are typically from higher-income groups. They have used scarce public funds for purposes that private money could have covered. And they made particularly little human development or economic sense when much of the population is illiterate.

There have been similar problems in health services. Spending is often skewed towards high-tech hospitals offering high standards of treatment for affluent patients, leaving others without even the most basic health care, particularly in rural areas.

Poor quality of education and health services are among the problems related to the inefficiency of public spending in Arab countries. With respect to education, studies from Egypt show that competency in language and mathematical skills are only 30 and 40% of the levels expected from primary-school students. In an international study of the educational achievements of eighth- grade students in 1996, Kuwait, which spends generously on education, came in 39th out of 41 countries at different levels of development. Jordan, often praised for high-quality education, was the only Arab country to participate in the same study in 1995, and ranked lowest among sixteen countries.

Bad policies have distorted the output of the educational systems to become grossly out of tune with the requirements of the labor market. This contributed to the high rate of unemployment among the educated in the region—a reflection of the mismatch between excess supply from tertiary education and the demands of the economy. It also contributed to a steady decline in overall productivity of 0.2% a year between 1960 and 1990—a period when, in contrast, productivity was growing at a little less than 2% in East Asia.

Food subsidies

Food-subsidy programs are another area of public spending where inefficiencies could be reduced. Universal food subsidy programs have been extensively used for nutritional and income transfer purposes. In Egypt, for example, in the early 1980s, food-subsidy allocations constituted about 20% of public expenditures, among the highest in the world. Universal food-subsidy schemes have contributed to nutritional improvements, though lacked cost-effectiveness as their benefits were disproportionate to their high budgetary cost. In Egypt, Morocco, Sudan, and Tunisia they helped raise caloric intake but contributed less to nutrition due to poor hygiene, sanitation, and other complements to food intake. Moreover, a greater share of their benefits went to the rich than to the poor. Because they were universal rather than rationed or targeted, the rich bought more of the subsidized goods than the poor, who could only afford small quantities.

Today, despite reductions in food-subsidy outlays (facilitated partly through targeting), the daily per capita supply of calories and protein in the Arab states is higher than in any other developing region. Syria and Egypt have the second- and third-highest daily per capita caloric supply in the developing world, respectively, after Turkey. Yet malnutrition persists amid obesity; 18% of children under the age of five are underweight, and about a quarter suffer from stunted growth.

Social assistance

Inefficiencies in welfare and social assistance programs also persist. Egypt's social assistance program is focussed on poor beneficiaries, has a fairly large coverage (2.7 million people), but pays minuscule benefits (5% of the poverty line) at a high administrative cost of 12% of total outlays. Tunisia's program of direct transfers to pre-schoolers, the handicapped, and to the needy includes some targeting, and serves a significant proportion of these beneficiaries. However, it still costs three times as much as would be needed to give all the poor the equivalent of the poverty-line income each year (assuming perfect targeting).[13]

Military spending

This is another area that needs to be reconsidered. In a vicious circle of cause and effect, military tensions have both led to and resulted from enormous resources being directed to the acquisition and development of arms and armies. The estimated financial losses to Arab countries from the first (Iran-Iraq) and second Gulf wars and the Lebanese and Yemeni civil wars are estimated at US$904 billion, of which Iraq's share was US$422 billion.[14] In Lebanon, material losses—in terms of infrastructure destroyed or decayed during the sixteen years of war—were estimated at between US$25 billion and US$30 billion, equivalent to between ten to twelve times the national income of the country at the end of the war.

Military expenditures in the region were about 7% of GDP in 1996, significantly higher than in any other region of the world, and nearly three times the global average. Compared to other regions of the world, the ratio of military expenditures to health and education expenditures—at 108%—was the highest in 1990–91.

Gender Inequality

Despite rapid progress in building women's capabilities, wide disparities persist between males and females in the Arab region. Compared to other regions, only

South Asia suffers greater gender inequalities in education. Though school combined first-, second-, and third-level enrollment rates improved compared to male rates, they still stood at only 85% of male enrollment in 1997.

While Arab women have expanded their capabilities through more education, health gains, lower fertility, etc., their access to opportunities is still very limited. In general, women have been more successful in overcoming barriers to building their capabilities than in surmounting obstacles to using these capabilities. Though Arab women's participation in the labor force increased, only 19.2% of Arab women above the age of fifteen were economically active in 1997. This is significantly lower than the proportion of women's participation in the region with the second-lowest female economic activity rate, South Asia.

Even lower is women's share of decision-making positions in government and business. Women hold 3.7% of seats in Arab countries compared to a still very low world average of 12%. In the nine Arab countries for which data is available they constitute only 8.6% of administrators and managers, and 31% of professional and technical workers. Lack of political and economic participation is reflected in the low rankings of Arab countries, according to the Gender Empowerment Measure (GEM), which accounts for women's share of parliamentary seats, administrative, managerial, professional, and technical jobs as well as income (Annex Table 8). Arab countries for which data is available are among the lowest third of the 102 countries ranked according to the GEM.

Lack of political commitment to address gender inequality is evident at various levels. Only a few countries have made an investment in closing gender gaps among the priorities of their social plans. Nine Arab countries have neither signed nor acceded to the Convention on the Elimination of all Forms of Discrimination Against Women. Arab countries represent one third of the countries that have not ratified this convention. Arab women still face legal inequalities. For example, women in some Arab countries need their husbands' consent to earn income outside the home and to travel abroad. Arab women married to foreigners cannot transfer citizenship to their husbands, though men in similar situations can.

Policy Recommendations

Arab countries need to correct development imbalances in order to more effectively translate wealth into human development, to sustain progress and carry it further. Gains of the past are threatened due to a slow-down of growth.

Political commitment to people-centered development that translates into greater capabilities and opportunities for citizens of Arab countries is critical.

The commitment should be to well-defined and monitorable human development and poverty-reduction objectives.

Nietzsche observed that the most common human error is not being clear about what the objective of human action is. What is the objective of development in the Arab states? Is it to increase national wealth? To accelerate growth? Or to enhance human development in order to ensure people's capabilities and well-being?

From a human development perspective the answer is clear. Development aims at expanding the choices available to people, including living a long and healthy life, receiving education and knowledge, and enjoying a decent standard of living. Of course increasing wealth and income are critically important.

Box 4

Egypt: Addressing Regional Disparities in Human Development

Egypt's National Human Development Reports (NHDRs) have used disaggregated HDIs and other disaggregated human development indicators to analyze rural-urban inequalities, regional disparities, and gender gaps. The Reports became useful decision-support tools for national and sub-national policy making, for resource allocation and for the monitoring of progress. Since the country published its first report, all 26 of its governors have been meeting to jointly examine disparities in human development among and within governorates, and they have come up with fresh strategies to reduce them. They shifted development priorities and reallocated resources to under-served areas. The governors established a Platform for Action and Monitoring to assess progress in reducing human development disparities using the findings and indicators in the National Human Development Reports a basis for analysis. It is also worth noting that the reports are used as a source of policy analysis by the People's Assembly and the Shora Council, the two Egyptian houses of parliament.

Turkey was the first country to use disaggregated HDIs. Today NHDRs for several Arab states present disaggregated HDIs, including Lebanon and Jordan's forthcoming NHDR.

Most people gain from reform that seeks to advance human development and reduce poverty. There are also bound to be those who rightly or wrongly perceive that they will lose from such reform, at least in the short-term. Policy research and analysis can help inform and mobilize potential beneficiaries to support reform. In many cases these people are unorganized/unmobilized or simply unaware of their potential gains. Of course there are individuals and groups who support human development for the public or moral good rather than for securing their own rights or vested interests. They are natural allies of reform for human development.

Resistance to human-development reform comes from those who perceive that they will lose from it. Analysis and research for human development should also help address misperceptions of those who wrongly expect to lose from reform. There are also reforms for human development where everyone wins now and in the future. It is important to identify such positive-sum cases that are often perceived as zero-sum. They should be accorded the high priority they deserve.

However, they are necessary but not sufficient conditions. They are means to more important ends.

To effectively reduce poverty there is a need for mobilizing broad support, by drawing on the strengths and capabilities of an extensive network of actors in government, academia, the media, the private sector, voluntary and non-governmental organizations, and social services. The power of ideas has been underestimated so often. Political commitment needs to be backed by research and policy analysis that identifies problems, diagnoses their causes, and presents options for policy makers highlighting the trade-offs and costs of each option. An increasingly dynamic and constructive civil society in the Arab region, including public and non-governmental think tanks and research institutions, promises to effectively provide intellectual and analytical ammunition for operationalizing the commitment to human development. Many of these institutions contribute to studies, reports, and publications as well as advocacy that seeks to contribute to national debates and impact policy. The thirteen National Human Development Reports that UNDP has supported in the region since 1994 are a case in point. The analysis, analytical tools, and indices presented in these reports can assist policy makers. For example, the analysis made possible by the use of the disaggregated HDIs should help guide policy and action to address gaps and inequalities by refocusing public expenditure (or aid allocations) to regions with low HDI rankings, as has happened in Egypt (Box 4).

In addressing the political economy obstacles and in building coalitions for human development and poverty reduction, it is useful to recognize that governments and institutional agents for development within and outside governments are not monolithic. They often include both potential winners and potential losers. Five essential actions are needed to accelerate human development and poverty eradication:

Empowerment
Empowering individuals, households, and communities to gain greater control over their life and resources by:

Ensuring access to assets as a protection against vulnerability
Access to credit and other financial services is vital, as is security of tenure, especially for housing and land. Credit, and particularly formal credit, is hardly accessible to most of the poor as they are asset-deprived and hence with little or no collateral. Credit remains overly concentrated on larger enterprise. In Lebanon for example in 1993, a very small fraction of borrowers (0.2%) received about 21.4% of loans, while 77% received only 6.5%. What hinders the access of many small-scale entrepreneurs and mini-firms to credit is their

inability to provide bank requirements such as feasibility studies and business plans. In Egypt, for example, about 95% of small enterprises do not even have a bank account. Poor women are doubly disadvantaged due to social norms. Access to credit is only marginally improved by social (including kinship) networks, and the expansion of formal banking facilities and state-funded rural credit. The poor largely have no alternative to informal credit facilities that provide them with an important coping mechanism against vulnerability. However, most of these mechanisms are costly.

The misperception that supporting micro-enterprises requires the provision of credit at interest rates below market rates is pervasive in the region. This raises the costs of micro-credit schemes and undermines their reach, scale, and sustainability. In Egypt, for instance, assistance from government-sponsored schemes, NGOs, and outside donors reaches only 5% of possible beneficiaries. While subsidizing credit limits its coverage and makes it attractive for political manipulation, it ignores the fact that market interest rates are not the constraint binding micro-entrepreneurs from accessing credit. Lacking access, they often pay interest as high as 100%. In comparison, an unsubsidized interest rate of 28% is cheap.

Countries such as Lebanon are trying to use retail financing through banks or companies, operating in a competitive environment to enhance the access of micro and small entrepreneurs to credit. This is the most likely to be effective, as shown by recent developments.[15] Establishing public guarantors of small and medium loans, as is happening in Lebanon at the national level and in Egypt under the social fund, should be approached with caution because it carries the risk of moral hazard and unsustainability.

One means of easing this constraint is to find better mechanisms to account for the poor's assets in order to use them as collateral. De Soto estimates that informal assets in Egypt account for $240 billion or three times annual GDP. The poor have no formal titles to these assets that include dwellings. Mobilizing even a fraction of these assets for credit purposes would help the poor access credit.

Land reforms that swept through the region after World War II helped improve land distribution. Inequality of land distribution as measured by the Gini has been reduced in a number of Arab countries since the 1950s. Between the 1950s and 80s, the Gini coefficient of land ownership in Egypt, for example, declined from 0.50 to 0.35, and in Iraq it declined from 0.76 to 0.35. This has contributed to the decline of inequality. However, the reforms were less effective in reducing poverty as they primarily benefited the rural middle or lower-middle classes rather than the poor. Most of the poor are left with no land or unproductive land, as over 90% of the land in Arab states is arid or semi-arid. Desertification further undermines the availability of land. In

Yemen, for example, 97% of the land suffers from desertification, albeit to different degrees.

Land redistribution does not seem to be an option, due to political considerations and the fact that fragmentation of ownership, largely due to inheritance laws, is already a problem hindering optimal exploitation of land. A more promising means to enhance poor people's benefits from land would be to improve the security of tenure to induce more sustainable use of land and facilitate its use as collateral. De Soto's above-mentioned recommendations seem relevant. However, they should be applied selectively to avoid cases where formalizing land tenure might hurt poor people, e.g. common lands in the Horn of Africa that do not have ownership titles and are used by the poor through traditional rights. Strengthening land markets that are nearly non-existent in many Arab countries should also help poor people sell land in time of hardship and purchase it in time of prosperity as an investment.

Land-reclamation plans such as those in Upper Egypt promise to fill part of the gap. The opportunity cost of the large investments they require needs to be given special consideration. Government action is needed to improve access to, and control over, resources such as agricultural research and extension, and the supply of agricultural inputs—needed for the efficient utilization of existing land by poor people.

Food security

Ensuring food security for households and all their members is a basic aspect of human development. For many years, policies aiming at food security in the region have focused on increasing the supply of foodstuffs rather than improving poor people's access to food by raising their entitlements and securing even geographical distribution of foodstuffs. Famines in Sudan in the 1980s were partly a consequence of policies fixated on increasing production and supply rather than securing access, entitlements, and distribution. While western Sudan suffered a famine, food stocks lingered elsewhere in the country.

A less dramatic variation on the theme of overemphasis on food supply at the expense of access and entitlements is evident in the very high levels of caloric and protein intake in many Arab countries that are incommensurate with their low nutritional levels. There is a need now to re-orient policy towards focussing on poor people's access and entitlements rather than just supply. This calls for a more balanced approach, and does not imply that food supply and production are not immensely important.

Food production in the region is still far below population needs. High caloric intake levels come at a considerable cost. The Arab region remains heavily dependent on food imports. It is estimated that by the year 2000, the per capita share of food imports will rise from $100 to $300 annually. Although the Arab states account for 4% of the world's population, they import 13% of the food and 20% of the cereals traded in international markets.

Consumer food subsidies have been a major means for enhancing food security in many Arab countries. Their objectives have varied from securing universal access to basic foodstuffs (Egypt and Morocco), to reducing poverty by protecting the purchasing power of the poor, to improving their nutritional levels and providing them with in-kind transfers (Tunisia since the early 1990s).

To enhance the effectiveness of food subsidies in combating poverty there is a need to identify poverty reduction as a primary goal; to integrate food-subsidy programs into national development and poverty-reduction strategies; and to apply targeting mechanisms, particularly self-targeting (using goods with negative income elasticity as vehicles for food subsidies). Tunisia and Egypt have gained considerable experience with self-targeting that could be useful not only for targeting food subsidies but also for other types of public spending, e.g., on the social sectors to increase their coverage of poor people and reduce leakage to the non-poor. Replacing food subsidies with income transfers could also be considered, since the latter allow the poor to spend the government's assistance on whatever they need most rather than limiting their choices to food. Income transfers are more useful in countries that have the capacity to target transfers through administrative means, e.g., by using means testing.

Education and health

Ensuring education and health for all, along with access to reproductive health care, family planning,, and safe water and sanitation are major human-develop-

Table 7.4. Some Arab countries have already reached some of the
     human development goals for 2000 and beyond

Goal	*Number of Arab states reaching goal*
Life expectancy above 70 years	6
Under-five mortality rate below 70 per 1000 live births	13
Net primary enrollment ratio of 100%	2
Girl's primary enrollment equal to or greater than boys'	3
Countries in region	19

Note: The life expectancy goal is for 2005 (ICPD 1994), the under-five mortality goal for 2000 (WSSD 1995), the enrollment goal for 2000 (UNESCO 1996c), and the girls' primary enrollment goal for 2005 (WSSD 1995).

Source: For life expectancy, UN 1996, for under-five mortality rate, UNICEF 1997; and for net enrollment, UNESCO 1996.

ment objectives. These goals need to be achieved within a decade or two, not post-poned for another generation. Commitments made at UN—sponsored confer-ences during the 1990s, such as the World Summit for Social Development, pro-vide what. Arab governments need to accord these commitments the priority they deserve. Some Arab countries have already reached their targets (Table 7.4).

Governments need to adopt targets that better reflect their resources and aspirations. For example, the goal of nine years of basic education for all chil-dren seems to be feasible for most Arab countries. By 2010 in all countries, minimum enrollment rates should reach 100% for primary school, 70% for secondary school, and 25% for higher education. The annual cost of achieving this expansion (adjusted for population growth, higher teacher salaries, and modest quality improvements) is about US$16 billion in Egypt, Jordan, Morocco, and Tunisia in 2010—three times their spending in 1990.[16]

To enhance the impact of social spending on human development there is a need to increase the share of investments, as opposed to recurrent expenditures in social spending. In Yemen, for example, expenditures to cover recurrent costs absorbed the lion's share of spending on education (93% on average between 1992–96 compared with only 7% for investment in education).[17] On average 90% of recurrent education expenditures in the region are allocated to human resources.

In Arab countries with middle and low human development, there is a strong case to be made for restructuring public spending on education to refocus on the primary and secondary levels, and public spending on health to ensure full coverage of preventive health measures. Resources re-allocated towards basic education should be targeted to the poor and to enhance the quality and effec-tiveness of public education. Resources could be focussed on human develop-ment priorities through intra-sectoral re-allocations (e.g., from tertiary to basic education) and inter-sectoral re-allocations (e.g., from military expenditures to human development priority concerns) and by privatization of loss-making inefficient public enterprises. Since the resource position is tight, a lot can be achieved by sidestepping prestigious development projects and by focussing instead on essential development priorities. Subsidies should be reserved for social programs that reach the masses rather than benefit a few—i.e., primary health care services instead of urban hospitals, basic education instead of uni-versities. In Lebanon's education sector this is already taking place (where high-er education is mostly private), and to a lesser extent in Jordan as well, where one-fifth of tertiary-education enrollments are in private institutions.

The 20/20 initiative supported by UNDP calls for the allocation of 20% of public spending to basic social services and 20% to aid allocations. Public expenditure reviews undertaken as part of this initiative, as in Lebanon, or as part of National Human Development Reports, as in Egypt, have often revealed imbalances in social-sector allocations as well as the significance of private spending. In Lebanon, for example, 50% of expenditures on health care were found to be private (around 12% of GDP)[18] and two-thirds of pre-university students were enrolled in private schools.[19] There is a need to increase private sector involvement in the social sectors. Yemen's *National Human Development Report*, for example, calls for the private sector to contribute 3–40% of private investments in education.

Social safety nets

Another priority is strengthening social safety nets to prevent people from falling into destitution, and to rescue them from disaster. Safety net and welfare programs usually include subsidies on basic consumer goods such as food, water, and energy, as well as direct assistance in the form of family allowances and cash transfers. As mentioned above, some programs have substantial leakage and limited impact on the poor because they do not establish a link between eligibility and poverty. State retrenchment in the last decade has strained safety net programs.

Government action is needed to improve the efficiency of social safety nets and welfare programs through improved targeting to the poor. Self-targeting by focusing subsidies on inferior goods or services, is particularly promising because of its low administrative costs.

Private philanthropy, emanating from the religious and cultural traditions of the region, could be more effectively tapped and targeted for the eradication of poverty. Currently much of private philanthropy goes to charitable transfers, in kind or in income, that are used for consumption rather than for investments contributing to lasting, sustainable benefits.

In assessing and publicizing performance in advancing food security, health, education, social safety nets, etc., governments need to refocus on results and outcomes rather than inputs. Overemphasis on the latter seems to prevail currently. This is manifest in government plans and progress reports, which often focus on how much was spent or constructed in one social sector or another, e.g. how many schools were built. While important, it is equally if not more important to monitor the results and benefits accruing to people from these inputs, e.g. to what degree did the new schools reduce the school dropout rate or improve literacy.

Gender Equality

Improving gender equality to empower women and to release their vast under-used energy and creativity is another priority. Because of significant gender gaps in the region, poverty eradication without gender equality is impossible and a contradiction in terms. Among key priorities are equal access to education and health, to job opportunities, and to land and credit, and actions to end domestic violence. Upholding gender equality is not an act of benevolence but is needed for the progress of the Arab states. The Arab people cannot succeed with half their population denied equal capabilities and opportunities. To accelerate the pace of progress on gender issues, Arab countries should adopt a strong agenda for policy action. Action is needed especially for: setting a firm timetable to end legal discrimination and establishing a framework for the promotion of legal equality; taking concrete action to restructure social and institutional norms; fixing certain threshold targets to gain momentum for complete gender equality; implementing key programs for universal female education, improved reproductive health and more credit for women; and mobilizing national and international efforts to target programs that enable people—particularly women—to gain greater access to economic and political opportunities.

Re-allocating resources to the advancement of women's education and economic participation offers one of the easiest ways to reduce poverty, as the recent experience of Morocco and Tunisia has shown. Poor human development indicators can be attributed partly to neglect of female education and the failure to capture the considerable externalities from educating girls—in health and economic growth. The financial cost of closing the gender gap in education in the Arab region is estimated at less than 1% of GDP.[20]

Empowering women should have positive-multiplier effects on other aspects of human development. Studies show that income is more likely to be spent on human development when women control the cash. The fact that even in one of the most gender-equal societies in the region, Lebanon, salaries of males are between 27% and 50% higher than salaries of females does not contribute to improving women's autonomy.[21]

The greatest challenge for policy aiming at gender equality lies in advancing women's equal rights and political and economic participation. As mentioned before, progress in advancing women's political participation has lagged behind progress in advancing their capabilities. Experience during the past few months in Kuwait, Egypt, and Morocco highlights the challenges facing gender emancipation within democratic systems in the region. In the three cases, parliaments resisted bills introduced by governments to allow women to participate in elections in Kuwait, and to enhance personal rights in Egypt and Morocco.

Pro-Poor Growth
Higher growth is essential for sustaining human development and reducing poverty. Moving from zero growth to 1% annual growth rate would reduce the

number of poor in the region by about seven million over the next decade. Without faster growth and with the continuation of past growth patterns, the number of people living on less than US$1 a day would rise to about fifteen million by 2010. The World Bank estimates that a minimum of 1.2% average annual growth in real consumption is needed for the MENA region to halve poverty (i.e., percentage of the population living on less than US$2 per day) in 25 years.[22]

The pattern and type of growth is as important as its rate. In several Arab countries in the past few decades, growth has coincided with increasing poverty. In Egypt, for example, between 1981–96 and in Sudan between 1968–78, moderate growth (0–4% in GDP per capita) has coincided with rising poverty.[23] Arab countries cannot afford growth that is jobless, voiceless, ruthless, rootless, and futureless.

Job creation is critical if income growth is to effectively improve peoples' lives. Public policy promoting labor intensive growth is needed. Otherwise, income growth does not automatically contribute to employment opportunities. An analysis of the experience of about one hundred countries during the eighties showed that in only about a third was growth associated with an expansion in employment opportunities (measured as the difference between the growth rate of employment minus the growth rate of the labor force). In about a fifth of the cases employment opportunities contracted despite growing income.[24]

Employment creation and opportunity expansion are high priorities of economic policy. Jobs for about 50 million new entrants into the Arab work force will have to be found by 2010. If current trends continue, the number of unemployed will more than double to fifteen million by then. New job-seekers will have to compete with the more than half a billion entrants into the world's labor force. Most of the latter will be earning wages below the average for the Arab region, nearly all of them will have attended primary school, and more than 150 million of them will have completed secondary school. The outcome of the competition will be determined to a large extent by the effectiveness of human development efforts in the Arab region. In order to maintain living standards, Arab countries will have to improve labor productivity and raise female participation in the labor force. All this highlights the strong link between human resource development and globalization. The link needs to be strengthened by addressing the mismatch between the outputs of the Arab education systems and the demands of national and international markets.

Globalization

Since 1981 growth of merchandise trade in the Arab states has been lower than in any other region, and the terms of trade have deteriorated faster than in other regions, except Latin America and the Caribbean.

In 1997–98, the share of Arab countries in international trade declined to less than 3%. For Arab countries, the share of manufacturers in their total reports has been picking exports up slowly. However, it is still miniscule with 260 million people. The value of Arab-manufactured exports is equal to that of Finland, which has a population of only five million people.

Arab countries have been unable to use national capital domestically (capital from the region invested abroad is about US$600–800 billion). They attracted only less than 3% of foreign investment.

Selective management of liberalization is needed that gives priority to the interests of poor people, rather than to liberalization dogma. Trade and capital flows need to be managed more carefully, and national governments should exercise more discretion when adopting policies of liberalization. A selective approach to the global market would follow the example of most East Asian economies—with time-bound, performance-related protection for potentially viable industries, some industrial intervention and some management of foreign capital flows. This should help increase and diversify exports, which will help meet future import requirements, such as food, and to reverse past trends.

To increase their share of international financial flows, Arab countries need to streamline and clarify their regulations, and put needed financial information in the international arena to attract investors. Easing unnecessary restrictions while building a system that addresses the needs of national and foreign investments is essential in most countries.

The prospects for reducing the debt burden of highly indebted Arab countries through inter-Arab or international agreements should be explored. Arrangements by which the Paris Club creditors of Poland and Egypt agreed to reduce their debt service commitments by half, provides a precedent worth repeating.

Strategy

A strategy for poverty eradication must focus not only on what needs to be done, but on how to ensure that action is taken as well. This requires such fundamental reforms as the promotion of political participation by all, ensuring accountability and transparency in government, preventing the criminalization of politics, promoting a free flow of information and freedom of the press, and ensuring a strong role for community groups and NGOs in policy-making and legislative decision-making. The legitimacy and strength of the state are based on its capacity to mobilize and be mobilized in the fight against poverty.

Mainstreaming human development and poverty reduction within national economic policy is needed. The economic priorities of structural adjustment sideline too often human development and poverty reduction. Countries that have reduced poverty while adjusting have shown that poverty reduction should be part of the goals and the process of structural adjustment (Box 5). This has now been accepted as a principle of international policy on adjustment, though it is not yet always practiced.

Various countries follow, and should follow, different paths for making policy and plans to improve human development and reduce poverty. Several elements are usually essential. At the World Summit for Social Development (WSSD) in 1995, most Arab countries committed themselves to address the following elements of a poverty-reduction strategy. Compared to other regions, Arab states by 1998 had the lowest rate of implementation of some of the most important poverty-reduction commitments made at the Social Summit.

Estimating the incidence of poverty

This is an important step towards assessing the problem and mobilizing the commitment and resources to address it. Four years after the WSSD, only half of the Arab states had poverty estimates. Some of the countries that have figures, such as Morocco and Sudan, still rely on estimates made in the early 1990s (Annex Table 11).

Estimating the incidence of poverty requires the identification of poverty and poor people. This should help address the ambiguity that has often shrouded the problem of poverty in the region. Government pronouncements and the media often skirt the issue. While terms such as "people with limited income" (*mahdoudi al-dakhl*) are commonly used, direct reference to poor people is rarely made.

Planning for poverty eradication

Arab governments also committed themselves to the goal of eradicating poverty and to "formulate or strengthen as a matter of urgency, ... national policies and strategies geared to substantially reducing overall poverty in the shortest possible time, reducing inequalities and eradicating absolute poverty." Three years later in 1998, only four Arab countries had explicit national poverty plans in place and another six had national poverty plans under-development (Table 7.5). Experience shows the value of developing plans and programs of action focused on priority groups and priority sectors.

Poverty plans should be backed by national assessments of the main causes of poverty, together with a strategy document that identifies targets and sets out the policies and actions needed to eradicate poverty. Experience shows the value of developing programs of action focused on priority groups and priority sectors, and of budgetary commitments to the allocation of resources needed to keep the strategy on track. A priority is to enhance the effectiveness of spending aimed at reducing poverty both to improve its impact and as the best argument for increasing such spending. Plan implementation needs to be monitored against targets to assess progress, guide corrections when the strategy goes off track and maintain public awareness and support.

Table 7.5. Poverty Planning

Explicit National Poverty Plan in Place		Explicit National Poverty Plan under Development		No Plan, but Poverty Reduction in National Planning	
130 dev'g countries	15 Arab countries	130 dev'g countries	15 Arab countries	130 dev'g countries	15 Arab countries
43	4	40	6	35	2
33%	27%	31%	40%	27%	12%

Setting targets

For poverty-reduction efforts to be activated and monitored and for resources to be allocated, there is a need for objectives to be set through a participatory process. A core set of measurable and time-bound targets is critical for mobilizing support and monitoring implementation. Setting such targets is also a major commitment made by most Arab countries at the Social Summit. The Arab states have the lowest rate of implementation with only one eighth having set poverty reduction targets.[25] Three Arab states adopted targets for extreme-poverty reduction and another three for overall poverty reduction (Table 7.6).

Targets should be set to reduce human poverty also, not only income poverty. While most policy-makers in the region and their national and foreign advisers agree that poverty is multidimensional, the measures they use for identifying

Table 7.6. Poverty Targets

Target for Extreme Poverty Reduction		Target for Overall Poverty Reduction	
130 dev'g countries	15 Arab countries	130 dev'g countries	15 Arab countries
44	44	45	3
34%	320%	35%	20%

Box 5

Structural Adjustment with a Tunisian Face

With one of the lowest rates of absolute poverty in the developing world, Tunisia's progress in reducing deprivation has been impressive. Its continuation during a period of stabilization and adjustment has been particularly remarkable. Stabilization and adjustment started in 1986 to reverse the growth of budget and balance of payments deficits, which grew, respectively, to 5.6% and 7.9% of GDP between 1980 and 1986. By 1986 a balance of payment crisis seemed imminent. To avert the crisis, the current account deficit was reduced through demand management (tighter fiscal and monetary policies and exchange rate adjustment). The stabilization program was largely successful not only in balancing the budget and the current account but also in resuming growth. Devaluation of the exchange rate and a fall in investment narrowed the current account deficit from 8% of GDP in 1986 to 4% in 1993. The net budget deficit was more than halved from 5.6% of GDP in 1986 to 2.6% in 1993. Despite lower investment, annual GDP growth was higher in 1987–93, at 4.7% than during 1980–86, at 3.6% a year.

The poor were largely protected from the rise in unemployment, which accompanied the contractionary policies. Many poor people benefited as changes in incentives associated with adjustment promoted growth in sectors relying on unskilled labor (textiles, clothing, leather products, tourism and simple offshore activities). Most jobs generated were at low wages and for unskilled and temporary workers.

Moreover, the poor benefited from an increase in well targeted social spending, which the government managed while achieving fiscal adjustment. While the government was halving the budget deficit from 5.3% of GDP in 1986 to 2.6% in 1993, it was increasing per capita social spending between 1987 and 1993/94 by 14% in real terms—from 47.5% to 52.5% of gross government expenditures. As a share of GDP, social spending rose from 18.3% to 20.9% during the most severe period of stabilization, 1987–89.

All this contributed to an improvement income distribution, which further helped poverty reduction. The Gini coefficient fell from 43.4% in 1985 to 40.1% in 1990. In 1985, the richest decal of the population accounted for 33.9% of total expenditures, and the bottom decal for only 2.2%. In 1990, this disparity was reduced, with the richest decal accounting for 30.5% and the poorest for 2.3%.

Moreover, in 1990, average expenditures for both groups were closer to mean expenditures than in 1985. Real consumption expenditure per capita increased by 10% during 1985–90. Roughly two-thirds of the decrease in poverty is attributable to the growth in mean consumption, and the rest to improved income distribution.

Unlike many countries implementing stabilization and structural-adjustment policies, Tunisia succeeded in combining them with sustained human development and poverty reduction. In Tunisia structural adjustment had a human face. And future prospects are promising. Based on the current poverty line standards, a moderate increase in the rate of growth of mean consumption of about 2.5% a year, combined with continued improvement in equality consistent with recent trends, could eliminate income/consumption poverty in Tunisia by the year 2000.

Sources: UNDP 1996, World Bank 1995, Bedouin and Gouia 1995.

and aggregating poverty and for setting targets for its reduction are unidimensional—based on income (or expenditures) only. Income-based measures of poverty are particularly inappropriate for the region because, as mentioned before, human poverty in terms of the Human Poverty Index (HPI) is much higher than income poverty at regional and national levels.

Policies in the Arab states should aim at creating a virtuous cycle of growth sustaining human development and human development sustaining economic growth. The path to a virtuous circle starts with a focus on people. The backlog of deprivation must be tackled if growth is to be resumed on a sustainable basis. The need for tackling this deprivation is particularly urgent in the case of the Arab countries with low human development. As the 1996 *Human Development Report* shows, every country that was able to combine and sustain both rapid human development and rapid growth did so by accelerating advancements in human development first, as in the case of China and Indonesia, or simultaneously with economic growth, as in the case of Botswana. In contrast, countries that relied primarily on economic growth to get them to a situation where growth and human development became mutually reinforcing failed in their efforts, as lack of human development kept undermining their growth process. Human development is a precondition for sustained economic growth. And poverty reduction is needed for both.

Glossary of Poverty and Human Development

Human Poverty
Denial of choices and opportunities most basic to human development, reflected in a short life, lack of basic education, lack of material means, exclusion, and a lack of freedom and dignity. Human poverty is:

- Multidimensional rather than unidimensional;
- People-centered, focusing on the quality of human life rather than on material possessions.

Human Poverty Index
The human poverty index (HPI) measures deprivation in basic human development in the same dimensions as the HDI. The variables used to show these dimensions are the percentage of people expected to die before age 40, the percentage of adults who are illiterate, and the overall economic provisioning in terms of the percentage of people without access to health services and safe water and the percentage of underweight children under five.

Human Development
The process of expanding people's choices and the level of well-being they achieve are at the core of the notion of human development. Such choices are neither finite nor static. But regardless of the level of development, the three essentials include the ability to lead a long and healthy life, to acquire knowledge, and to have access to the resources needed for a decent standard of living. Human development does not end there, however. People also highly value political, economic, and social freedom, opportunities for being creative and productive, self-respect and guaranteed human rights. Income is a means, with human development the end.

Human Development Index
A composite index, the HDI measures the average achievements in a country through three basic dimensions of human development: longevity, knowledge and a decent standard of living. The variables used to show these dimensions are life expectancy, educational attainment and real gross domestic product per capita.

Gender-Related Development Index
The gender-related development index (GDI) measures achievements in the same dimensions and variables as the HDI does, but takes account of inequali-

ty in achievement between women and men. The greater the gender disparity in basic human development, the lower a country's GDI compared with its HDI. The GDI is simply the HDI adjusted downward for gender inequality.

Gender Empowerment Measure

The gender empowerment measure indicates whether women are able to actively participate in economic and political life. It focuses on participation, measuring gender inequality in key areas of economic and political participation and decision-making. It thus differs from the GDI, an indicator of gender inequality in basic capabilities.

Incidence of Poverty

The incidence of poverty is an estimate of the percentage of people below the poverty line. It does not indicate anything about the depth or severity of poverty and thus does not capture any worsening conditions of those already in poverty.

Poverty Lines

Poverty lines for international comparison

A poverty line set at US$1 a day per person is used by the World Bank for international comparison. This poverty line is based on consumption of goods and services. A poverty line of $2 a day is suggested for Latin America and the Caribbean. For Eastern Europe and the republics of the former Soviet Union, a poverty line of $4 a day has been used. For comparison with industrialized countries, a poverty line corresponding to the US poverty line of $14.40 a day per person has been used.

National poverty lines

Developing countries that have set national poverty lines have generally used the "food poverty" method. These lines indicate insufficient economic resources to meet basic minimum food needs. In industrialized countries, national poverty lines are used to measure relative poverty. The European Commission has suggested a poverty line for these countries as half the median, adjusted personal income.

Table A7.1. Human Development Index and Aspects of Human Development

	Human Dev Index rank 1997	Human Dev. Index 1997	Life Exp (yrs) At Birth 1977	Adult Literacy Rate (%) 1997	Combined 1st, 2nd, 3rd level Gross Enrollment Ration (%) 1997	Real GDP per capita (PPP$) 1997	Real GDP per capita (PPP$) Rank Minus HDI Rank (a)
High Human Development							
Kuwait	35	0.833	75.9	80.4	57	25,314	-30
Bahrain	37	0.832	72.9	86.2	81	16,527	-8
Qatar	41	0.814	71.7	80	71	20,987	-23
United Arab Emirates	43	0.812	74.8	74.8	69	19,115	-18
Medium Human Development							
Libyan Arab Jamahiriya	65	0.756	70	76.5	92	6697	-6
Lebanon	69	0.749	69.9	84.4	76	5940	-4
Saudi Arabia	78	0.74	71.4	73.4	56	10,120	-37
Oman	89	0.725	70.9	67.1	58	9960	-47
Jordan	94	0.715	70.1	87.2	66	3450	2
Tunisia	102	0.695	69.5	67	70	5300	-34
Algeria	109	0.665	68.9	60.3	68	4460	-31
Syrian Arab Republic	111	0.663	68.9	71.6	60	3250	-11
Egypt	120	0.616	66.3	52.7	72	3050	-14
Iraq	125	0.586	62.4	58	51	3197	-22
Morocco	126	0.582	66.6	45.9	49	3310	-27
Low Human Development							
Sudan	142	0.475	55	53.3	34	1560	-7
Yemen	148	0.449	58	42.5	49	810	18
Djibouti	157	0.412	50.4	48.3	21	1266	-7
Somalia*	175	0.184 – 0.159	42	15.5	10.5	650	—
All developing countries		0.637	64.4	71.4	59	3240	—
Arab States		0.626	65.1	58.6	59	4094	—
World		**0.706**	**66.7**	**78.0**	**63**	**6332**	—

Note: * UNDP, *Somalia National Human Development Report, 1998* (Figures are for 1995–97)

Source: UNDP, *Human Development Report 1999*

Table A7.2. Poverty

HDI rank 1997	Human poverty index (HPI-1) 1997 Rank	Value(%)	National Estimate Extreme	National Estimate Overall	Survey year	Population below $1 a day %	International Poverty Line Poverty gap at $1 a day %	Population below $2 a day %	Poverty gap at $2 a day %
High Human Development									
35 Kuwait	—	—					—		—
37 Bahrain	10	9.8					—		—
41 Qatar	—	—					—		—
43 United Arab Emirates	27	17.7					—		—
Medium Human Development									
65 Libyan Arab Jamahiriya	22	16.4					—		—
69 Lebanon	14	11.3					—		—
78 Saudi Arabia	—	—		35% (1996)*			—		—
89 Oman	39	23.7	7% (1993)				—		—
94 Jordan	9	9.8		21% (1993)	1992	2.5	0.5	23.5	6.3
102 Tunisia	38	23.1	6% (1997)		1990	3.9	0.9	22.7	6.8
109 Algeria	52	28.8	6% (1995)	14% (1995)	1995	<2	—	17.6	4.4
111 Syrian Arab Republic	32	20.1					—		—
120 Egypt	57	33.0	7% (1996)	23% (1996)	1990–91	7.6	1.1	51.9	15.3
125 Iraq	—	—					—		—
126 Morocco	67	39.2	7% (1990/91)	13% (1990/91)	1990–91	<2	—	19.6	4.6
Low Human Development									
142 Sudan	61	36.8		85% (1992)			—		—
148 Yemen	78	49.2	16% (1998)	30% (1998)			—		—
157 Djibouti	69	40.8	10% (1996)	45% (1996)			—		—
All developing countries		27.7							
Arab States		32.4							
World		—							

Source: Columns 1–2: UNDP, *Human Development Report 1999*; Columns 3–4: UNDP, *Poverty Report*, Forthcoming; Columns 5–9: World Bank, *World Development Indicators*, 1999

* Unsatisfied Basic Needs

Table A7.3. Progress in Survival

HDI rank 1997	Life expectancy at birth (years)		Infant mortality rate (per 1,000 live births)		Under-five mortality rate (per 1,000 live births)	
	1970	1997	1970	1997	1970	1997
High Human Development						
35 Kuwait	65.9	75.9	49	12	59	13
37 Bahrain	61.8	72.9	67	18	93	22
41 Qatar	60.9	71.7	71	16	93	20
43 United Arab Emirates	60.7	74.8	61	9	83	10
Medium Human Development						
65 Libyan Arab Jamahiriya	51.5	70	105	22	160	25
69 Lebanon	64.1	69.9	40	30	50	37
78 Saudi Arabia	51.8	71.4	118	24	185	28
89 Oman	46.9	70.9	126	15	200	18
94 Jordan	54	70.1	77	20	107	24
102 Tunisia	53.7	69.5	135	27	201	33
109 Algeria	53	68.9	123	34	192	39
111 Syrian Arab Republic	55.5	68.9	90	27	129	33
120 Egypt	50.9	66.3	157	54	235	73
125 Iraq	54.9	62.4	90	94	127	122
126 Morocco	51.6	66.6	120	58	187	72
Low Human Development						
142 Sudan	42.6	55	107	73	177	115
148 Yemen	40.9	58	175	76	303	100
157 Djibouti	40	50.4	160	111	241	156
All developing countries	54.5	64.4	111	64	170	94
Arab States	50.6	65.1	125	53	192	70
World	59.1	66.7	98	58	149	85

Source: UNDP, *Human Development Report 1999*

Table A7.4. Food Security and Nutrition

HDI rank 1997	Daily per capita supply of calories 1970	1996	Daily per capita supply of protein Total (grams) 1996	Change (%) 1970–96	Daily per capita supply of fat Total (grams) 1996	Change (%) 1970–96	Food production per capita index (1989–91 =100) 1997	Food imports (as % of merchandise imports) 1997	Food consumption (as % of total household consumption) 1980–85
High Human Development									
35 Kuwait	—	3,075	98.3	31.1	97.1	38.3	157	16	—
37 Bahrain	—	—	—	—	—	—	117	12	—
41 Qatar	—	—	77.9	—	—	—	137	—	—
43 United Arab Emirates	3,196	3,366	104.8	—	108.3	40.7	190	—	—
Medium Human Development									
65 Libyan Arab Jamahiriya	2,439	3,132	71.8	19.7	112.6	50.1	101	18	—
69 Lebanon	2,330	3,279	82.6	40.0	107.4	67.6	119	17	—
78 Saudi Arabia	1,872	2,735	77.9	62.3	74.4	125.4	90	—	—
89 Oman	—	—	—	—	—	—	101	—	35
94 Jordan	2,415	2,681	69.2	4.8	79.4	32.3	151	11	37
102 Tunisia	2,221	3,250	87.6	43.6	84.9	49.2	150	32	—
109 Algeria	1,798	3,020	80.6	70.8	71.0	97.7	108	—	—
111 Syrian Arab Republic	2,317	3,339	86.7	35.5	92.1	50.8	133	—	49
120 Egypt	2,352	3,289	87.9	37.3	57.5	22.5	133	26	—
125 Iraq	2,254	2,252	45.2	-25.9	86.3	100.2	90	—	—
126 Morocco	2,404	3,244	85.8	32.0	65.1	51.6	95	17	38
Low Human Development									
142 Sudan	2,167	2,391	73.5	20.5	72.5	—	146	17	60
148 Yemen	1,763	2,041	54.3	6.5	38.2	31.8	121	—	·
157 Djibouti	1,842	1,920	39.0	-7.1	53.9	46.1	83	—	—
All developing countries	2,129	2,628	66.4	30.1	57.7	92.9	132	—	—
Arab States	2,206	2,907	77.4	27.2	70.2	51.1	120	—	—
World	2,336	2,751	73.5	26.5	70.4	79.0	124	—	—

Source: UNDP, *Human Development Report 1999*

Table A7.5. Education

HDI rank 1997	Adult literacy rate (%) 1997	Net enrolment ratio		Children not reaching grade 5 (%) 1992–95
		Primary (as % of relevant age group) 1997	Secondary (as % of relevant age group) 1997	
High Human Development				
35 Kuwait	80.4	65.2	63.2	—
37 Bahrain	86.2	98.2	87.2	1
41 Qatar	80.0	83.3	73.3	1
43 United Arab Emirates	74.8	82.0	77.8	2
Medium Human Development				
65 Libyan Arab Jamahiriya	76.5	99.9	99.9	—
69 Lebanon	84.4	76.1	—	11
78 Saudi Arabia	73.4	60.1	58.7	4
89 Oman	67.1	67.7	66.6	2
94 Jordan	87.2	—	—	9
102 Tunisia	67.0	99.9	74.3	6
109 Algeria	60.3	96.0	68.5	6
111 Syrian Arab Republic	71.6	94.7	42.3	6
120 Egypt	52.7	95.2	75.1	—
125 Iraq	—	74.6	42.9	—
126 Morocco	45.9	76.6	37.7	22
Low Human Development				
142 Sudan	53.3	—	—	—
148 Yemen	42.5	—	—	—
157 Djibouti	48.3	31.9	19.6	21
All developing countries	—	85.7	60.4	22
Arab States	—	86.4	61.7	10
World	—	87.6	65.4	—

Source: UNDP, *Human Development Report 1999*

Table A7.6. Resource Use

HDI rank 1997		Public expenditure on education (as % of GNP)		Public education expenditure				Public expenditure on health		Military expenditure (as % of GDP)	
				As % of GNP	As % of total government expenditure	Primary and secondary (as % of all levels)	Higher (as % of all levels)	As % of GNP	As % of GDP		
		1985	1996	1993–96	1993–96	1993–96	1993–96	1960	1995	1988	1996
High Human Development											
35	Kuwait	4.9	5.7	5.7	8.9	50.6	29.9	—	3.5	8.2	11.9
37	Bahrain	4.1	—	—	12.8	73.1	—	—	—	5.5	5.4
41	Qatar	4.1	3.4	3.4	—	—	—	—	—	—	—
43	United Arab Emirates	1.7	—	—	16.7	—	—	—	2	6.7	4.5
Medium Human Development											
65	Libyan Arab Jamahiriya	7.1	—	—	—	—	—	1.3	—	—	—
69	Lebanon	—	2.5	2.5	8.2	68.9	16.2	—	—	—	6.3
78	Saudi Arabia	6.7	—	—	17.0	82.2	17.8	0.6	—	17.6	13.2
89	Oman	4	—	—	17.8	98.8	—	0.6	—	20.1	13.2
94	Jordan	5.5	7.3	7.3	19.8	64.5	33.0	0.6	3.7	11.4	8.8
102	Tunisia	5.8	6.7	6.7	17.4	79.7	18.5	1.6	—	2.7	1.8
109	Algeria	8.5	5.2	5.2	16.4	95.3	25.9	1.2	—	1.9	3.4
111	Syrian Arab Republic	6.1	4.2	4.2	13.6	71.7	33.3	0.4	—	7.9	6.7
120	Egypt	6.3	—	—	—	66.7	—	0.6	—	4.5	—
125	Iraq	4	—	—	—	—	—	1	1.7	—	—
126	Morocco	6.3	5.3	5.3	24.9	83.4	16.5	1	—	4.1	3.9
Low Human Development											
142	Sudan	—	—	—	9.0	69.8	21.1	1	—	2	1.6
148	Yemen	—	6.1	6.1	20.8	—	—	—	1	—	—
157	Djibouti	2.7	—	—	12.7	—	—	—	—	—	—
	All developing countries	3.9	3.6	3.6	14.8	—	—	0.9	1.8	3.1	2.4
	Arab States	5.9	—	—	15.8	—	—	1	—	8.2	—
	World	4.9	4.8	4.8	12.7	—	—	—	5.5	4	2.4

Source: UNDP, *Human Development Report 1999*

Table A7.7. Gender-Related Development Index

Gender-related development index (GDI) rank	GDI Value	Life expectancy at birth (years) 1997		Adult literacy rate (%) 1997		Combined first, second and third-level gross enrolment ratio(%) 1997		HDI rank minus GDI rank (a)
		Female	Male	Female	Male	Female	Male	
High Human Development								
Kuwait	35	0.825	78.2	74.1	77.5	83.1	59	56	-1
Bahrain	38	0.813	75.3	71.1	80.7	89.9	84	79	-2
Qatar	41	0.796	75.4	70	81.2	79.6	74	69	-2
United Arab Emirates	45	0.79	76.5	73.9	76.8	73.9	72	66	-4
Medium Human Development								
Libyan Arab Jamahiriya	68	0.732	72.2	68.3	62.9	88.7	92	92	-9
Lebanon	66	0.734	71.1	68.1	78.3	91.2	77	76	-4
Saudi Arabia	78	0.703	73.4	69.9	62.5	81	53	58	-9
Oman	85	0.686	73.3	68.9	55	76.9	57	60	-8
Jordan	—	—	71.5	68.9	81.8	92.2	—	—	—
Tunisia	87	0.681	70.7	68.4	55.8	78.1	68	72	-2
Algeria	93	0.642	70.3	67.5	47.7	72.7	64	71	-1
Syrian Arab Republic	95	0.64	71.2	66.7	56.5	86.5	56	63	-1
Egypt	103	0.603	67.9	64.7	40.5	64.7	66	77	-2
Iraq	—	—	63.9	60.9	—	—	44	57	—
Morocco	106	0.565	68.5	54.8	32.7	59.3	42	55	-2
Low Human Development								
Sudan	117	0.453	56.4	53.6	41.3	65.4	31	37	0
Yemen	128	0.408	58.4	57.4	21	64.2	27	70	-6
Djibouti	—	—	52	48.7	35	62.2	17	24	—
All developing countries	—	0.360	66.1	63.0	62.9	80.0	55	64	—
Arab States	—	0.609	67.1	64.2	46.4	70.6	54	64	—
World	—	0.700	68.9	64.7	71.1	84.3	60	67	—

Source: UNDP, *Human Development Report 1999*

Table A7.8. Gender Empowerment Measure

	Gender Empowerment Measures (GEM)		Seats in Parliament held by women (as % of total)	Female administrators and managers (as % of total)	Female professional and technical workers (as % of total)	Women's real GDP per capita (PPP$)
	Rank	Value				
High Human Development						
Kuwait	72	0.355	0.0	5.2	36.8	13,481
Bahrain	—	—	—	—	—	5512
Qatar	—	—	—	—	—	5193
United Arab Emirates	96	0.239	0.0	1.6	25.1	4544
Medium Human Development						
Libyan Arab Jamahiriya	—	—	2.3	—	—	2373
Lebanon	—	—	—	—	—	2793
Saudi Arabia	—	—	—	—	—	2284
Oman	—	—	2.5	4.6	28.7	2339
Jordan	98	0.220	7.4	12.7	35.6	1429
Tunisia	75	0.353	3.8	5.9	27.6	2742
Algeria	92	0.245	10.4	2.9	37.0	1896
Syrian Arab Republic	81	0.317	2.0	16.4	28.4	1397
Egypt	86	0.275	6.4	—	—	1800
Iraq	—	—	0.7	25.6	31.3	970
Morocco	84	0.301				1909
Low Human Development						
Sudan	97	0.227	5.3	2.4	28.8	741
Yemen	—	—	0.7	—	—	579
Djibouti	—	—	0.0	—	—	—
All developing countries			10.0	—	—	2088
Arab States			3.7	—	—	1730
World			12.0	—	—	4523

Source: UNDP, *Human Development Report 1999*

Notes

1 This should not discount the pioneering efforts of countries such as Morocco, Lebanon, Jordan, and Yemen
2 Generalizations about the Arab region are bound to blur important national and sub-regional specificity. Regional generalizations in this chapter should be approached with caution. From a human development perspective, countries in the region can be sub-divided into three groups: high human development (Kuwait, Bahrain, Qatar, and the United Arab Emirates); medium human development: (Libya, Lebanon, Saudi Arabia, Oman, Jordan, Tunisia, Algeria, Syria, Egypt, Iraq, and Morocco); and low human development (least-developed) (Sudan, Yemen, Djibouti, Somalia).
3 Many of the statistics cited here, though from internationally reputable sources, might be criticized for inaccuracy. There is no room for discussing data weaknesses here. Suffice it to consider Anthony Long's metaphorical warning: we should not use statistics as a drunkard uses a lamppost for support. Instead statistics should be used for enlightenment.
4 The levels are higher for East Asia when China is excluded.
5 UNDP 1994.
6 Van Eeghen 1996.
7 Hamdan 1996.
8 UNDP 1999.
9 Among Arab countries, only Jordan and Yemen have real GDP per capita rankings lower than their HDI rankings—an indication that they are using their economic resources efficiently to advance capabilities and well-being.
10 As measured by the reduction in the shortfall of the non-income components of the HDI (life expectancy and educational attainment).
11 World Bank 1999.
12 National Human Development Report for Egypt, 1998.
13 World Bank 1995.
14 Kossaifi 1999.
15 Zafiris Tzannatos. 1999. Social Protection in the Middle East and North Africa: A Review. World Bank.
16 World Bank 1995.
17 National Human Development Report for Yemen, 1998.
18 Nadeem Karam for UNDP. 1999. Lebanese National Budget Allocations for Basic Health Services.
19 Lebanon, Ministry of National Education, Youth and Sports (1996).
20 Ibid.
21 Estimates of female/male wage differences from Lebanon: National Employment Agency et al. 1997 and Central Administration of Statistics 1998.
22 World Bank 1999.
23 UNDP 1998.

24 UNDP. 1996. Human Development Report.
25 UNDP forthcoming.

___

References

Ahmad, Ziauddin. 1991. "Islam, Poverty, and Income Distribution." Leicester: The Islamic Foundation.

Bedoui, Mongi, and Ridha Gouia. 1995. "Exclusion: Concept and Causes— Study Case:Tunisia." Mimeo.

Berry, Albert, Susan Horton, and Dipak Mazumdar. 1997. "Globalization, Adjustment, Inequality and Poverty." Background Paper for Human Development Report 1997. Mimeo.

Bremner, Robert H. 1994. *Giving: Charity and Philanthropy in History.* New Jersey: Transaction Publishers.

Bir-Zeit University. 1996/97. *Palestine Human Development Profile.* UNDP.

El-Mahdi, Alia. 1997. *Aspects of Structural Adjustment in Africa and Egypt.* Report by the Center for the Study of Developing Countries. Giza: Cairo University.

Economic and Social Commission for Western Asia (ESCWA). 1995. Selected Proceedings ofthe Expert Group Meeting on Human Development in the Arab World. Cairo. December 6–9, 1993.

ESCWA. 1996. "Poverty in Western Asia: A Social Perspective." United Nations. Amman.

Gordon, David. 1996. "CROP Poverty Glossary." School of Policy Studies, University of Bristol. Mimeo.

Hamdan, Kamal. 1996. "Poverty in the Arab World." In *Preventing and Eradicating Poverty.* A Report by UNDP and UN Department for Development Support and Management Services.

Institute of National Planning (INP). 1994. *Egypt Human Development Report.* Cairo: INP and UNDP.

INP. 1995. *Egypt Human Development Report.* Cairo: INP and UNDP.

INP. 1996. *Egypt Human Development Report.* Cairo: INP and UNDP.

INP. 1997/98. *Egypt Human Development Report.* Cairo: INP and UNDP.

Iraqi Economists Association. 1995. National Human Development Report for Iraq. Baghdad:UNDP.

Ministry of Planning and UNDP. 1997. National Human Development Report for Kuwait.

Richards, Alan, and John Waterbury. 1996. *A Political Economy of the Middle East.* Boulder: Westview Press.

UNDP. 1994. *Human Development Report 1994*. New York: Oxford University Press.

UNDP. 1995. *Iraq Human Development Report 1995*. Baghdad: Iraqi Economists Association.

UNDP. 1996. Évolution de la Perception de la Pauvreté et Evaluation des Programs de Promotion Sociale en Tunisie. Version Provisoire.

UNDP. 1996. *Economic Growth for Human Development*: Arab States. New York: UNDP.

UNDP. 1996. *Human Development Report 1996*. New York: Oxford University Press.

UNDP. *Preventing and Eradicating Poverty*, Volumes 1 & 2. New York: UNDP.

UNDP. 1997. *Human Development Report 1997*. New York: Oxford University Press.

UNDP. 1997. National Human Development Report for Morocco 1997. Rabat: Imrpim Elite.

UNDP. 1997. Human Security for the New Millennium: Elements for a Poverty Eradication Strategy in the Arab States. Mimeo.

UNDP. 1998. *Human Development Report 1998*. New York: Oxford University Press.

UNDP. 1998. Human Development Report for Lebanon 1998. Beirut.

UNDP. 1998. *Poverty Report*. New York:United Nations.

UNDP. 1998. The National Human Development Report, Lebanon. Beirut: UNDP & CDR.

UNDP. 1998. Human Development Report: State of Bahrain. Manama:UNDP.

UNDP. 1999. *Human Development Report 1999*. New York: Oxford University Press.

UNDP. (Forthcoming). Poverty Report.

Van Eeghen, Willem. 1996. "Poverty in the Middle East and North Africa." In *Preventing and Eradicating Poverty*. Report by UNDP and UN Department for Development Support and Management Services.

World Bank. 1995. Republic of Tunisia—Poverty Alleviation: Preserving Progress while Preparing for the Future (in two volumes).

World Bank. 1995. *Claiming the Future*.

World Summit for Social Development (WSSD). 1995. "Report on The Preparatory Expert Group Meeting on The Arab Declaration on Social Development." Amman. September 19–22, 1994.

8

Enhancing Women's Economic Participation in the MENA Region

Valentine M. Moghadam

Introduction

Due to significant changes in the world economy, women's labor force participation rates, and female shares of the labor force, have increased almost everywhere. The female share of the world's labor force grew from 38% in 1970 to 41% in 1996 (ILO 1997, 8). At the global level, the classic M-shape of women's labor market participation is flattening out and rising, particularly in the industrialized countries. In developed countries, women have made inroads into all types of occupations and professions—including many that previously were the exclusive domain of men. In many developing countries, women are still attached to the agricultural sector, home-based work, and the urban informal sector, but a growing proportion of the female economically active population is engaged in work in modern services and manufacturing. This is partly the result of higher educational attainment of women, partly the result of changing household needs, and partly the result of growing demand for more "flexible" (and cheaper) labor in import industries and services (Moghadam 1999a, 1999b; UN, 1999, 2000).

Many studies have documented how educated and employed women have contributed to household well-being, lower fertility rates, long-term economic growth, and industrial development (e.g., Goldin 1986; Hopkins 1983; INSTRAW/Joekes 1987; Buvinic and Lycette 1994). In the United States, women's work as teachers contributed to both social development and economic growth. By teaching for lower wages than men, women helped to expand mass education, raise the stock of education per laborer, and increase real U.S. national income (Carter 1986, citing Denison 1962). The participation of women in export manufacturing contributed to industrial development and growth of the manufacturing sector in South Korea, Thailand, Singapore, Hong Kong, Malaysia, and Mexico. Women's access to paid work contributes to economic and social development, but it is also crucial for the advancement of women. Women's economic participation is associated with heightened social and gender consciousness, which has led to the growth of women's organizations, women's political participation, and their contributions to civil society.

While these trends are all positive, there is much that remains problematic with respect to women's economic participation worldwide. Problems include: the continuing exclusion of women from certain occupations and professions; the gender-based wage gap; hostile work environments, including sexual harassment; the absence of national legislation or firm-level policies that facilitate employment and family life (e.g., paid maternity leave, quality childcare facilities, flexible work schedules); the often adverse effects of restructuring and globalization on women's jobs and wages; and the dearth of women in decision-making positions. These and related issues were taken up at the Fourth World Conference on Women (Beijing, 1995); they are also the focus of women's organizations throughout the world.

In the Middle East and North Africa (MENA), female participation rates and occupational shares are growing, but they remain among the lowest and smallest in the world. The under-utilization of half the human resource base is a cause for concern, particularly in light of the imperatives of a globalizing world. How, then, can women's participation be enhanced to productively utilize this potential for economic development?[1] The changing political economy in the MENA region raises additional questions. How will economic restructuring and globalization affect women's labor force participation and patterns of employment? Will economic liberalization in MENA countries increase demand for women workers and job opportunities for women across different sectors? Will the education and training of women receive more attention, and what kinds of jobs are likely to be available to women?

These questions are the focus of the present chapter. I will address them first by discussing the global context; second by describing the characteristics of the female labor force in the region; and third by examining recent developments in women's employment. Using Iran as a case study, I will illustrate the problems and prospects of women's economic participation. I will end by offering a number of recommendations for enhancing women's economic participation in the region. The focus of this chapter is on women's non-agricultural economic participation.[2]

The Global Context

In the current global environment of open economies, new trade regimes, competitive export industries, and expanding services, globalization relies heavily on the economic participation of women. This participation is both waged and unwaged, in formal sectors and in the home, in manufacturing and in public and private services. Around the world there has been a tremendous increase in women workers, professionals, and entrepreneurs. Much has been written about the growth of a female working class engaged in export manufacturing during the 1980s (e.g., INSTRAW/Joekes 1987; Ward 1990). But there has been also an expansion of women in public and private services. During the 1980s and 1990s, certain sectors which tended to be female-dominated, such as services, expanded; meanwhile others—such as heavy industry—mainly employing men, declined. This altered patterns of labor demand. At the same time, women's growing educational attainment enabled them to enter new occupations and professions. For example, in the 1990s, women's share of jobs in finance, real estate, and business services increased throughout the world; in 1994, the female share was 36% in Malaysia and 40% in Cyprus (ILO 1997, 9). There also was a noticeable growth of the female share of public service employment, where, for example, women constituted 52% of public service jobs in Venezuela in 1993 (Standing 1989, 1999). Moreover, women constitute an ever-growing share of managerial and administrative jobs, especially in the public sector. In Venezuela, Costa Rica, Paraguay, Finland, Ecuador, Uruguay, Switzerland, Norway, the Philippines, Australia, and the U.S., their shares range from 23% to 43% (ILO 1997, 15).

Globalization, flexibilization, and feminization appear to be interrelated. The feminization of employment has occurred in the context of globalization and the pursuit of flexible forms of labor; feminization, therefore, is often accompanied by, and sometimes preceded by, stagnating salaries or de-unionization. Moreover, the growth of women's employment has not been accompanied by a redistribution of domestic, household, and childcare responsibilities. Indeed, during the 1990s protective legislation for working women came under attack or was streamlined in many countries. Women remain disadvantaged in the new labor markets, in terms of wages, training, and occupational segregation (Anker 1998). They are also disproportionately involved in the non-regular forms of employment that have increased: temporary, part-time, casual, or home-based work. Such forms of unstable and precarious employment are characterized by low wages and the absence of social insurance.

In developing countries, women workers include urban dwellers, recent rural migrants, immigrants, and foreign contract workers. They may be young, single women, married women, or women maintaining households alone. Nevertheless, social policies, labor legislation, and the urban infrastructure have not kept up with the large-scale entry of women in urban labor markets. Education and training programs for women are not extensive, leaving women workers vulnerable to recession, increasing labor-market competition, and redundancies. Existing legislation providing social protection for women workers tends to be limited in scope and coverage, with benefits reaching a relatively small proportion of the total urban female labor force.[3] At the same time, such legislation, including maternity leave provisions, childcare facilities, and affirmative-action-type programs to encourage the employment of women, have come under scrutiny in the context of the expansion of neoliberal economic policies. As a result, some countries have streamlined or eliminated the entitlements and programs geared to women in the work force. Apart from the harm done to children and families, cutbacks limit women's ability to participate fully in market activities and to compete fairly with men in the labor market.

Along with the growth in female employment, there has been a growth in female unemployment—itself the result of economic recession, economic restructuring, and low growth. Unemployment rates have been very high by international standards in Algeria, Jamaica, Jordan, Egypt, Morocco, Nicaragua, Poland, the Slovak Republic, and Turkey (World Bank 1995a, 1995c, 29; ILO 1996, 145, 147). Unemployment is often higher for women (Moghadam 1995, Figures 8.1–8.4; UN 1995, Chart 5.13, 122; UN 2000, Chart 5.10, 120). Many unemployed women are new entrants to the urban labor force, who are seeking but not finding jobs; others lost jobs as a result of restructuring (as in Malaysia in the mid-1980s, Viet Nam in the late 1980s, and Morocco, Tunisia, and Turkey more recently).[4] The 1998 financial crisis in southeast Asia hit women workers especially hard (Ghosh 1998; UN 1999).

Unemployment, deteriorating real incomes, and the "feminization of poverty" have distinct effects on women. In the 1980s and 1990s, declining household incomes compelled women in many developing countries to seek paid jobs or engage in informal sector activity (Beneria and Feldman 1992; Meer 1994). But financial pressures within households can also result in exclusion or devaluation of female members. For example, girls can be withdrawn from school and sent to work; wives may have to endure domestic violence; young women may be prostituted.

The effects of economic restructuring and globalization have been taken up by women's organizations. Local women's groups and transnational women's networks have criticized downsizing, restructuring, poverty, growing income gaps, and increasing pressures on women. Women in many countries are seeking better representation in trade unions, or are building their own unions (Martens and Mitter 1994). In some industrialized countries, especially the United States, Australia, and the Nordic countries, women have been the largest growing union constituency (Eaton 1992; Hastings and Coleman, 1992). In India, the Working Women's Forum and the Self-Employed Women's Association (SEWA) work to improve the lives of very poor women economically and socially, and to make them self-reliant. SEWA, which started in 1972, operates as a trade union, a bank, and a women's rights organization of over 200,000 women.

The Situation in the Middle East and North Africa

The MENA region faces economic restructuring and the challenges of a global economy with its own distinct features. One feature is the centrality of oil to countries such as Algeria, Iran, Iraq, Libya, Saudi Arabia, and the Gulf sheikhdoms. Another distinct feature pertains to the structure of the female labor force.

One of the region's longstanding labor force characteristics has been the low rates of female labor force participation, compared with other regions in the world economy, and compared with male participation rates.[5] A second, related characteristic, again relative to other regions and to men, has been the limited access of women to wage employment. Women generally constitute a small percentage of the total salaried work force in these countries.[6] A third feature is that female non-agricultural employment has been concentrated in public sector professional jobs, a function of the correlation between educational attainment and female labor force participation.[7] A fourth feature is that women have been conspicuously absent from certain occupations—especially in private sales and services and in the sector of hotels, restaurants, and wholesale and retail trade—at least according to official statistics for wage employment (Doctor and Khoury 1991, 28; Moghadam 1993, 45–51; Anker 1998, 166).[8]

These characteristics are a result of both political economy and culture. The regional oil economy and its place in the global economy, along with resource endowments, development strategies, and state policies of particular countries, help to explain patterns of women's employment (and non-employment) in the region.[9] Apart from the generally small size of the population of employees in the region, capital-intensive technologies and relatively high wages for men during the oil era precluded a deeper involvement of women in the labor force

(Moghadam 1993, ch. 2; Karshenas 1997). A comparison of women's employment across oil and non-oil economies, labor-poor and labor-surplus countries, and rich and poor countries indicates that generally, the more open the economy and the less dependent on oil revenues, the greater women's involvement in the labor force. Thus in Tunisia and Morocco in 1990, women comprised 22–30% of the work force, whereas in Algeria and Iran, women comprised about 10% of it. State policies and the legal framework also have been important in explaining differences in women's access to paid work across the region.

Culture also matters. The region has been characterized by what I call a "patriarchal gender contract," a set of social relationships between men and women predicated upon the male breadwinner/ female homemaker roles, in which the male has direct access to wage employment or control over the means of production, and the female is largely economically dependent upon male members of her family. The patriarchal gender contract also determines the occupations and professions that are considered suitable for women. During the oil boom, the patriarchal gender contract was made possible and indeed financed by the regional oil economy, the wealth of the oil-producing states, and the high wages obtained during the oil era. (Although Turkey was not strictly speaking a part of the regional oil economy, other features described here, such as the limited access of women to paid employment, apply to that case as well.) The patriarchal gender contract is also codified in law, especially in the region's family laws. Currently, family laws in many countries require women to obtain the permission of fathers or husbands for employment, seeking a loan, starting up a business, or undertaking business travel. They also give women a lesser share of inheritance of family wealth.

Both political economy and culture have resulted in MENA women's limited participation in paid employment, and in the region's rather large gender gaps in literacy and educational attainment.[10] In a cross-regional study of gender and jobs, Anker notes the following about his six sample countries from the Middle East and North Africa: "the female share of non-agricultural employment is small;" although it has been increasing, and "the number of years of schooling is low for both men and women in this region" (Anker 1998, 145). In another recent comparative study, Horton (1999) concludes that women's economic participation has decreased in MENA countries, although she also states that the data are difficult to interpret.[11]

Table 8.1 gives some indication of the cross-regional differences in women's occupational activity and the under-representation of MENA women in nearly all occupation groups. Table 8.2 illustrates the problems in the area of educational attainment, compared with other countries that are at similar stages of economic development or at similar income levels.[12]

Table 8.1. Women's Share in Major Occupational Groups, 1990, by Region

	Prof./Tech. & related	Admin./ manag.	Clerical & service	Sales workers	Production workers
Developed countries					
Western Europe	50	18	63	48	16
Other	44	32	69	41	22
Eastern Europe	56	33	73	66	27
Developing countries					
Sub-Saharan Africa	36	15	37	52	20
Oceania	41	18	52	53	17
Latin America	49	23	59	47	17
Caribbean	52	29	62	59	21
Eastern Asia	43	11	48	42	30
Southeast Asia	48	17	48	53	21
Southern Asia	32	6	20	8	16
Western Asia*	37	7	29	12	7
North Africa	29	9	22	10	10

Note: Western Asia refers to the Middle East.
Source: UN, *The World's Women 1995: Trends and Statistics*, Chart 5.16.

Table 8.2. Mean Years of Schooling, 25+, early 1990s, by Sex and Country

MENA country	Males	Females	Other developing countries	Males	Females
Algeria	4.0	0.8	Argentina	8.5	8.9
Egypt	3.9	1.9	Chile	7.8	7.2
Iran	4.6	3.1	China	6.0	3.6
Iraq	5.7	3.9	Colombia	6.9	7.3
Jordan	6.0	4.0	Malaysia	5.6	5.0
Kuwait	6.0	4.7	Mongolia	7.2	6.8
Lebanon	5.3	3.5	Philippines	7.8	7.0
Libya	5.5	1.3	Sri Lanka	7.7	6.1
Morocco	4.1	1.5	Thailand	4.3	3.3
Saudi Arabia	5.9	1.5	Viet Nam	5.8	3.4
Tunisia	3.0	1.2	Uruguay	7.4	8.2

Source: UNESCO, *Education for all: Status and Trends 1994*. Paris, UNESCO, 1994.

As in other regions, the MENA countries have turned from the previous economic development strategy of import-substitution industrialization to export-led growth, as a way to balance budgets and increase competitiveness. In the post-oil boom era, wages have eroded, especially in the public sector, and men have been taking on second and third jobs in the private sector and in the informal economy (World Bank 1995b, 3–4). Low productivity and inefficiencies pervade the labor markets (Karshenas 1995). Rising unemployment is the result of rapid growth of the labor force caused by high fertility rates, combined with poor economic growth (Shaban, Assaad, and Al-Qudsi 1995; ERF 1996). Countries have adopted structural adjustment policies, often with World Bank and IMF assistance, in order to rejuvenate growth. In this context, how could the changing political economy affect women's economic participation?

Let us imagine a positive scenario, in which economic liberalization and restructuring lead to more employment opportunities for women:

- Structural reforms often call for fiscal changes and the mobilization of domestic resources, through such measures as expanding the tax base and making taxation more efficient. Governments may reason that in order to increase the income-tax-paying population, policies would be needed to increase the size of the female labor force.
- Countries focus on making their labor forces more qualified, partly by raising education and skill levels. There is thus increased attention to improving education, vocational training, and skills-upgrading for women.
- There is a rising demand for women in the labor-intensive textiles and garments branches that are geared for export.
- Women's numbers rise in such expanding occupations as banking, insurance, accounting, computing, and business services.
- The expansion of tourism breaks down cultural proscriptions against women's employment in sales and private services, and in hotels, restaurants, and trade.
- As governments relinquish control over economic enterprises to focus on expanding and upgrading health, education, and social services, this enhances the participation of women in the social sectors.
- The emphasis on private sector development and entrepreneurship leads to support for women-owned or managed businesses.

A more negative scenario, however, is equally plausible. Here, stagnation continues, investments do not increase, inequalities widen and poverty grows, women face exclusion from paid work, and informal sector work grows. In addition, women continue to face the current constraints in access to paid employment:

- High population growth and fertility,[13]
- High illiteracy, especially among rural women and older age groups,

- Inferior or incomplete schooling and inadequate training that fail to prepare women for modern sector jobs,
- High male unemployment (especially of young men), which acts as a disincentive to hire women,
- The widespread perception of women as less reliable workers, coupled with a tendency to regard men as the real breadwinners and women as secondary earners only,
- Provisions in labor legislation that prohibit night work for women (interpreted in some places as the inability of women to apply for second-shift jobs in the industrial sector) or that require maternity leaves whose costs must be borne entirely by the employer,[14]
- Employment costs to women, including infrastructural deficiencies (such as poor roads and public transportation, which result in lengthy travel time), and inadequate social policies to help women balance wage work and family responsibilities,
- Lack of gender sensitivity and gender awareness on the part of government officials and planners, and absence of integration of a gender dimension in economic policy-making,
- The absence of influential women's organizations, including those that may focus on the problems of women in the labor force.

Some Recent Trends, Problems, Prospects

Let us now examine some of the ways that economic restructuring in countries of the Middle East and North Africa affected women's employment during the 1990s, or since adjustment began. As we shall see, aspects of both the positive and negative scenarios have been realized.

Women and Economic Need
We begin with economic need, poverty, and inequalities, which affect women's economic participation in very basic ways. According to a 1994 official report on the Arab region (ESCWA 1995a, 15):

> Despite the lack of accurate gender-disaggregated data on poverty in the Arab States consistent with the indicators adopted by the United Nations Commission on the Status of Women, it is obvious that the effect of global economic recession combined with structural adjustment policies and programmes in some Arab States, the transition to a market economy and the associated shrinking in the role of the public sector in creating job opportu-

nities and providing social services, as well as the exacerbation of the problem of foreign debt and its servicing and the dwindling of revenues and financial resources for development, have undermined the capacity of Governments to provide for the basic needs of their populations, and as such have undermined anti-poverty initiatives, especially those benefiting women and children.

Much of the literature on women and work in the MENA region has focused on women's educational attainment as the main factor behind their employment, but economic need is increasingly important. In Lebanon, 35% of the respondents to the Working Women's Survey indicated that the main reason for their employment was economic need (Al-Raida 1998). Elsewhere, growing income inequalities and poverty have increased the supply of job-seeking women—many of whom have to accept low-wage jobs, sometimes in thriving export sectors. Growing urban inequalities and female-headed households have made women's poverty more visible.

In Egypt, Iran, Jordan, and Syria, poverty increased during the 1990s, in part due to the sharp decline in wages when these countries underwent large adjustments. In Egypt, wages fell drastically, especially in sectors where women predominate, such as textiles and garments, and the government sector (World Bank 1991). The "working poor" in Egypt include government employees, manufacturing workers, and the self-employed. In the early 1990s there was a decline in school enrollments and an increase in drop-outs among girls in Egypt and Morocco, and this was attributed to the introduction of user fees and growing pressures on low-income families. In Jordan, poverty increased after economic reforms began in the early 1990s (World Bank 1994a; Khuri-Tubbeh 1996), and a trend noted by researchers is the growing visibility of poor women (El-Solh 1994, 19).

In Morocco and Tunisia, the growth of income inequalities and urban poverty was due largely to the growth of low-wage jobs in the booming export sectors (World Bank 1995b, 3). During 1984–89 employment in the export sector in Morocco expanded by 25% a year while real wages declined by 2.6%. It was during this period that female employment in the industrial sector saw a dramatic increase. The most competitive sectors—clothing, food, leather, shoes, where women were concentrated—had low and declining capital intensity and offered very low wages (World Bank 1994b, vol. I, 33). Poor women received as little as half the wage rate per hour earned by poor males. Morocco and Tunisia (along with Egypt and Yemen) report relatively high rates of female-headed households in both urban and rural areas: in 1994, 17.3% in Morocco and 11.3% in Tunisia (ESCWA 2000, Annex 10). Such households tend to have higher-than-average rates of economic activity.

Tunisia has spent more on poverty-reduction programs, but as in Morocco, there has been a growth in temporary, low-wage and low-skill employment (World Bank 1995d). One-half of all new jobs in textiles and in tourism created in 1985–90 were of this nature. Moreover, in these two sectors, wages for temporary workers fell more than did wages for permanent workers. Thus the labor market in tourism and textiles—the latter being predominantly feminized—has become characterized by increasing "flexibility."

In 1994, Algeria became unable to service its US$26 billion foreign debt, which was consuming 93.4% of export earnings, and had to resort to an IMF and World Bank SAP in exchange for debt relief (Layachi 1999). The SAP led to a 40% devaluation of the dinar, the lifting of subsidies on basic food, and the liberalization of foreign trade. Between 1994 and 1998, 815 public enterprises were dissolved, and Public Economic Enterprises laid off 60% of their workers (Layachi 1999). The retrenchments affected mainly men, but women's livelihood was adversely affected. More women sought jobs to augment deteriorating household budgets, thus contributing to higher economic activity rates. However, gender biases as well as structural economic problems have foreclosed employment opportunities, and this has raised women's unemployment rates to high levels.

Women and the Informal Sector
Little systematic work has been done on women's roles in the informal sector in the MENA region, or on the relation between the formal and informal sectors, but good ethnographic studies offer important insights. Lobban (1998, 9) notes that women are involved in: small-scale retailing of food and clothing; weekly markets and street sales; household and domestic sales and services; informal or illegal sexual services; loan pools and cooperatives; and "the survival economy." Early (1998, 133) found that women in Cairo were engaged as vendors, merchants, midwives, seamstresses, tattooers, bread bakers, henna-appliers, and bath attendants. Among Palestinians in the West Bank, much of the textile work is done by home-based women (Hindiyeh-Mani 1998, 24).[15] In Iran, anecdotal evidence and research by Poya (1999) suggest an increase in urban women's informal sector activity, especially in light of limited employment opportunities after the 1979 revolution. In particular, there seems to have been a growth of home-based personal/beauty services, in part a response to the closing down of many beauty salons (not barber shops) after the revolution.

In Tunisia, surveys conducted in 1989 and 1991 found that the informal sector employed nearly 35% of total urban wage earners. About half of the informal sector workers (mainly apprentices and *aides familiaux*) had a salary significantly lower than the minimum wage (World Bank 1995d, 26). The types of informal sector work encountered by Berry-Chikhaoui (1998, 218) in Tunisia seemed to represent three forms of responses: to poverty, to traditions and food needs, and to modern aspirations. In each category women were a minority, but they were most represented in the second category. Berry-Chikhaoui found women working as seamstresses, public bath attendants, hairdressers; potters, and scribes; and she found them engaged in small-scale food production, small-scale metal work, textiles, leather; artisanal crafts, and street food sales. These sectors "rely heavily on young women and low wages to sustain them" (Lobban 1998, 31). Other ethnographic studies and small-scale surveys on women in the informal sector (e.g., Khuri-Tubbeh 1996), suggest that increasing income inequalities, growing unemployment among men, rising prices, and household survival strategies may be propelling more women into informal sector work and self-employment.

Women in Manufacturing
Tunisia and Morocco prioritize exports of textiles and clothing; consequently, official statistics indicate a relatively large proportion of the female labor force in the manufacturing sector. In contrast to the rest of the region, Tunisian women are disproportionately represented in the manufacturing sector (Anker 1998, 167). Tunisia's 1989 census found that most of the female labor force was located in manufacturing, and that 43% of the manufacturing work force was female (ESCWA 1995b; Moghadam 1998, 56). In Morocco in 1991, 37.4% of the manufacturing work force was female (ILO 1994). These numbers suggest that the recruitment of cheap female labor in the export sector has contributed to the competitiveness of Morocco's and Tunisia's garments industries. Elsewhere, there is an important role for women workers in the manufacturing sector in Turkey (25% female in 1992) and Egypt (17.6% in 1989). Jordan's manufacturing sector absorbed about 35% of female recruitment between 1988 and 1990 (Khuri-Tubbeh 1996, 88).

But the data show disconcerting trends as well, such as declines in women's involvement in manufacturing, a high incidence of non-regular and non-salaried activity among women in this sector, and a wide gender gap in earnings. In Palestine, 90% of all home-based workers in the textiles and clothing industry were women, and 35% of them were unwaged (Mehra and Gammage 1999, 541). In Iran, women's role in modern, urban manufacturing is marginal; the registered female manufacturing work force is largely rural and non-waged.

In Tunisia there was a registered decline in women's share of manufacturing between 1984 and 1989, from 48% to 43% (Moghadam 1998, 68). Nearly half the women in Tunisia's manufacturing sector in 1989 were non-salaried (that is, unpaid family workers or own-account workers in the informal sector). Still, a larger proportion of Tunisia's working women remain in manufacturing (43.4%) compared to men (31.5%), according to a recent study (République Tunisienne/PNUD 1999, 97). In Syria, between 1981 and 1991 the share of female labor in manufacturing, electronics, construction, trade, finance, and community services decreased, while their share of agriculture increased. According to Alachkar (1996, 107): "If we remember that the process of economic liberalization has led to increasing the role of the private sector in manufacturing, we will deduce that this liberalization has negative effects on women's participation in the labor force [in Syria]." There is conflicting data for Egypt. ILO data suggest that women's access to paid employment in manufacturing may have decreased, from 12.2% in 1990 to 10% in 1996 (ILO 1997, Table 2E), while Assaad's 1998 survey shows an increase (see Assaad 1999). In Turkey, the decline in real wages in manufacturing helped raise the competitiveness of Turkey's exports in the 1980s (Hansen 1991; Karshenas 1995), but it also widened the gender gap in earnings. According to Kasnakoglyu and Dayioglu (1996), women on average earn 60% of male earnings. Furthermore, ILO data show a decline in women's share of paid employment in manufacturing, from 25% in 1992 to 17% in 1996 (ILO 1997, Table 2B). (See Figure 8.1.) Anecdotal evidence suggests a growth of home-based work in Turkey at the expense of paid work in the modern manufacturing sector.

Figure 8.1. Male and female employed share in manufacturing, 1988–1996, Turkey

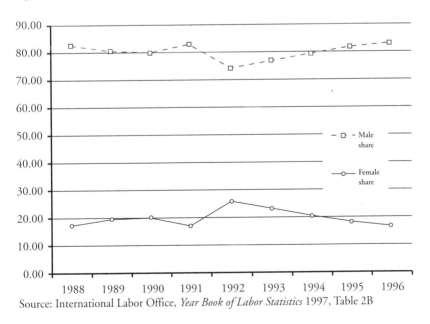

Source: International Labor Office, *Year Book of Labor Statistics* 1997, Table 2B

Women in Sales and Services

As mentioned above, a characteristic of MENA labor markets has been the low participation of women in sales and service occupations. This is certainly due to political economy and culture, but it also may be a methodological matter. There has been a longstanding difficulty in measuring sales and services activities, indicating the need for improved enumeration methods and labor force surveys. Much economic activity in this sector (and in agriculture) is unrecorded (Anker 1995). Another problem is the non-comparability of data, as different methods of enumeration yield different results. Thus in Egypt, the female share of employment in trade, restaurants, and hotels was only 7.3% according to the 1986 census, but 17.7% according to the 1989 Labor Force Sample Survey (ILO 1994; Moghadam 1998, 115).[16]

In the 1990s, MENA women remained underrepresented in sales and services, although their participation seemed to be increasing. According to official statistics, the Tunisian female labor force is strikingly under-represented in services—despite the importance of the tourism sector. Iranian women's participa-

Table 8.3. Female Service Employment by Subsectors, Selected MENA Countries (female share)

Country	Trade, restaurants, and hotels		Transport, storage, and communications		Finance, insurance, real estate, business services		Community, social and personal services	
	1980	1990–94	1980	1990–94	1980	1990–94	1980	1990–94
Algeria	2.7	3.7	3.4	4.2	16.4	12.4	19.4	19.9
Bahrain	4.1	6.9	9.9	11.9	27.1	12.3	21.9	31.4
Egypt	5.7	17.7	3.3	5.9	18.8	18.1	17.6	26.1
Iran, Islamic Rep.	2.0	1.7	2.2	1.4	9.4	9.2	18.9	13.6
Iraq	7.2	11.4	2.8	5.4	16.3	40.0	9.0	11.9
Jordan	2.1	2.1	0.6	0.6	15.9	15.9	13.8	13.8
Kuwait	3.2	4.6	4.9	5.8	14.2	16.2	25.1	36.1
Lebanon		4.4	0.0	3.4		10.8		20.3
Libya		1.4		0.8		8.3		10.5
Morocco	4.8	3.9	2.9	2.4	27.9	23.7		
Qatar		1.4		3.8		9.7		18.8
Saudi Arabia		0.7		0.5		0.6		9.7
Syria	2.7	2.9	2.4	2.6	14.7	12.3	16.8	21.2
Tunisia	6.0	8.1	5.3	21.9	24.6	24.6	21.0	21.0
Turkey	4.6	7.0	4.9	4.7	25.8	29.3	14.8	19.2
United Arab Emirates	2.8	4.0	2.3	3.3	11.0	11.2	11.3	20.5

Source: United Nations, Women's Indicator and Statistics Database (WISTAT), 1994

tion in sales and private services is also insignificant, despite anecdotal evidence of many home-based services. According to the 1996 census, Iranian women remain under-represented in clerical work, wholesale and retail trade, and finance/real estate/business services. Table 8.3 and Figures 8.2–8.4 illustrate the low representation of women in the service sectors. But they also indicate some growth.

In the long run, economic liberalization and current policies that prioritize expansion of the tourism sector could lead to increases in the demand for and supply of female labor in trade, restaurants, and hotels. Tourism is a mixed blessing for countries, cultures, the environment, and women. But it is a sector that could promote women's employment. Already hotel management schools are training young women in a number of MENA countries; women employees are seen in the large hotels of Turkey, Tunisia, and Egypt, and a trend in Turkey is the hiring of young women in the fashionable cafés of Istanbul and Ankara. In Jordan, young women are now working in the upscale Safeway supermarket in Amman. Can it be long before the Filipina women imported to work as waitresses in Jordan (because this occupation is considered inappropriate for Jordanian women) are eventually replaced by nationals?

Figure 8.2. Trade, restaurants, and hotels (female share)

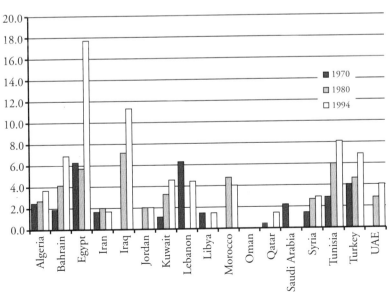

Source: United Nations, Women's Indicator and Statistics Database (WISTAT), 1994

Figure 8.3. Finance, insurance, real estate business services (female share)

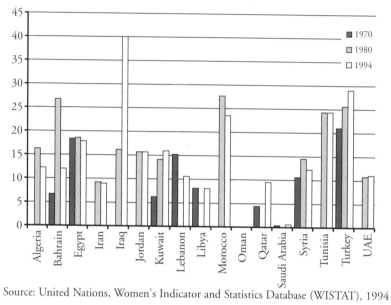

Source: United Nations, Women's Indicator and Statistics Database (WISTAT), 1994

Figure 8.4. Community, social and personal services (female share)

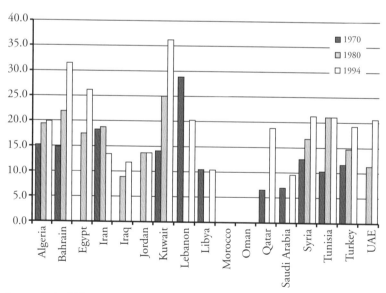

Source: United Nations, Women's Indicator and Statistics Database (WISTAT), 1994

In other services—and especially in community, social, and personal services—some growth in women's participation has been registered. The data on finance, insurance, real estate, and business services shows a mixed picture, and a regional pattern or trend is difficult to discern. Some countries show declines between the 1980s and 1990s, but female shares of over 20% are encouraging. It is likely that in the latter part of the 1990s, the female shares grew in Tunisia, Morocco, Jordan, and possibly Turkey. If so, these countries will be following the global trend.

Women and Public Services
In most countries of the region, women's share of salaried employment steadily increased between 1970 and 1990 (see Table 8.4.). This share is expected to grow further, mainly due to women's growing share of public-sector employment. Women continue to seek employment in the government sector, despite low incomes, because of job security and the availability of social insurance. In Egypt this is the preferred sector for women, in part because gender-based earnings discrimination is low at all wage quartiles (Said 1998). Given the underdevelopment of the private sector and lack of women-friendly policies there, the public sector is preferred by women in many MENA countries. Thus in Jordan, while most men (60%) are in the private sector, among women, 55% are in the

Table 8.4. Female Share of Total Employees, Selected Countries,
       1970–90

Country	1970	1980	1990
Algeria	5	8	10
Egypt	9	9	16
Iran	15	12	10
Iraq	—	8	11
Jordan	—	9	10
Kuwait	8	14	21
Morocco	—	18	25
Syria	10	9	15
Tunisia	6	15	17
Turkey	14	15	18

Sources: UN, *WISTAT* CD-ROM, 1994
Note: In the 1990s, female shares are as follows: Bahrain 10% in 1995; Egypt 17.7% in
       1995; Jordan 11% in 1993; Morocco 22% in 1992; Syria 17% in 1991; Tunisia
       23% in 1994 (ILO, 1996, 1997, Table 2E). According to Iran's *Statistical
       Yearbook 1375/1996*, women were 12 percent of the salaried population in 1996
       (IRI, 1997, Table 3.4, p. 74, and Table 3.9, p. 81). On Lebanon, see Al-Raida,
       special issue on Women in the Labor Force (vol. XV, no. 82, summer 1998),
       which reports that women's share of employment is 20 percent (p. 16)

government sector compared with 41% in the private sector (Khuri-Tubbeh 1996, 82).

The public sector—especially government employment—has seen both a stabilization of recruitment and a feminization of employment. In Syria, the female share of government employment increased from 18.7% in 1980 to 26.9% in 1992 (Alachkar 1996). In 1994 in Turkey, women represented 35% of all public sector employees (UNDP-Ankara 1996, 54–55). The proportion of women in the government sector in Iran reached 31% in 1991 (Islamic Republic of Iran 1995). In 1995, permanent-contract women employees in the government sector (that is, those subject to labor law and social insurance) were 38.6% (Islamic Republic of Iran 1997). Among the Gulf countries, the shares range from a high of 39% in Kuwait to a low of 9% in Qatar (see Table 8.5.).

The field of education has always been open to women's employment, although not necessarily at the highest levels. The percentage of female teaching staff at institutes of higher education ranges from 18% in Saudi Arabia and 20% in Syria, to 28% in Tunisia and 30% in Egypt. This compares with a high of 50% female teachers in Thailand. But the MENA region actually compares well in this regard with other developing countries (ILO 1997, 50). Clearly, teaching is a growing sector for women (and for men).

It appears that as men gravitate towards the expanding and more lucrative private sector, more jobs in the public sector are available to women.[17] Thus, although the concentration of the non-agricultural female labor force in public sector professional jobs is in keeping with a pre-existing trend, one may con-

Table 8.5. Women's Share of Public Service Employment in
     Selected MENA Countries

Country	Year	Percent Female
Iran	1986	30
	1991	31
	1996	38
Kuwait	1983	31
	1994	39
Morocco	1989	29
	1991	31
Qatar	1988	9
Syria	1980	19
	1992	27
Turkey	1994	35

Sources: Alachkar 1996; UNDP-Ankara 1996; IRI 1995, 1997;
     Standing 1999

clude that economic liberalization, restructuring, and privatization are leading to the feminization of public sector employment.

Women's Share of Administrative and Managerial Jobs, and Participation in Governance
Women's economic and political participation at high levels is increasingly seen as a measure of women's advancement and of a country's efforts towards gender equality in decision-making (UN 1995, 1996; UNDP 1995, 1999). There is also the perception that women at high-level positions can be effective advocates, policy-makers, and decision-makers on issues pertaining to women, work, and family.

In the MENA region, women are generally under-represented in administrative and managerial jobs. However, some MENA countries seem to be more receptive than others to greater female participation at higher levels; in this respect, Morocco stands out. In Turkey, women's share is 10% (30% in total employment), while in Egypt, women's share is 12% (20% in total employment) (ILO 1997, 15). In the Turkish public service, in 1996, some 32% of division chiefs (middle-management positions) were women. At higher levels, they held 12% of general directorships and just over 2% of under-secretary positions (ILO 1997, 22).

Table 8.6. Women's Participation in Administration, Management, and Governance, 1997

Country	Female Share of Administrative and Managerial Positions	Female Share of Parliamentary Seats
Algeria	5.9	3.2
Bahrain	n.a.	n.a.
Egypt	11.5	2.0
Iran	3.5	4.9
Iraq	n.a.	n.a.
Jordan	4.6	1.7
Kuwait	5.2	0
Morocco	25.6	0.7
Oman	n.a.	—
Qatar	n.a.	—
Saudi Arabia	n.a.	—
Syria	2.9	9.6
Tunisia	12.7	6.7
Turkey	10.1	2.4
Yemen	n.a.	n.a.

Source: UNDP, *Human Development Report 1998*. Table 3, 134

Women's participation in governance is still rather limited across the region, and this is reflected in the low female shares of parliamentary positions (see Table 8.6.). Some progress has been registered, however. In Iran, four women were hired for high-level government posts under President Khatami, and in Morocco, Prime Minister Youssefi appointed four women to top government positions, including two cabinet posts.

Women-Owned Businesses

Self-employment ranges from dead-end survival activities to more stable endeavors and enterprises that have the potential for growth and development. Similarly, women-owned businesses range from poverty-alleviating micro-enterprises funded by micro-credits (e.g., a one-woman sewing enterprise in an impoverished household), to small enterprises funded by small loans, to large and modern businesses that are self-sustaining and profitable. There is a need for more data on women's participation in and experience with self-employment, including home-based work, in the MENA region. There are, of course, several well-known businesswomen in the MENA region who have helped build large firms and some who have successfully entered the global corporate world.[18] However, for non-elite women, entrepreneurship entails financial and legal obstacles.

In Jordan, women-owned businesses still represent a tiny proportion of the total, but there has been a relative increase in the numbers of women business owners—from 211 in 1979 to 250 in 1985, and to 1043 in 1991 (Jordan Coordinating Office 1995, 23). Women's SMEs range from home-based sewing and embroidery to catering and desk-top publishing. In Egypt, women-owned businesses are growing, but many potential owners are blocked by the reluctance of banks to lend to women. In Lebanon, where the vast majority of the female labor force is found in the private sector, some 45% of women workers are employed in SMEs. Among them is a mix of highly educated women running professional services, and "those with low qualifications and educational status" involved in the informal sector (Al-Raida 1998, 16).

Throughout the region, there is a great need for businesses that are owned and operated by women and that cater to women.

Women and Unemployment

The high rates of unemployment among women in the MENA region indicate that the supply of job-seeking women is growing, but women are encountering barriers to their participation (see Table 8.7.). Unemployed women appear to be mainly new entrants (with secondary school education, as well as poorer women with only primary school education), but include previously employed women who have lost jobs with enterprise restructuring or privatization, especially in

Jordan, Morocco, and Tunisia (World Bank 1995b, 3). In Turkey, the majority (63%) of registered unemployed women are in the age group 15–24 (ILO 1996, Table 3B). It appears that the most vulnerable persons in the labor market are women with incomplete education, although in Jordan educated women—and especially graduates of community colleges—can also expect high levels of unemployment. In Egypt, educated women are more likely to be unemployed than are educated men (Assaad 1999). Although in absolute numbers more men are unemployed, the rate of female employment is much higher, and disproportionately high, given women's smaller share of the labor force. Clearly there has been a feminization of unemployment in the region.

Working Women and Social Policies
As in other regions, there has been an ongoing debate in MENA countries on social policies for working women. The majority of economically active women are not beneficiaries of employment-related social insurance programs or labor legislation. However, the small numbers of women who are employed in the formal sector and are entitled to maternity leaves and childcare benefits have to confront widespread perceptions of them as less reliable than men, uncommitted to their work, and "expensive labor." According to the World Bank (1995b, 17):

> Regulations intended to protect women have backfired in many countries, and now constrain many young, educated women seeking jobs in the formal private sector. In the past mandates such as low retirement age and generous maternity benefits encouraged women to stay in school and to work in the public sector, where these advantages are well enforced .... But these advantages are costly, and reduce the demand for women's labor in the private sector.

In research I conducted in the early 1990s, I discovered reluctance on the part of many employers to hire women. This was in part due to their perception of women workers as less reliable than male workers, because of women's family responsibilities. It was also due to labor law requirements that employers provide women workers with paid maternity leaves and, in some cases, creches and nursing breaks.

This was especially the case in Egypt, where women public sector employees took full advantage of the generous and lengthy maternity benefits available to them (three months of paid maternity leave and up to two years unpaid maternity leave, available up to three times with no loss of seniority). Interviews conducted during fieldwork in Egypt in January 1995 confirmed that employers were very much opposed to lengthy maternity leaves. Moreover, a government

258   Valentine Moghadam

study stated: "... there seems to be implicit discrimination against female employment, especially in the private sector, mainly because of women's work discontinuity due to childbearing and rearing" (cited in Moghadam 1998,111). Private sector employers circumvent the labor law that requires creches and nursing breaks in enterprises with 100 or more women workers by deliberately hiring fewer than 100 women. Although Egypt has an anti-discrimination law,

Table 8.7. Unemployment Rates, Various MENA Countries, 1990s

Country	Year	Male	Female	Total
Algeria	1992	24.2	20.3	23.8
	1997	26.9	24.0	26.4
Bahrain	1991	5.5	13.4	6.8
Egypt	1995	7.0	22.1	10.4
Iran*	1991	9.5	24.4	15.0
Iraq	1987	4.3	7.4	5.1
Jordan	1991	14.4	34.1	17.1
	1994	12.9	28.3	15.0
	1997	11.7	28.5	14.4
Lebanon	1996	8.6	7.2	7.0[†]
Morocco (urban)	1992	13	25.3	16.0
	1998	17.4	22.9	18.7
Oman	1993	4.7	8.7	5.1
Palestine	1997			
West Bank		17.2	17.7	15.5
Gaza		26.5	29.8	26.2
Syria	1981	3.2	2.0	3.0
	1991	5.2	14.0	6.8
	1995	5.1	11.6	6.5
Tunisia	1993	14.7	21.9	16.1
Turkey**	1993	8.2	7.2	7.9
Yemen	1991	14.0	6.0	12.3
	1994	10.1	5.4	18.1

* According to Iran's Statistical Yearbook 1375/1996, the female unemployment rate was 12.5% in 1996 (IRI, 1997)
** Urban unemployment in Turkey in 1994 was 19.8% female and 9.1% male (SIS 1996)
† 22% new entrants
Sources: World Bank (1995b), p. 5; ERF (1996), p. 103; ILO (1996), Table 3A; Moghadam (1998), pp. 57, 118, 138, 147, 168, 183; ESCWA (2000); Moghadam (2001)

it is apparently not enforced, and compliance is not monitored. The labor law has been revised and unified to bring the public sector benefits in line with private sector benefits. For women this entails the reduction of the unpaid maternity leave to one year rather than two, taken twice instead of three times, and available to a woman employee after ten months of service. The maternity leave entitlement is now 50 days, at 100% of the salary.

In Iran, women represent a very small part of the salaried work force, with most employed in the government sector. Labor legislation on maternity leave follows the ILO minimal recommendation of twelve weeks leave at two-thirds pay (Moghadam 1998, 170). Currently, only employed women in urban areas and government employees are covered, which means that the majority of working women have no coverage. Another problem is that a maternity leave of three months is insufficient, and is in the interest of neither the baby's health nor the mother's labor force attachment.

A better solution for both Egypt and Iran would be to extend maternity leave to six months and entitle women to take it at full pay twice in their career. This may encourage more women to enter and remain in the labor force, while also taking into account population-stabilization concerns. Maternity leaves should also be financed through contributions from employer, employee, and general revenues.

The need for appropriate social policies for working women and an expansion of women's socioeconomic rights has been taken up by women's organizations. North African women's groups have been calling for the modernization of family laws and well as rights of working women. In 1995, a Roundtable on the Rights of Workers was organized by the Moroccan Democratic League of Women's Rights, and a committee structure was subsequently formed, consisting of twelve participating organizations. The objective was to revise the labor code to take women's conditions into account, to include domestic workers in the definition of wage-workers and the delineation of their rights and benefits, to set the minimum work age at fifteen, and to provide workers on maternity leave with full salary and a job-back guarantee. In a highly publicized incident, Moroccan feminist groups came to the assistance of factory women who went on strike over sexual harassment.[19] In Tunisia, the National Commission on Working Women was created in July 1991 within the Tunisian General Federation of Workers.

The Jordanian National Committee for Women forwarded the following economic demands (JNCW 1993):

> Increasing the participation of women in the labour force, and guaranteeing that they are not discriminated against in employment

in all spheres and sectors of work. Extending the necessary assistance to encourage women's entry and continued participation in the labour market by encouraging and developing support services.

In the same document, they specify the need for:

> … making available the necessary support services to working women, and in particular encouraging the establishment of nurseries and kindergartens that are to be provided with improved levels of supervision. These facilities would encourage women to opt for and continue in the job market, making use of the various legislative provisions contained in the Labour Law.

Educating Women for a Globalizing Economy

The good news in the MENA region is that more young women are entering into higher education fields of study such as engineering, medicine, law, commerce, and finance (Moghadam 1998, ch. 2). They are also increasingly graduating with degrees in mathematics and computer sciences. In Turkey, the proportion of women in universities almost doubled, from 19 to 37%, between 1968 and 1990. But it increased even faster in engineering (7 to 22%), in mathematics and natural sciences (22 to 46%), and in agriculture and forestry (10 to 33%). In 1994–95, Turkish women were awarded 45% of the undergraduate and 33% of the postgraduate degrees in mathematics and computer science (ILO, 1997: 44). Egypt has a high proportion (30%) of women engineering students at the university level (ILO 1997, 43). In the early 1990s, the percentage of business administration students at the third level who were women was 70% in Bahrain, 39% in Jordan and Tunisia, and 35% in Turkey. Countries with respectable percentages of women receiving first university degrees in mathematics and computer sciences in 1994–95 included Iran (33%), Jordan (45%), Saudi Arabia (28%), Tunisia (22%), and Turkey (45%). Women are also a larger proportion of graduates in media and information fields. This is especially true in Algeria, Egypt, Lebanon, and Tunisia, where they are the majority, and in Iran and Jordan, where women are 34–40% of graduates in third-level mass communications and documentation studies (UN 2000, Chart 4.13, 97).

Such graduates can contribute significantly to the economic and social development of their countries—as teachers, administrators, business-owners, and social commentators.

A Case Study of Women's Economic Participation: Iran

In some ways, Iran's pattern of women's economic participation is a special case, in that it has been affected by a highly politicized revolutionary and religious climate. Nevertheless, Iranian women's employment patterns and Iran's public policies are not substantially different from those found across the region. This section, therefore, will put the spotlight on patterns of Iranian women's economic participation, according to labor force data from the 1996 national population census.

The Islamic Republic's second ten-year census was completed in November 1996. It showed some continuity and some changes with the patterns and trends in women's socioeconomic participation since the 1970s. In summary: women's share of the total economically active population was 12.7%; of the urban economically active population, 11.7%; of the urban employed population, 11.2%; of total public sector wage-earners 16.4% (a slight increase over 1986). Thus women's labor force shares were still under 20% and therefore low by international standards. They were lower than in 1976 (Iran's third census round prior to the revolution), but higher than in 1986 and 1991. Women's unemployment rate was 12.5%—much lower than in 1986 and 1991, but still higher than men's (8.3% in 1996).[20]

Who were the unemployed women? Of the 271,565 unemployed women, 53% were urban and 47% were rural. Some 38% of the rural unemployed women had completed primary education; 51% of urban unemployed women had a high school education, and 12% had higher education. A higher proportion of educated women were without employment compared with educated men; 27% of urban unemployed men had a high school degree, and only 4.7% had higher education.

The 1996 labor force data showed that women continued to work in the public sector, and that the private sector remained underdeveloped, traditional, and rural, at least as far as women's involvement is concerned. Women's manufacturing activity remains overwhelmingly rural and traditional, whereas men's manufacturing is urban and more modern. Furthermore, public and private sector employees in Iran are highly divided by educational attainment; women (and men) tend to have at least a high school education or more in the public sector, whereas the majority in the private sector have completed only primary or intermediate school. Outside of agriculture (where women's involvement continues to be undercounted) and manufacturing (where women's work is largely rural), women remain over-represented in urban professional jobs (primarily in education and health) and under-represented in all other occupational categories (such as sales and services). Figures

8.5, 8.6, 8.7, and 8.8 illustrate these patterns not only for 1996, but also over time. The salient characteristics of Iranian women's economic participation at the threshold of the twenty-first century may be delineated as follows:

- Although most of the female labor force (55%) was engaged in the private sector (compared with 39.5% in the public sector), the vast majority of women private-sector workers (86.4%) were in the rural areas. In contrast, the majority of women public sector workers (63.3%) are urban.
- Of all economically active women, 28% were working in professional fields; in the urban areas, 46% of employed women were in professional fields.
- Women's share of the field of education was 44% for the total country, but much higher in urban areas (48.6%) than in rural areas (22%).
- Women's share of employment in the health services was 39.3% for the total country, though higher in urban areas (40.4%) than in the rural areas (33%).
- Some 21.6% of working women were in manufacturing—a higher percentage than in 1986, but mostly in the rural areas where they are non-wage-earners.[21] Their share of manufacturing was 22.8% for the total country, but significantly higher (45.2%) for rural areas.
- Women were still underrepresented in administration and management, technical and related jobs, clerical work, service and sales work, and agriculture.[22] They were also underrepresented in agriculture, urban manufacturing, wholesale and retail trade, finance, and real estate/business services.
- The female share of total private sector employment was 10% (mainly rural), and the share of private sector wage-earners is 7.6%. In contrast, women's share of public sector wage-earners was 16.4%.[23]
- Women's civil service employment had increased since 1991, and in 1996 women were 38.6% of all civil service employees covered by social insurance. (Their share of total public sector employment was lower, however, because of their marginal involvement in state-owned industries, hotels, etc.) Women were concentrated in the ministries of Education (44% female) and Health (43% female). In the Ministry of Justice, women made up about 27% of employees.
- Ministries with relatively low female involvement, given their mandates, include: Culture and Higher Education (20%), Labor and Social Security (11.3%), Agriculture (7.2%), Development and Housing (13.7%), Commerce (12% female), and Culture and Islamic Guidance (17.8%).

Figure 8.5. Female share of economically active and non-active
           population (10 years and above), Iran, 1956–1996

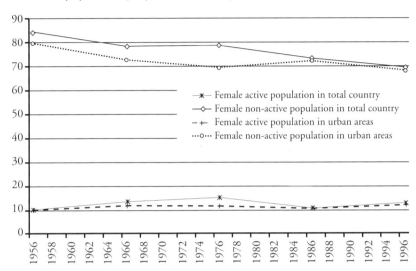

Source: *Statistical Yearbook of Iran*, Statistical Center of Iran, Plan and Budget Organization,
          Islamic Republic of Iran, 1997, Table 3-1, p70

Figure 8.6. Share of employed population (10 years and above) by
           gender, Iran, 1956–1996

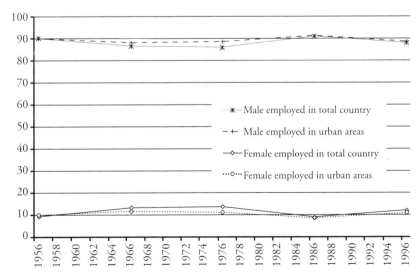

Source: *Statistical Yearbook of Iran*, Statistical Center of Iran, Plan and Budget Organization,
          Islamic Republic of Iran, 1997, Table 3-1, p70

Figure 8.7. Female share of employed population (10 years and above), Iran, 1956–1996

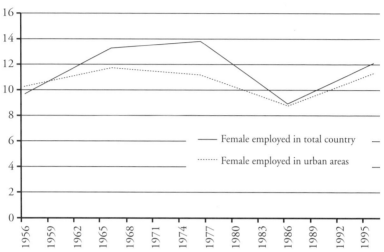

Source: *Statistical Yearbook of Iran*, Statistical Center of Iran, Plan and Budget Organization, Islamic Republic of Iran, 1997, Table 3-1, p70

Figure 8.8. Female employees, (10 years and above), share of major occupations, Iran, Nov.1996

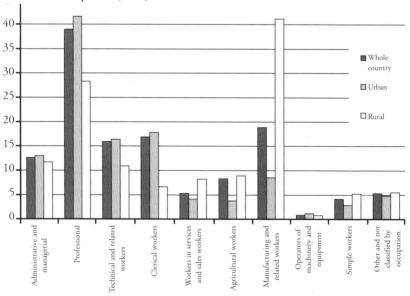

Source: *Statistical Yearbook of Iran*, Statistical Center of Iran, Plan and Budget Organization, Islamic Republic of Iran, 1997, Table 3-8, p80

Enhancing Women's Economic Participation: Some Recommendations

The changing political economy, women's rising educational attainment, and economic need could result in increased availability of women for employment. Still, if the MENA region is to meet the challenges of a globalized world economy, countries should implement a long-term strategy for human resource development that includes investments in women and proactive policies to encourage women's economic participation. Investing in the education and employability of women could contribute to greater domestic resource mobilization through enhanced taxation of its working population (as well as other forms of taxation). Some of the MENA countries, such as Iran, are among the lowest-taxed economies in the world (see, e.g., Karshenas 1995). By encouraging more women to enter the labor force and by introducing fiscal reform to make the system of income taxation more efficient, governments can mobilize increased domestic resources to finance investments in infrastructural development, improvements in the quality of education, and future structural reforms, industrial restructuring, and adjustment.

Since the 1995 Fourth World Conference on Women, some countries have adopted national action plans to implement the Beijing Platform for Action (see, e.g., discussion of Tunisia, below). However, in most countries of the region, women are not yet seen as breadwinners or as contributors to economic growth. Their economic participation is not taken as seriously as that of men, and employment-generation for women is not an official objective. In this final section, we offer recommendations for governments, NGOs, the private sector, and donors that entail institutional initiatives, infrastructural development, resource allocations, legal reform, new public policies, and research.

Gender Mainstreaming
This has been the focus of much discussion internationally, and many international organizations have adopted gender mainstreaming as a matter of policy. Gender mainstreaming can take three forms: (1) the establishment of the equivalent of a Ministry for Women and Family; (2) the establishment of WID units in all ministries and government agencies, including the line ministries; and (3) the integration of gender issues, including women's employment, in policies, programs, and projects at all levels and in all sectors. In many countries (e.g., Turkey and Tunisia), the Women and Family Ministry is the coordinating body for the implementation of the post-Beijing national action plan. Such a ministry should be funded adequately. WID offices should be established in all ministries and government agencies, but it is especially important,

given the paucity of data, that they be established in the central statistical offices and the ministries of labor, agriculture, and industry, and the planning bureau. These WID offices should have some oversight over policies, projects, and research. Working with the Women's Ministry, the WID offices can determine the strategies necessary to enhance women's economic participation within each ministry, in the economy, or throughout the society. These could include, for example, surveys on working women; or a chapter on women in the national development plan; or media campaigns concerning women, work, and family issues.

Cooperation between government and women's NGOs. Implementation of action plans pertaining to women should entail partnership with NGOs, as specified in the Beijing Platform for Action. Enhancing women's economic participation in the MENA region offers an opportunity to strengthen the institutions of civil society and to improve state-society relations. Women's NGOs could be involved in project development and implementation, in monitoring and evaluation, and in research.

The Private Sector and Women
In many countries the private sector is not seen as "women-friendly;" thus most women prefer to work in the public sector. The private sector can be involved in enhancing women's economic participation in several ways. First, small and medium-sized businesses should be fostered, and women should be encouraged to start their own enterprises. There are many kinds of enterprises that women can run, and that can be very useful to other women and to children: sewing, food preparation, catering, appliance repairs, childcare services, transportation services, and public baths. Second, banks should be involved in lending and credit programs for women. Around the world there exist many micro-credit and lending institutions that focus on low-income women (and men): ACCION, the Grameen Bank, Women's World Banking, Banco de Sol, and Bank Rakyat Indonesia, among others. More commercial banks should be involved to help support SMEs. Third, larger private sector businesses can be involved in national plans to promote women's employment. For example, in return for hiring women workers at decent wages and with social insurance, businesses may receive tax incentives.

Supporting Women-Owned Businesses
Privatization and liberalization could promote a cultural climate and a financial and regulatory environment conducive to women-owned or managed businesses. In various countries in the region there are policies to improve women's self-employment opportunities by providing them with training, credits, and loans to set up small- and medium-sized businesses, and to provide them with booths

to display and market their products. Certainly the extension of credit and training for low-income women would contribute to poverty alleviation of households. Training programs and credits for women should be enhanced, and should not be limited to traditional types of self-employment (e.g., garment-making or carpet-weaving).

According to the World Bank (1995b, 17), there are many kinds of community, social, and personal services that could benefit from women's enhanced participation. Women should be encouraged—perhaps through the equivalent of a Small-Business Bureau, a special fund for women entrepreneurs, or credits and loans from various lending institutions—to start their own businesses. Some types of businesses that could be especially socially useful as well as culturally appropriate are childcare centers, nursery schools, and kindergartens. Other types of businesses include shops, restaurants, cleaning services, food processing and catering services, health clubs, childcare centers, dental clinics, urban transport services, bookstores, career and counseling centers, etc. Here, governments, NGOs, the private sector, and donors can be very effective.

Facilitating women's self-employment in productive, profitable, and socially useful work would serve many purposes. It would tackle poverty and reduce women's unemployment. Not only would this expand women's participation as owners and managers of such businesses and provide additional job opportunities for women, but it would also expand the range of women-friendly and child-friendly services available.

Because most start-up capital comes from family funds, women's self-employment could be encouraged by removing the legal obstacles that exist in civil law, such as the lesser share of family wealth that women receive, and the husband's right to prevent his wife "from engaging in a profession or trade unfit to the family's welfare or prestige."

Supporting the Development of a Non-Profit Sector with the Participation of Women

What is sometimes referred to as the "third sector," the "voluntary sector" or the "NGO sector" consists of not-for-profit organizations and services that foster the development of civil society, citizenship, and national solidarity. Women and women's organizations can play a central role in developing this sector. They can serve as advocates for women and local communities. They can implement, monitor, or evaluate poverty alleviation, community development, or WID programs and projects. And with the support of banks, donors, or government agencies, they can establish vital non-profit services such as women's health clinics, shelters for women, adult learning centers, or camps for children.

Enhancing Women's Participation in the Tourism Sector
This is another area that could, in the context of economic restructuring, see greater participation by women. Many MENA countries are now further developing their tourism sectors, while also seeking to improve data, including data on tourism-related income and employment.[24] In order for the tourism sector to become amenable to women tourists, it needs to have women employees providing services for women traveling alone, and for women with families. At present, only 15% of the tourism work force are female in Turkey.[25] For this percentage to increase, and for the quality of the work force to be raised there and in other countries, incentives such as training, good wages, and good benefits need to be offered to women. A media campaign could assist in making the case that this sector is an appropriate one for women. Both the government and the private sector could be involved in offering training, placement, good salaries, and benefits for women to work in hotels, shops, restaurants, travel agencies, taxi and bus services, banks, etc. Women-owned businesses could be involved in the tourism sector as well.

New Information Technologies and Women
The introduction of information technologies is changing the nature of work around the world, and it offers possibilities for women's employment in the MENA region. A wide range of services and manufacturing industries have converted previously white-collar occupations into new forms of home-based work. 'Telework' has the potential to gain in importance, and it could be a significant source of women's employment. This kind of work includes typing, word and data processing, invoicing, editing, and translating. For educated women, 'telework' holds the promise of more flexible and family-friendly employment.

Infrastructural Development
Infrastructural development, both social and physical, can increase women's willingness to enter and remain in the formal sector labor force. For example, women-friendly and affordable transportation, along with childcare facilities in the community or at the workplace, can reduce the employment costs to women. Street lighting is also important for women working at night. The government and private sector can take the initiative in these endeavors, with NGOs involved at the planning and project-implementation stages.

Maternity leaves should be offered to working mothers for a period of six months, fully paid, and taken at most twice. Both mothers and fathers should have the option of an additional unpaid leave of six months. Such a policy will benefit the child, keep the family intact, and allow working mothers to balance employment and family life. Moreover, inconsistencies in maternity leave policies should be ironed out. For example, in Lebanon some working women are entitled to 40 days maternity leave, and others, two months. In Egypt, the previous labor law only benefited women in the public sector. Maternity leave policies should be unified, and ideally they should be funded by general revenues, or by some combination of employer, employee, and government contributions.

Improving the Workplace Environment
Public policies should be introduced to make the workplace a healthy and welcoming environment for women. In this regard, there is a role for government, the private sector, trade unions, and NGOs. National and firm-level policies against sexual harassment should be introduced. These already exist in Morocco and Egypt, but they need to be enforced, as well as monitored by trade unions and women's NGOs. Equal-opportunity employment legislation should be considered as well. An equal-opportunity employment policy is a commitment to engage in employment practices and procedures which do not discriminate, and which provide equality between individuals of different groups or sex to achieve full, productive, and freely chosen employment (ILO 1997, 65). Such legislation convinces women that there are real opportunities for them in both the public and private sectors. A media campaign could assist in spreading a positive message concerning women-friendly workplace environments.

Preventing the Feminization of Poverty and Eliminating Poverty
Poverty is not conducive to economic participation; it is, in fact, a form of exclusion. The poverty of women and of girls is related to national or household poverty, but it has distinct correlates and costs. Programs to tackle women's poverty or to prevent the feminization of poverty should be part of a national poverty-eradication program, as was recommended by the World Summit for Social Development (Copenhagen, March 1995) and by the Fourth World Conference on Women (Beijing, September 1995). As the Beijing Platform for Action states:

> Sound and stable macroeconomic policies should be designed and monitored with the full and equal participation of women, and with the goal of people-oriented sustainable development [para. 58 (c)]; public expenditures should be restructured to promote women's economic opportunities and equal access to productive resources [para. 58 (d)]; governments should provide access to and control of land, appropriate infrastructure and technology in order to increase women's incomes and promote household food security [para. 58 (n)].

Increasing Educational Attainment and Implementing Educational Reform
As we saw above, women's participation is increasing in fields of study that should enhance their employability. Women with higher education degrees are less likely to be unemployed. However, women with high school diplomas or with incomplete education are at a disadvantage in the labor market, and it appears that their unemployment rates are very high in many countries. With the emergence of a more women-friendly private sector, high school graduates should be able to find employment opportunities there, while women with incomplete education should be able to receive vocational training that could prepare them for, and place them in, appropriate occupations.

The long-term goal should be the attainment of universal literacy and higher rates of educational attainment. To help accomplish this, universal, compulsory education should be enforced, until at least the tenth grade. (Concomitantly, the minimum age of marriage for girls should be raised to at least sixteen.) Training of women teachers should receive some priority, given relatively low female shares. Attractive salaries or benefits should be offered to teachers who will serve in rural or urban disadvantaged areas. It may be necessary to review textbooks and other educational materials for their portrayals of women's roles.[26]

Historically, *fertility* declines have followed from female educational attainment and labor force participation. This is bound to occur in the MENA region as well, but in the meantime, the availability of contraception for married women, along with raising the legal age of marriage, will accelerate the process. With higher educational attainment and fewer children, more married young women will be available for employment.

Improving Labor Force Data
It is well known that outside the formal sector, data on women's economic participation in the region lack exactitude. And it is very difficult to determine needed policies on the basis of unreliable data. Labor force data are not comparable, due to differing enumeration techniques over time, not only across countries but also within countries. For example, Algeria's 1977 census counted the labor force over age twelve, but in 1987 it counted the labor force over age six. Iraq records the economically active population over age seven, Tunisia tallies age fifteen and over, and Turkey counts age twelve and over. The Iranian census of 1986 showed a drastic decline in women's agricultural participation, compared with 1976. In Egypt, the labor force sample survey of 1989 showed much-higher rates of female participation in sales and services and in agriculture, compared with the 1986 census. Clearly there is a need for standardization and harmonization of surveys, and more precision with respect to female labor

force participation and employment patterns. This goal should be realized by governments (and their WID offices) in partnership with women's NGOs, and with donors who may wish to help fund the establishment of gender-aware data-collection methods. Donors may also fund surveys or other data-collection projects by independent research institutes.

Policy-Oriented Research
There is a need for research around certain topics. Almost everywhere, more information is needed on women's roles in the urban informal sector, the agricultural sector, and in rural manufacturing. Surveys can be carried out to determine attitudes towards women's employment and employers' attitudes towards women employees. Research is also needed on the situation of low-income women; on women's experiences with SMEs; on the status of women managers and administrators; on experiences with, or the need for, employment services. Other research topics are country-specific. For example, research is needed on the status of women in rural carpet-production in Iran, given the importance of carpet exports in Iranian manufacturing, and given the large numbers of women workers in this sector. In Iran the carpet industry earns huge amounts of foreign currency that rival those of the oil industry and exceed those of (non-oil) industrial exports. It would be worthwhile to investigate women's employment status, work conditions, and income received for this culturally important and financially lucrative product. Also important for both policy and social justice is how the income is controlled and spent within the rural household.

Like reliable census and labor force data, quality research helps to guide policy. Government agencies, WID offices, women's NGOs, and donors can work in tandem to conduct research that will add to our knowledge of women's economic positions, and inform policies to enhance women's economic participation and their contribution to development and growth.

Implementing ILO Standards
Creating a legal environment more conducive to women's economic participation would be facilitated by the implementation of ILO standards. These include: Discrimination (Employment and Occupation) Convention (No. 111) and Recommendation (No. 111); the Equal Remuneration Convention (No. 100) and Recommendation (No. 90); the Convention (No. 156) and Recommendation (No. 165) concerning workers with family responsibilities; Convention No. 3 and No. 103 on maternity protection; the Home Work Convention (No. 177) and Recommendation (No. 184). The WID offices of relevant ministries, including the Labor Ministry, should be involved in publicizing and monitoring the implementation of these standards.

Tunisia: A Positive Example

Tunisia has committed itself to enhancing women's economic (and social) participation. It has established policies, mechanisms, and funding priorities that can serve as models for other countries in the region. For example, its national action plan for implementing the Beijing Platform for Action is being carried out by the government in partnership with eleven women's NGOs that represent a cross-section of women in trade unions, research, business, agriculture, and politics. The primary agency responsible for implementation is the Ministry of Women and Family. The ministries of Agriculture, Education, and Justice have mainstreamed gender concerns into their policies. The Ministry of Women and Family and the Center for Research, Study, and Documentation of Information on Women (CREDIF) have the authority to submit measures for adoption by the legislature.

The women's NGOs involved in the national action plan include the National Commission of the Working Woman, the Tunisian Association of Democratic Women, the Association of Tunisian Women for Research and Development, the National Chamber for Women Heads of Enterprises, the National Federation of Tunisian Women Farmers, the Tunisian Association for Mothers, and the Tunisian League of Human Rights, Women Section. Priorities include increasing women's access to finance and credit, alleviating women's poverty, and improving data collection on women. The budget for women's programs has increased since 1995 by 15%, and the government allocates 20% of its annual budget to implementing the platform.[27]

Notes

1   The Beijing Platform for Action, to which nearly all MENA countries are signatories, calls for action by governments, in cooperation with the private sector and NGOs, to "facilitate women's equal access to resources, employment, markets and trade." Similarly, the Barcelona Declaration of November 1995 for a Euro-Mediterranean Partnership stresses that the signatories agree to "recognize the key role of women in development and undertake to promote their active participation in economic and social life and in the creation of employment". It further states that the partners "recognize the importance of social development which ... must go hand in hand with any economic development. They attach particular importance to respect for fundamental social rights, including the right to development." In February 2000 a Euro-Mediterranean Conference on the Promotion of Women in Economic Development took place, at the initiative of Belgium, Portugal, Morocco, the Palestinian Authority, and Tunisia.

2   This paper draws in part on research described in Moghadam (1998). In addition

to examining the relevant secondary sources, I undertook research travel to Algeria, Morocco, Tunisia, Egypt, Iran, Jordan, and Turkey in 1990, 1994, 1995, and 1996. There I obtained official statistics on women's employment and interviewed statisticians, government officials, enterprise managers, working women, and women activists. For the present paper I have also consulted recent ILO studies, the 1996 Iranian census data, and reports on country-level implementation of the Beijing Platform for Action.

3   For a description of current maternity leave benefits, see UN (2000), Table 5.C, pp. 140–143.

4   According to ILO researcher Lin Lean Lim, more than half the total number retrenched between 1983–85 were from the two most feminized industries, electronics and textiles, while in administrative services the largest employment cuts were among clerks, another feminized occupation. See Moghadam (1995) for details. In 1991 and 1992 in Vietnam, "more than 8,000 people had to leave their jobs in state enterprises and organs, and 60 % of them were women" (Li Thi, 1995:50).

5   The female share of the total labor force in various regions in 1995 was as follows: 17% in the Arab region, 37% in Sub-Saharan Africa, 24% in South Asia, 25% in South Asia, 43% in East Asia, 37% in Southeast Asia, and 27% in Latin America and the Caribbean. The average for all developing countries was 35%. See UNDP (1995), Table 39, p. 216.

6   However, because women's informal sector, home-based work, and agricultural work is generally undercounted, a higher proportion of the measured female labor force is gainfully employed, statistically.

7   Indeed, according to Anker (1998: 164), "women's share of employment in [the professional and technical group] is two and a half times their share in the non-agricultural labour force. Turkey, an OECD member, follows the typical pattern of Middle Eastern countries where a large proportion of working women are in a professional or technical occupation. ... Social and cultural factors do ensure that most adult women in the Middle East and North Africa region do not work in the non-agricultural labour force, but for the relatively few who do, an unusually high percentage (by world standards) have a professional or technical job (often teacher or nurse)."

8   Lebanon may be an exception to this general rule.

9   This despite some diversity across countries in the region. The GCC countries have very small labor forces and have traditionally imported labor, including female labor. Even so, there are differences today between, on the one hand, Kuwait, and a certain extent Bahrain, both of which have higher recorded female employment, and on the other hand, the other GCC countries, with their very small female labor force. Countries with large agricultural sectors (e.g., Turkey, Syria, Iran, Egypt) may constitute a distinct type, inasmuch as a larger proportion of their female economically active population is found in the rural/agricultural sector (whether they are enumerated as such or not). Countries with successful

export manufacturing sectors (Morocco, Tunisia, Turkey) similarly may constitute a distinct type, as a larger proportion of their female labor force may be found in manufacturing (which is especially true of Morocco and Tunisia). Finally, Lebanon may be a distinct case, as its economy is largely comprised of private sector services. Consequently, 74% of the Lebanese female labor force is found in private services.

10 In 1995, the Arab region's human development index—which includes life expectancy, adult literacy, combined first, second- and third-level enrollment, and real GDP per capita was, at 0.6443, higher than that of South Asia or Sub-Saharan Africa, but lower than that of Southeast Asia and Latin America. See UNDP (1995), Table 39, p. 216.

11 As I shall explain presently, methodological problems—and in particular the inconsistency in enumerating women in agriculture, rural manufacturing, and the urban informal sector—may be partly responsible for the statistical declines.

12 With reference to the data in Table 2, the World Bank (1995b: 17) provides higher mean years of schooling for Arab countries, but they are for all age groups, not only the population aged 25 and above, as with the UNESCO data above. Thus, in 1995, mean years of schooling were: 6.37 in Algeria, 6.23 in Bahrain, 5.90 in Iraq, 7.05 in Kuwait, 6.66 in Syria, and 4.22 in Tunisia. The booklet notes that the majority of women are still illiterate in Algeria, Egypt, Morocco, and Saudi Arabia (p. 18).

13 Among Arab countries, the population growth rate for 1992–2000 is, at 2.9% per annum, the same as in Sub-Saharan Africa, and higher than that of South Asia (2.5). The total fertility rate is 4.8 for the Arab countries, 3.4 in Turkey and 5.0 in Iran. These rates are of course considerably higher than those of Latin America and Southeast Asia. Data from UNDP, Human Development Report 1995.

14 See Moghadam (1989), especially chapters on Egypt and Jordan.

15 Hindiyeh-Mani (1998:27) makes the interesting, if disconcerting, point that Palestinian women who work at home for a subcontractor report that their wages are paid directly to their husbands—not to themselves.

16 It was about 14% in 1998, according to the ELMS 98 (see Assaad, 1999, Table A13).

17 Men are also more likely to suffer from privatization of state-owned enterprises, given women's limited participation in such enterprises. As men lose jobs in SOEs and move toward the private sector, the private sector becomes even more masculine while the public sector becomes more feminine.

18 For example, Egypt's Neveen El Tahri, who heads a securities company, and Turkey's Umit Boyner, whose company is among the world's largest textiles firms.

19 This is described in detail in Moghadam (1998), pp. 72–73, and p. 213. Full references may be obtained there.

20 Data from Iran Statistical Yearbook 1375/1996 (IRI, 1997), Table 3-1, p. 70.

21 Ibid., Table 3-4, p. 74.

22 Ibid., Table 3-8, p. 80.

23 Ibid., Table 3-9, p. 81.
24 See ERF, Forum, vol. 6, no. 2, July/August 1999.
25 "The Turkish Tourist Industry: A Model Success Story", by Ozen Dalli, in ERF (ibid), p. 10.
26 Costa Rica may be a model. There, a 1990 law prohibits any educational content, methodologies, and pedagogical instruments that assign men and women social roles contrary to the social equality and complementarity of the sexes, or which depict women as subordinate. Furthermore, it requires the state to promote the concept of shared responsibility with regard to family rights and obligations, and of national solidarity. These values must be incorporated in all educational material, programs, and teaching methods (ILO, 1997: 46).
27 "Tunisia", in Mapping Progress: Assessing Implementation of the Beijing Platform 1998 (New York: WEDO, 1998).

———

References

Alachkar, Ahmad. 1996. "Economic Reform and Women in Syria." In Khoury and Demetriades, eds., *Structural Adjustment, Economic Liberalization, Privatization, and Women's Employment in Selected Countries of the Middle East and North Africa*. 99–114.

Al-Raida. Summer 1998. Special issue on Women in the Labor Force (Lebanon) 15 (82). Beirut: Institute for Women's Studies in the Arab World, Lebanese American University.

Anker, Richard. 1998. *Gender and Jobs: Sex Segregation of Occupations in the World*. Geneva: ILO.

Anker, Richard. 1995. "Measuring Female Labour Force with Emphasis on Egypt." In Nabil F. Khoury and Valentine M. Moghadam, eds., *Gender and Development in the Arab World: Women's Economic Participation, Patterns, and Policies*. London: Zed. 148–176.

Assaad, Ragui. 1999. "The Transformation of the Egyptian Labor Market: 1988–1998." Presented at the Conference on Labor Markets and Human Resource Development in Egypt. November 29–30, 1999. Cairo.

Beneria, Lourdes, and Shelley Feldman, eds. 1992. *Unequal Burden: Economic Crises, Persistent Poverty, and Women's Work*. Boulder: Westview Press.

Berry-Chikhaoui, Isabelle. 1998. "The Invisible Economy at the Edges of the Medina of Tunis." In Lobban, ed., *Middle Eastern Women and the Invisible Economy*. 215–31.

Buvinic, Mayra, and Margaret Lycette. 1994. *Women's Contributions to Economic Growth in Latin America and the Caribbean: Facts, Experience, and Options*. Washington, DC: International Center for Research on Women.

Carter, Susan B. 1986. "Comment." (on "The Female Labor Force and American Economic Growth" by Claudia Goldin). In Stanley Engerman and Robert Gallman, eds., *Long Term Factors in American Economic Growth.* Chicago: The University of Chicago Press.

Doctor, Kailas and Nabil Khoury. 1991. "Arab Women's Education and Employment Profiles and Prospects: An Overview." In Nabil F. Khoury and Kailas C. Doctor, eds., *Education and Employment Issues of Women in Development in the Middle East.* Nicosia: Imprinta Publishers. 13–45.

Early, Evelyn. 1998. "Nest Eggs of Gold and Beans: *Baladi* Egyptian Women's Invisible Capital." In Lobban, ed., *Middle Eastern Women and the Invisible Economy.* 132–147.

Eaton, Susan C. October 1992. "Women Workers, Unions and Industrial Sectors in North America." IDP Women Working Paper No. 1. Geneva: International Labour Office.

El-Solh, Camillia. 1994. "Women and Poverty in the ESCWA Region: Issues and Concerns." Paper prepared under commission for ESCWA for the Arab Regional Preparatory Meeting for the FWCW. November 6–10, 1994. Amman.

Economic Research Forum (ERF). 1996. *Economic Trends in the MENA Region.* Cairo: ERF.

Economic and Social Commission for West Asia (ESCWA). 1995a. "Arab Regional Preparatory Meeting for the Fourth World Conference on Women." November 9–10, 1994. Amman. Final Report High-Level Segment. New York: UN.

ESCWA. 1995b. "Arab Women in the Manufacturing Industries." Studies on Women in Development, No. 19. New York: UN.

ESCWA. 2000. *Women and Men in the Arab Region: A Statistical Portrait 2000.* Amman: ESCWA.

Ghosh, Jayati. July 1998. "Women and Economic Liberalization in the Asian and Pacific Region." *WINAP Newsletter* 22. Bangkok: UN Economic and Social Commission for Asia and the Pacific (ESCAP).

Goldin, Claudia. 1986. "The Female Labor Force and American Economic Growth." In Stanley Engerman and Robert Gallman, eds., *Long Term Factors in American Economic Growth.* Chicago: University of Chicago Press.

Handoussa, Heba, and Gillian Potter, eds. 1991. *Employment and Structural Adjustment: Egypt in the 1990s.* Cairo: The American University in Cairo Press.

Hansen, Bent. 1991. *The Political Economy of Poverty, Equity, and Growth: Egypt and Turkey.* Oxford and New York: Oxford University Press.

Hastings, Sue, and Martha Coleman. December, 1992. "Women Workers and

Unions in Europe: An Analysis by Industrial Sector." IDP Working Paper
No. 4. Geneva: International Labour Office.

Hopkins, M. 1983. "Employment Trends in Developing Countries: 1960–80
and Beyond." *International Labour Review* 122 (4).

INSTRAW/Joekes, Susan. 1987. *Women in the Global Economy: An
INSTRAW Study.* New York: Oxford University Press.

International Labour Office. 1995. *World Employment 1995.* Geneva: ILO.

International Labour Office. 1996. *World Employment 1996/97: National
Policies in a Global Context.* Geneva: ILO.

International Labour Office. 1994, 1996. *Yearbook of Labour Statistics.*
Geneva: ILO.

International Labour Office. 1997. *Breaking Through the Glass Ceiling: Women
in Management.* Geneva: ILO.

Islamic Republic of Iran. 1995. *National Report on Women in the Islamic
Republic:* Prepared for the Fourth World Conference on Women. Tehran:
Bureau of Women's Affairs.

Islamic Republic of Iran. 1376 (1997). *Statistical Yearbook 1375 (1996).*
Tehran: Statistical Center of Iran.

Jordan Coordinating Office for the Beijing Conference. 1995. *The Jordanian
Women: Past and Present.* Amman.

Jordanian National Committee for Women. September 1993. *The National
Strategy for Women in Jordan.* Amman.

Karshenas, Massoud. 1997. "Female Employment, Economic Liberalization,
and Competitiveness in the Middle East." Working Paper. Cairo: Economic
Research Forum.

Karshenas, Massoud. 1995. "Structural Adjustment and Employment in the
Middle East and North Africa." School of Oriental and African Studies,
Department of Economics, Working Paper Series No. 50.

Kasnakoglu, Zehra, and Meltem Dayioglyu. July 1996. "Education and
Earnings by Gender in Turkey." Economic Research Center Working Paper
No. 96/10. Ankara: Middle East Technical University.

Khoury, Nabil, and Evros Demetriades, eds. 1998. "Structural Adjustment,
Economic Liberalization, Privatization, and Women's Employment in
Selected Countries of the Middle East and North Africa." Proceedings of a
Seminar Held in Nicosia, Cyprus, November 1995. Nicosia: Department
of Statistics and Research, Ministry of Finance.

Khuri-Tubbeh, Taghrid. 1996. "Liberalization, Privatization and Women's
Employment in Jordan." In Khoury and Demetriades, eds., *Structural
Adjustment, Economic Liberalization, Privatization, and Women's Employment
in Selected Countries of the Middle East and North Africa.* 71–98.

Layachi, Azzedine. November 1999. "Reform and the Politics of Inclusion in the Maghreb." Paper presented at the annual meeting of the Middle East Studies Association, Washington, DC.

Li, Thi. August 1995. "Doi Moi and Female Workers: A Case Study of Hanoi." In Valentine M. Moghadam, ed., *Economic Reforms, Women's Employment, and Social Policies*. Helsinki: UNU/WIDER, World Development Studies 4.

Lobban, Richard A., ed. 1998. *Middle Eastern Women and the Invisible Economy*. Gainesville: University Press of Florida.

Martens, Margaret Hosmer, and Swasti Mitter. 1994. *Women in Trade Unions: Organizing the Unorganized*. Geneva: ILO.

Meer, Fatima, ed. 1994. *Poverty in the 1990s: The Responses of Urban Women*. Paris: UNESCO.

Mehra, Rekha, and Sarah Gammage. 1999. "Trends, Countertrends, and Gaps in Women's Employment." *World Development* 27 (3): 533–50.

Moghadam, Valentine M. 1993. *Modernizing Women: Gender and Social Change in theMiddle East*. Boulder: Lynne Rienner Publishers.

Moghadam, Valentine M. 1995. "Gender Aspects of Employment and Unemployment in a Global Perspective." In Mihaily Simai, ed., *Global Employment: An Investigation into the Future of Work*. London and Tokyo: Zed Books and the United Nations University Press.

Moghadam, Valentine M, ed. 1996. *Patriarchy and Development: Women's Positions at the End of the Twentieth Century*. Oxford: Oxford University Press.

Moghadam, V. M. 1998. *Women, Work, and Economic Reform in the Middle East and North Africa*. Boulder: Lynne Rienner Publishers.

Moghadam, V. M. 1999a. "Gender and the Global Economy". In Myra Marx Ferree, Judith Lorber, and Beth Hess, eds., *Revisioning Gender*. Thousand Oaks: Sage.

Moghadam, V. M. 1999b. "Gender and Globalization." *Journal of World-Systems Research* 5 (2): 301–14.

Moghadam, V. M. 2001. "Globalization and Women's Unemployment in the Arab Region." Prepared for CAWTAR-Tunis.

Poya, Maryam. 1999. *Women, Work and Islamism: Ideology & Resistance in Iran*. London: Zed Books.

République Tunisienne et PNUD. 1999. *Rapport National sur le Développement Human en Tunisie—1999*. Tunis.

Said, Mona. 1998. "The Distribution of Gender Differentials and Public Sector Wage Premia in Egypt." Prepared for the ERF Fifth Annual Conference. August 31–September 2. Gammarth.

Shaban, Radwan, Ragui Assaad, and Sulayman Al-Qudsi. 1995. "The Challenge of Unemployment in the Arab Region." *International Labor Review* 135 (1): 65–81.

SIS (State Institute of Statistics). 1996. *1994 Household Labor Force Summary Results*. Ankara: SIS.

Standing, Guy. 1989. "Global Feminization Through Flexible Labour." *World Development* 17 (7): 1077–95.

Standing, Guy. 1999. "Global Feminization Through Flexible Labour: A Theme Revisited." *World Development* 27 (3): 583–602.

United Nations. 1999. *1999 World Survey on the Role of Women in Development: Globalization, Gender and Work*. New York: UN.

United Nations. 1995. *The World's Women 1995: Trends and Statistics*. New York: UN.

United Nations. 2000. *The World's Women 2000: Trends and Statistics*. New York: UN.

United Nations. 1994. *Women's Indicators and Statistics Database (WISTAT)*, Version 3, CD-ROM. New York: UN

United Nations Development Program (UNDP). 1995, 1998, 1999. *Human Development Report*. New York: Oxford University Press.

UNDP. 1996. *Human Development Report 1996: Turkey*. Ankara: UNDP.

UNESCO. 1994. *Education for All: Status and Trends 1994*. Paris: UNESCO.

Ward, Kathryn, ed. 1990. *Women Workers and Global Restructuring*. Ithaca: ILR Press.

WEDO. 1998. *Mapping Progress: Implementing the Beijing Platform for Action*. New York: WEDO.

World Bank. 1995a. *Claiming the Future: Choosing Prosperity in the Middle East*. Washington, DC: The World Bank.

World Bank. 1995b. *Will Arab Workers Prosper or be Left out in the Twenty-first Century?* Washington, DC: The World Bank.

World Bank. 1995c. *World Development Report 1995: Workers in an Integrating World*. New York: Oxford University Press.

World Bank. 1995d. *Republic of Tunisia: Poverty Alleviation: Preserving Progress While Preparing for the Future*. Washington, DC: World Bank.

World Bank. 1991. *Egypt: Alleviating Poverty during Structural Adjustment*. Washington, DC: The World Bank.

World Bank. 1994a. *Hashemite Kingdom of Jordan Poverty Assessment*. Washington, DC: World Bank.

World Bank. 1994b. *Morocco: Poverty, Adjustment, and Growth*, Vols. I and II. Washington, DC: World Bank.

MDF Partners

Hani Hourani
Founder and Director General
Al-Urdan Al-Jadid Research Center
P.O. Box 940631
Amman 11196, Jordan
Tel. 962-6-553-3113/4
Fax. 962-6-553-3118
Email: info@ujrc-jordan.org

Imed Limam
Deputy Director General
Arab Planning Institute
PO Box 5834
Al Safat 13059, Kuwait
Tel: (965) 484-3459, (965) 484-3130
Fax: (965) 484-2935
E-mail: ilimam@api.org.kw
Website: www.kuwait.net/~api

Hisham Awartani
Project Director
Center for Palestine Research and Studies (CPRS)
PO Box 132
Nablus, Palestine
Tel: (972-9) 238-0383
Fax: (972-9) 238-0384
E-mail: cprs@cprs-palestine.org
Website: www.cprs-palestine.org

Heba Handoussa
Managing Director
Economic Research Forum for the Arab
Countries, Iran and Turkey
7 Boulos Hanna St.
Dokki, Cairo, Egypt
Tel: (20-2) 337-0810, (20-2) 748-5553
Fax: (20-2) 761-6042
E-mail: erf@idsc.net.eg, hhandousa@erf.org.eg
Website: www.erf.org.eg

Ahmed Galal
Executive Director
The Egyptian Center for Economic Studies
World Trade Center
1191 Corniche El Nil, 14th Floor
Cairo, Egypt 11221
Tel: (20-2) 578-1202, Direct: (20-2)579-1731
Fax: (20-2) 578-1205
E-mail: agalal@eces.org.eg
Website: www.eces.org.eg

Faycal Lakhoua
Conseiller
Institut Arabe des Chefs d'Entreprises
77, Boulevard de l'Union du Maghreb Arabe
2036, La Soukra
Tunis, Tunisia

Tel: (216-1) 759-166, (216-1) 759-155
Fax: (216-1) 759-247
Email: iace@planet.tn

Salim Nasr
General Director
Lebanese Center for Policy Studies
Tayyar Center
Box 55215
Sin al- Fil
Beirut, Lebanon
Tel: (961-1) 490-561 /6
Fax: (961-1) 601-787
E-mail: snasr@lcps.org.lb
Website: www.lcps-lebanon.org

Ali Belhaj
President
Maroc 2020
5, rue Lieutenant Bergé
Casablanca, Morocco
Tel: (212) 22-22-82-24, (212) 227-39-63
Fax: (212) 22-22-82-69, (212) 227-39-55
E-mail: abelhaj@mbox.azure.net

Nabil Sukkar
Managing Director
Syrian Consulting Bureau for Development &
Investment
Wahat Al-Fardos Building, Suite 501
Al-Fardos Street, PO Box 12574
Damascus, Syria
Tel: (963-11) 222-5946
Fax: (963-11) 223-1603
E-mail: SCB@net.sy
Website: www.scb-nsukkar.org

Taciser Belge
Turkish Economic and Social Studies Foundation
Fenerli Turbe Sok. No: 6
Rumeli Hisarustu
80815 Istanbul, Turkey
Tel: (90-212) 263-19-28, (90-212) 287-32-13
Fax: (90-212) 257-76-25
E-mail: info@tesev.org.tr, tesev@superonline.com
Website: www.tesev.org.tr

Chantal Dejou
Coordinator, MENA Region
World Bank Institute, The World Bank
1818 H Street NW
Washington, DC 20433
Tel: (1-202) 473-3357
Email: cdejou@worldbank.org
Website: www.worldbank.org/mdf

In this series:

Institutional Reform and Economic Development in Egypt
Edited by Noha El- Mikawy and Heba Handoussa

The Egyptian Labor Market
Edited by Ragui Assaad

Human Capital: Population Economics in the Middle East
Edited by Ismail Serageldin

Economic Trends in the Middle East and North Africa Region, 2002
Edited by The Economic Development Forum for the Arab Countries, Iran and Turkey